Sea Kay~~~~ ~g
Coastal
MASSACHUSETTS
From Newburyport to Buzzards Bay

Also available from
Appalachian Mountain Club Books

PADDLING GUIDES

    AMC River Guide: Maine

    AMC River Guide: Massachusetts/Rhode Island/Connecticut

    AMC River Guide: New Hampshire/Vermont

    Classic Northeastern Whitewater Guide

    Quiet Water Canoe Guide: Maine

    Quiet Water Canoe Guide: Massachusetts/Rhode Island/Connecticut

    Quiet Water Canoe Guide: New Hampshire/Vermont

    Quiet Water Canoe Guide: New York

    River Rescue

    Sea Kayaking along the Mid-Atlantic Coast

    Sea Kayaking along the New England Coast

    Whitewater Handbook

TRAIL GUIDES

    AMC White Mountain Guide

    AMC Hiking Guide to Mount Washington and the Presidential Range

    AMC Massachusetts and Rhode Island Trail Guide

    AMC Maine Mountain Guide

    AMC Southern New Hampshire Trail Guide

    North Carolina Hiking Trails

    West Virginia Hiking Trails

    High Huts of the White Mountains

MULTI-RECREATIONAL GUIDES

    Discover Acadia National Park

    Exploring in and around Boston on Bike and Foot

    Exploring the Hidden Charles

    Exploring Martha's Vineyard by Bike, Foot, and Kayak

Sea Kayaking
Coastal
MASSACHUSETTS
From Newburyport to Buzzards Bay

Lisa Gollin Evans

APPALACHIAN MOUNTAIN CLUB BOOKS
BOSTON, MASSACHUSETTS

Cover Photograph: Robert Harrison
All photographs by the author unless otherwise noted
Cover Design: Elisabeth Brady
Book Design: Carol Bast Tyler
Illustrations: Paul Mirto

Distributed by The Globe Pequot Press, Inc., Guilford, CT.

Library of Congress Cataloging-in-Publication Data
Evans, Lisa Gollin, 1956-
    Sea kayaking coastal Massachusetts : from the North Shore to
    Buzzards Bay / Lisa Gollin Evans.
        p.   cm.
    Includes bibliographical references (p.) and index.
    ISBN 1-878239-84-8 (alk. paper)
    1. Sea kayaking — Massachusetts — Guidebooks.
    2. Massachusetts — Guidebooks. I. Title.

GV776.M4 E82 2000
917.44—dc21   00-034989

The paper used in this publication meets the minimum requirements of the American National Standard for Information Sciences—Permanence of Paper for Printed Library Materials, ANSI Z39.48–1984.∞

**Due to changes in conditions,
use of the information in this book
is at the sole risk of the user.**

Printed on recycled paper using soy-based inks.
Printed in the United States of America.

10 9 8 7 6 5 4 3 2   03 04 05

To my husband, Frank,
with love and gratitude always.

The smaller one feels on the earth, dwarfed by
mountains and assailed by weather, the more respectful
one has to be—and unless we are very arrogant,
the less likely we are to poison or destroy it.

—Paul Theroux,
The Happy Isles of Oceania: Paddling the Pacific

CONTENTS

IV. ENVIRONMENTALLY SOUND KAYAKING 53

The Massachusetts Coastal Environment 53
Kayakers as Environmental Stewards 57

V. KAYAKING TRIPS:
NEWBURYPORT TO IPSWICH

CAPE ANN AND THE NORTH SHORE

BOSTON HARBOR

THE SOUTH SHORE

CAPE COD BAY

NANTUCKET SOUND AND ENVIRONS

BUZZARDS BAY

MAP LEGEND

———	road
+++++	railroad
⧓	bridge
～⌒	river/creek
〰	tide rip
≈≈≈	waves/strong current
⊥	marshy area
✳	rock (in water)
⊛	submerged rock
🄻	primary put-in
🄻*	primary put-in with parking
L	alternate put-in
L*	alternate put-in with parking
Ⓡ	rest stop/picknicking
⍭	lighthouse
▲	camping
🗼	tower
🏃	scenic viewpoint
🄿	parking

STATE LOCATOR MAP

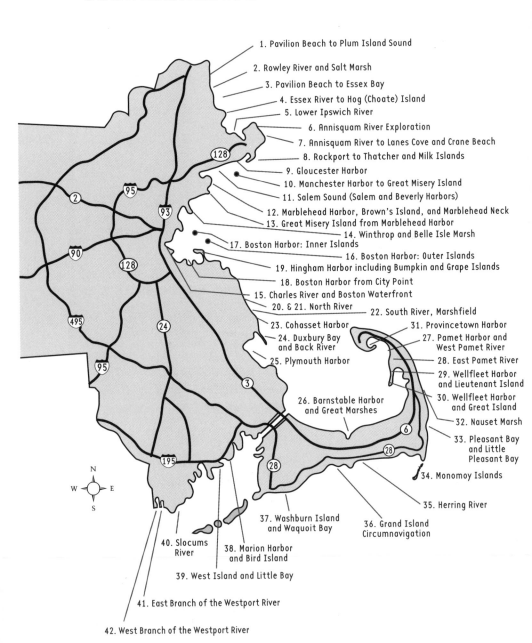

1. Pavilion Beach to Plum Island Sound
2. Rowley River and Salt Marsh
3. Pavilion Beach to Essex Bay
4. Essex River to Hog (Choate) Island
5. Lower Ipswich River
6. Annisquam River Exploration
7. Annisquam River to Lanes Cove and Crane Beach
8. Rockport to Thatcher and Milk Islands
9. Gloucester Harbor
10. Manchester Harbor to Great Misery Island
11. Salem Sound (Salem and Beverly Harbors)
12. Marblehead Harbor, Brown's Island, and Marblehead Neck
13. Great Misery Island from Marblehead Harbor
14. Winthrop and Belle Isle Marsh
17. Boston Harbor: Inner Islands
16. Boston Harbor: Outer Islands
19. Hingham Harbor including Bumpkin and Grape Islands
18. Boston Harbor from City Point
15. Charles River and Boston Waterfront
20. & 21. North River
22. South River, Marshfield
23. Cohasset Harbor
31. Provincetown Harbor
24. Duxbury Bay and Back River
27. Pamet Harbor and West Pamet River
25. Plymouth Harbor
28. East Pamet River
29. Wellfleet Harbor and Lieutenant Island
30. Wellfleet Harbor and Great Island
26. Barnstable Harbor and Great Marshes
32. Nauset Marsh
33. Pleasant Bay and Little Pleasant Bay
34. Monomoy Islands
35. Herring River
37. Washburn Island and Waquoit Bay
36. Grand Island Circumnavigation
40. Slocums River
38. Marion Harbor and Bird Island
39. West Island and Little Bay
41. East Branch of the Westport River
42. West Branch of the Westport River

BOSTON HARBOR ISLANDS

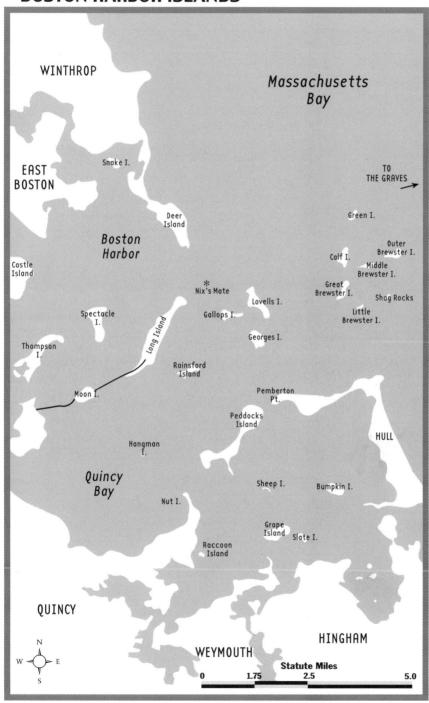

WINTHROP

Massachusetts
Bay

EAST
BOSTON

Snake I.

TO
THE GRAVES

Deer
Island

Green I.

Boston
Harbor

Outer
Brewster I.

Castle
Island

Calf I.

Middle
Brewster I.

Nix's Mate

Great
Brewster I.

Shag Rocks

Spectacle
I.

Lovells I.

Gallops I.

Little
Brewster I.

Long Island

Thompson
I.

Georges I.

Rainsford
Island

Moon I.

Pemberton
Pt.

Peddocks
Island

HULL

Hangman
I.

Quincy
Bay

Sheep I.

Bumpkin I.

Nut I.

Grape
Island

Slate I.

Raccoon
Island

QUINCY

HINGHAM

WEYMOUTH

N
W   E
S

Statute Miles

0   1.75   2.5   5.0

TRIP HIGHLIGHTS

Round-Trip Mileage	Type of Water	Recommended Tide	Camping	Sandy Beach	Island Hopping/ Picnicking	Hiking
8.4–14.6	protected	mid to high	Y	Y	Y	N
5.8–10.5	protected	mid to high	Y	N	Y	N
9.0	protected/open	mid to high	N	Y	Y	Y
8.0	protected	mid to high	N	Y	Y	Y
4–6	protected	high	N	N	N	N
4.2	protected	mid to high	Y	Y	N	Y
7.0–10.6	open	low to high	Y	Y	N	Y
6.6–9.0	open	low to high	N	N	Y	N
3.0–11.7	protected	low to high	N	Y	N	N
3.2–11.0	open	low to high	N	N	Y	Y
3.2–12.0	open	low to high	Y	Y	Y	N
3.5–5.1	protected/open	mid to high	N	Y	Y	N
13.9	open	mid to high	N	N	Y	Y
3.5	protected	high	N	N	N	N
7.0–10.0	protected	low to high	N	N	Y	N
6.7–11.5	protected/open	low to high	Y	Y	Y	Y
4.1–9.4	open	low to high	Y	Y	Y	Y
4.0–6.0	protected	mid to high	N	Y	Y	Y
7.2	protected	mid to high	Y	Y	Y	Y

Round-Trip Mileage	Type of Water	Recom- mended Tide	Camping	Sandy Beach	Island Hopping/ Picnicking	Hiking
11.1	protected	mid to high	N	Y	Y	N
4.5	protected	high	N	N	N	N
11.0	protected	mid to high	N	N	Y	N
4.0–8.0	open/protected	mid to high	N	Y	Y	N
4.0–11.0	open/protected	mid to high	N	Y	Y	N
5.8–13.8	open/protected	mid to high	N	Y	Y	N
9.0-10.0	protected	mid to high	N	Y	Y	N
3.5–9.0	open/protected	mid to high	N	Y	Y	N
2.5	protected	——	N	N	N	N
3.8–8.0	protected	high	N	Y	Y	N
4.0–10.0	protected	high	N	Y	Y	Y
3.7–15.0	protected	mid to high	N	Y	Y	N
6.5–15.9	protected	mid to high	N	N	Y	Y
5.5–10.3	protected	mid to high	N	Y	Y	Y
15.0	open	low to high	N	Y	Y	Y
4.0	protected	mid to high	N	Y	Y	Y
6.5	protected	mid to high	Y	Y	Y	Y
4.5–6.75	protected	mid to high	N	Y	Y	Y
7.0–11.5	open/protected	low to high	N	N	Y	N
6.5–9.0	open/protected	mid to high	N	Y	Y	Hiking
7.0–14.5	open/protected	mid to high	N	Y	Y	Y
7.0–14.0	protected	mid to high	N	N	N	N
7.0–11.0	protected	mid to high	Y	Y	Y	Y

ACKNOWLEDGMENTS

I AM INDEBTED to many for their help in creating this book. Without the expertise and generosity of the following individuals and organizations, I would definitely have been "up a creek." The following guided me on the water, reviewed portions of this book, or provided me with indispensable equipment and information. I sincerely thank Nick Dsylan and Necky Kayak for the opportunity to paddle the superb Looksha IVS and Amaruk; Bob Burnett and the North Shore Paddlers Network; Al Goldberg and the Boston Sea Kayak Club; Ernie Falbo and Karen Lundsgaard for the use of their beautiful home; Scott Szczepaniak, Dave Jacques and Charles River Canoe and Kayak; Derek Hutchinson for his expert instruction and book; Armand Santos of Buzzard Bay Kayaks; Carline McOsker, Anne Wachtmeister, and Liz Bradfield of Off the Coast Kayaks; Appy Chandler and Richard Osbourne of Essex River Basin Adventures; George Ward and Pat Long of Billington Sea Watercraft; Yvonne Sabourin of the Kayak Shack; Adam Bolansky, John Leonard, Leon Granowitz, Bryan Mitchell, Tom Scully of the Beverly Public Library; Jay Moore, Bob Speare, Carol Decker, and Dennis Murley of the Massachusetts Audubon Society; Christopher Husgen of the Parker River Wildlife Refuge; Fred Bull of Cape Cod Coastal Canoe and Kayak; Walter Chadwick of Edward's Boatyard; and Werner Paddle, Lotus Designs, and Stoltquist Water Ware for terrific, well-built, and reliable gear.

With great pleasure, I want also to thank the many kayaking partners who befriended and inspired me on paddling expeditions up and down the coast. This book would have been impossible (and much less fun) without them. They include my daughter, Gracie, and my friends, Julie, Ned, Laura, Peter and Katherine Strong, Willy Weygint, Maureen Ashley, Chris Perkins, Bob Baldridge, Roger Voeker, Hal Levine, David Schultz, and Amy Walker. I'd like to particularly credit once again the fine organizations of the North Shore Paddlers Network and Boston Sea Kayak Club through which I met many of these great kayakers. Heartfelt thanks also to Prisca Akene, who so ably helped me in a pinch when I needed her most.

Last but not least, thanks to Frank, Sarah, Gracie, and Lilly who put up with my frequent absences, dripping equipment, and gear-filled car. Special thanks to my husband for a summer's worth of babysitting so I could be on the water. And as always, thanks, Mom, thanks, Dad, thanks, Jimmy. Love you all.

INTRODUCTION

THIS BOOK DESCRIBES forty-two sea-kayaking trips along the coast of Massachusetts. The trips, averaging about eight miles round-trip, are chosen especially for novice to intermediate kayakers. Longer and more difficult trips can easily be assembled by combining two or three trips or by utilizing the "trip tips" listed at the end of some of the trip descriptions. For more experienced kayakers, additional access information is included to add more flexibility to trip design.

Those new to Massachusetts sea-kayaking will find valuable information in the book's first four chapters. Chapter 1 discusses how to choose a kayak and assemble essential gear. Safety, ocean hazards, and navigation are discussed in chapter 2. Chapter 3 covers coastal access issues in Massachusetts: and environmentally sound kayaking is explored in chapter 4.

The remainder of the book is filled with trip descriptions. Trips are divided into six sections by geographic location: Newburyport to Ipswich, Cape Ann and the North Shore, Boston Harbor, the South Shore, Cape Cod Bay, Nantucket Sound and environs, and Buzzards Bay. Each trip description includes information on the natural environment, safety considerations, and local history. Several useful appendices follow, including a bibliography of recommended reading, a primer on using tide and current tables, a glossary of kayaking terms, and a voluminous listing of local kayaking resources for Bay State paddlers.

WHO SHOULD USE THIS BOOK

This book is for *all* paddlers seeking superlative kayaking adventures off the Massachusetts coast. The intent of this book is to describe trips accessible to kayakers of *all* abilities. Its emphasis is on locating relatively protected waters and describing reasonably short routes that take kayakers to serene, scenic spots where paddlers can enjoy the nature, wildlife, and astounding beauty of the coast. Protected estuaries, winding marsh creeks, harbor pockets, and offshore islands have been documented for your pleasure. Use this book as a launching point. Greater coastal adventures are only strokes away.

HOW TO USE THIS BOOK

Trip Descriptions

For each trip, the following information is listed in summary form at the beginning of each description:

Level of Difficulty: Kayak trips are first rated *easy, moderate,* or *strenuous.* The level of difficulty takes into consideration mileage, conditions at the launch site, average wind and water conditions, and the paddling hazards likely to be encountered. This rating is subjective at best, and is useful only under average sea and weather conditions. Even the shortest and easiest paddle can turn difficult, or even deadly, in a gale. Paddlers should read the entire trip description carefully before departing to assess the level of difficulty of any particular trip.

Trips are also described as *protected* or *open* water, or a combination of both. Trips in protected water (rivers, marshes, small bays) are likely to have less surf, wind, and risk of dangerous water conditions. Even in "protected" waters, however, difficult conditions can develop. Local forecasts must always be consulted prior to *any* kayaking trip.

Round–Trip Mileage: An estimated round-trip mileage is given for each trip. Mileage is given in nautical miles; one nautical is roughly equivalent to 1.15 statute miles. Because this book is aimed at novice and intermediate paddlers, the estimated mileage assumes a conservative route paralleling the shoreline (rather than the most direct course). From the given mileage, one can roughly calculate the time required for each trip by using an average paddling speed of 3.0 to

3.5 miles per hour. Sea state, tidal current, wind speed, and the efficiency of the paddler will affect the actual time spent on the water.

Attractions: This section lists the special enticements of a trip, such as an isolated sandy beach, the presence of seals, good fishing, great sunsets, nearby hiking trails, camping, fabulous ice cream, etc.

Precautions: For each trip, paddlers are alerted to areas of rapid current, tidal rips or races, hazardous waves (boomers, dumpers, or clapotis), high-traffic areas, mud flats, difficult launching and landing, and areas of significant tidal rise and fall. Despite the author's best intentions, hazards can appear on paddling trips without warning. Kayakers must always be on the lookout for dangerous conditions while paddling.

Charts: This section lists the recommended National Oceanic and Atmospheric Administration (NOAA) chart(s) a kayaker should carry for each trip.

Tidal Information: For trips greatly affected by tidal flow, this section imparts critical information. It alerts readers to tidal range, tidal hazards, the appropriate tide table to consult, and recommended times for launching and landing.

Launch Site and Directions: The name of the recommended launch site and directions from the nearest major highway are given. When available, several alternate access points are included for each trip. Driving directions, as well as alternative launch sites, are found at the *end* of each trip description. Information on parking and launching fees is also included.

Camping: Camping opportunities are noted where applicable.

A NOTE ABOUT SAFE PADDLING

Kayaking is a dangerous activity. This sport must be approached with the utmost respect for the immense power and unpredictability of the sea. Avoid weather and water conditions that put you at risk. Paddling safely requires preparedness, skill, and intelligence.

Advice to the boater can be summarized as follows. To **PADDLE** safely, a kayaker must:

• **Pay constant attention.** A kayaker's momentary inattention can result in an unlucky and unnecessary capsize. While it takes only a few seconds to overturn, re-entry may take many life-threatening minutes. An observant paddler is less apt to be endangered by unpleasant surprises. Watch constantly for changes in weather and water conditions. Always be alert for rocks, obstructions, waves, boat wakes, other boats, and the deteriorating condition of paddling partners or equipment.

• **Always paddle with a fit partner, but depend on yourself.** It is *always* safer to paddle with companions. Novices should be especially hesitant to paddle solo, under any conditions. A partner offers another set of eyes to spot hazards and lends additional judgment to the decisions that need to be made at sea. Rescues are also immensely easier when assistance is available. While there is greater safety in numbers, numbers alone do not reduce risk. When choosing kayaking partners, make sure they are equipped with the skills and gear to help themselves and to assist you in an emergency. A novice partner lacking judgment, skills, or proper safety equipment can be a liability for any paddler.

Lastly, paddle with partners but make sure *you* have the equipment and skills necessary to keep you safe. Don't count on the skills or equipment of anyone else. You never know when you'll get separated or when your companions will be incapacitated. Be prepared to go it alone, but never do so intentionally.

• **Dress for the water.** Cold water kills, and hypothermia is a paddler's greatest threat. Consequently, dress for a swim every time you paddle. Although comfort above the water may be sacrificed, proper clothing greatly increases your chance of surviving a capsize. Always, always wear a personal flotation device (PFD). Simple possession is the law, but it is not good enough. A PFD can't help you if it's strapped to the deck.

• **Dare to be conservative.** Caution and conservatism are the watchwords of a wise kayaker. Know what situations you can and cannot handle. Until greater experience and skills are acquired, novices must avoid paddling unassisted into situations of great risk, including solo paddling, strong tidal currents, wind-swept shorelines, lengthy crossings, remote areas, long-distance trips, trips with difficult navigation, heavy weather, and paddling in winter and early spring. When conditions dictate (fatigue, bad weather, failing partners), have the courage and flexibility to act conservatively. Taking risks to adhere to a pre-existing float plan is not only foolhardy but dangerous.

• **Learn new skills and practice often.** New skills are a novice kayaker's ticket to safer, more exciting adventures. Take a class, join a kayaking club, attend a workshop, or paddle with more experienced kayakers. The more skills you gain, the more fun you'll have. And, just as with any other sport, practice is essential. Practicing and mastering solo and assisted rescues are especially essential to your safety.

• **Expect the unexpected.** Be prepared for the worst. Consider the "what ifs" each time you paddle. Equip your kayak with essential safety gear for each and every outing. Use a checklist to insure that you're properly equipped for each trip. Lastly, keep all essentials accessible, so they can actually assist you in an emergency. Flares stowed deep in a hatch can't possibly help you when you need them.

chapter
one

YOUR KAYAK
AND ESSENTIAL
GEAR

B **EFORE GETTING ON THE WATER,** you'll need a boat, the knowledge to operate it safely, and an understanding of your role as an environmental steward. This chapter guides you through the most frightening aspect of sea-kayaking: *buying your first boat*. Next you'll learn how to outfit it with essentials and, most importantly, how to prepare yourself to paddle *safely* in coastal waters.

SELECTING A KAYAK

Selecting your first kayak can be exciting, yet overwhelming. It requires familiarity with new terms (you will soon be speaking "kayak-ese," see glossary). The wealth of choices is astounding. But don't despair; the following information will greatly assist your purchase.

First, let's simplify the process. Number one: don't obsess. The first boat you buy will probably not be your last. As you become a better paddler, your needs and desires will change.

Secondly, spend as much time as possible in other peoples' boats before you buy your own. Rent, borrow, attend a symposium, accompany an outfitter, or patronize a retailer who lets you test paddle a variety of boats. The more kayaks you paddle the more you'll learn, both about kayaks themselves and about your own preferences as a paddler.

Third, narrow your choices to a reasonable number by deciding (or at least guessing) where, when, and how you'll use your boat. Different kayaks do different things well, and unfortunately no kayak does everything perfectly. Some boats are superb and compact travelers; others provide stable platforms for fishing, photography, birdwatching or scuba diving; others slip effortlessly through the water. Rank which features are most important to you. Do you want stability, performance, portability, durability, or speed? Will you be paddling solo or in tandem, camping, surf-riding, or exploring protected coves? Do you want to putter around or log miles? The more you know about your needs and goals, the easier it will be to choose a boat.

buying a good kayak on a limited budget

An excellent way to stretch your budget is to purchase a used kayak. Several Massachusetts outfitters sell off their fleets each year, offering discounts of at least 40 percent off the retail price on a wide variety of boats. These popular sales occur in fall, however, so you have to plan ahead. Used boats can also be found year-round in the *Want Advertiser*, on a few kayaking club websites, and perhaps in your local paper. (Check the outfitters and clubs listed in Appendix A for sales and website want ads.) When purchasing a used plastic boat, be sure to examine the hull carefully for heat or pressure damage. Examine fiberglass boats for tears, breaks, soft spots, poor repair jobs, and leaky seams.

THE DIFFERENT TYPES OF SEA KAYAKS

There are four principal types of sea kayaks: sit-on tops, recreational kayaks, touring kayaks, and surf skis. Read the descriptions below and consider how each type of kayak would meet your personal kayaking goals.

Sit-on-top, or open cockpit, kayaks are user-friendly, relatively stable kayaks that are great fun for paddling in surf and warm water. All sit-on-tops have open, self-bailing cockpits, and some can accommodate diving equipment and additional passengers. Children especially enjoy the freedom of a sit-on-top. Many sit-on-tops can be flipped over to create a stable platform for a variety of water games (and can even be paddled upside-down!). After capsizing, most are easily reboarded without assistance or rescue equipment. Lengths vary from a short and sporty 8 to nearly 15 feet. All are relatively wide, ranging from 26 to 34 inches. While fun to paddle and easy to transport, sit-on-tops have significant limitations in cold Massachusetts waters. Furthermore, since most lack a supportive seat and storage capacity, their comfort for long distance touring is questionable.

On the other hand, if you'll do all your paddling in July on the Cape and your kids would love this almost indestructible boat, a sit-on-top may be the kayak for you. Its simplicity can't be beat on a warm summer day. For touring, make sure that the kayak is long and narrow enough to track well and move easily through the water. You will also want to outfit the boat with the optional padded seat and thigh braces.

Most sit-on-tops are made from tough polyethylene (plastic). In fiberglass, you'll find a hybrid, sit-on top with built-in seats and a deeper passenger well.

Recreational (sport) sea kayaks are relatively short, wide, and stable boats that easily accommodate day-tripping paddlers and are particularly user-friendly for novices. They serve a variety of purposes well, from puttering around in protected coastal waters to longer day trips, and are especially good for paddlers interested in photography, bird-watching, and fishing. Usually constructed of durable rotomolded polyethylene (plastic), they are economical and withstand bumps, rough landings, and inadvertent collisions without serious repercussions. The length of a single recreational kayak runs generally from 9 to 16 feet and their width from 21 to 32 inches. Doubles are 12 to 17 feet long with an average width of about 31 inches. At the short end of the scale, the boats are light enough to be carried by a single person. Most recreational kayaks are not equipped with rudders, and many lack stern and bow hatches and bulkheads. The majority are designed to be paddled with

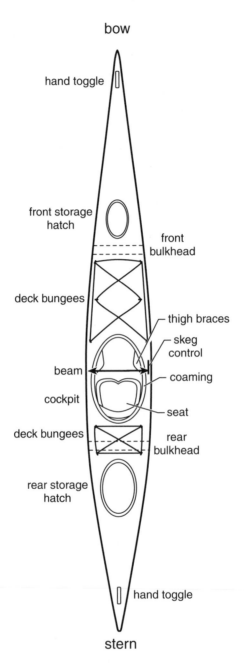

bow

hand toggle

front storage
hatch

front
bulkhead

deck bungees

thigh braces

skeg
control

beam

coaming

cockpit

seat

deck bungees

rear
bulkhead

rear storage
hatch

hand toggle

stern

Parts of a kayak

sprayskirts, but several, including the doubles, have extra-large cockpits which paddlers often leave uncovered.

These easy-to-paddle boats generally attract novices who desire a simple mode of transportation on protected waters. Most paddlers feel immediately comfortable in a recreational kayak. These boats are not geared for kayak enthusiasts who anticipate refining their skills or who are interested in open-water touring or multiday camping. Due to their relatively short length and wide beam, they do not track as well as longer boats, and some tend to yaw (swing right and left with each paddle stroke). In addition, the absence of a rudder makes recreational kayaks more difficult to paddle in windy conditions. (Some models can, however, have factory rudders installed.) Nevertheless, if paddling is merely a means to an end and your hobby calls for a stable, maneuverable, comfortable, and easily transportable boat, a recreational sea kayak may suit your needs perfectly.

Touring sea kayaks are relatively long, seaworthy boats built for paddlers interested in developing good paddling skills and in testing these skills in a variety of water and weather conditions. Touring kayaks are generally longer than recreational sea kayaks (averaging more than 16 feet) and have slender beams (averaging about 22 inches). Doubles run 17 to 21 feet long, with beams of 24 to 32 inches. The boats often have low to moderate initial stability but moderate to high secondary stability. Paddling a touring kayak requires at least a moderate amount of skill and attention to balance. Many have bulkheads and hatches at the bow and stern to provide storage for multiday touring. The often standard rudders or skegs found on touring kayaks make paddling in wind considerably easier. Touring kayaks can be found in rotomolded plastic, fiberglass, and Kevlar. Their cockpits are generally snug and are designed to be paddled with sprayskirts.

Touring kayaks have many advantages over recreational boats. Their length and sleek hull shape allow them to move swiftly, track well, and handle ocean wind and waves when paddled with the requisite skill. For paddlers looking to log miles in both protected and open ocean waters, touring kayaks are the right choice. These boats are also perfect for paddlers who want to improve their skills and master techniques like bracing and rolling.

Surf skis are extremely long, narrow kayaks, built for speed and wave riding. Their specialized racing design and limited stability make them a relatively poor choice for a beginner looking for a versatile touring boat.

KAYAK DESIGN 101

Even if you've narrowed your search to only one category of kayak, there is still a multitude of boats to consider. The following guidelines will help you understand the differences between kayaks. No kayak will have all the desirable traits you seek. Nevertheless, it is possible to find a happy compromise of the traits that are most valuable to your kayaking goals.

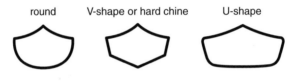

round   V-shape or hard chine   U-shape

Kayak hull shapes (cross-section)

Stability

The general rule is that wide boats are more stable than narrow boats. In fact, a wide, flat-bottomed boat in calm water can feel as stable as a couch. For many sea-kayakers, however, this high degree of initial stability is not always desirable. Initial stability is defined as the degree of resistance to minor amounts of heel. In other words, it describes a boat's resistance to leaning. Secondary stability is a hull's tendency to stabilize as it's leaned to one side. A boat with high or moderate secondary stability increasingly resists tipping as the hull enters the water above the normal waterline. Because the ability to lean a kayak is essential to developing good paddling skills and to staying afloat in rough water, most sea-kayakers look for a boat with good secondary stability but not necessarily high initial stability. A little roundness or **V** shape to the hull (rather than flat) makes the boat easier to lean and thus more seaworthy when encountering waves. A wide, flat-bottomed boat will sit flat on calm water but is liable to capsize if waves hit it broadside.

Maneuverability

The more *rocker* in the hull design (the curve in a boat's bottom as seen in profile), the easier the boat will be to turn. A short boat with significant rocker will be the most maneuverable. A long, flat-bottomed boat will require the most effort to turn. For general touring, a mid-length kayak with a slight degree of rocker suits most paddlers.

Tracking

The ability to track (keep a straight course) is usually a highly prized trait for sea kayaks. *Yawing* can be incredibly frustrating and tiring. The general rule is that longer boats track better than short ones, but there are other variables as well. A slight **V** shape to the hull aids tracking, and the addition of a rudder or skeg to a short boat can keep the boat on course. A boat that tracks very well (a long boat, for example) may be very difficult to maneuver in tight spaces.

Windage

All sea kayakers are interested in minimizing the impact of wind on their boats. Even more than wave action and current, wind is the force that most frustrates ocean kayakers. Many rudderless or skegless kayaks have a tendency to turn upwind, or *weather-cock*. A high bow or deck can catch the wind and make the boat hard to handle. A rudder or skeg can counter the annoying effects of weather-cocking. Boats without rudders or skegs must be well-designed to minimize the effects of wind. Fortunately, more and more sea-kayak designers are paying attention to minimizing windage and improving the tracking ability of rudderless and skegless boats. Look for features such as integral rudders or skegs and/or a slight **V** shape to the hull.

Speed

A general rule is that a long boat (up to about twenty feet) can reach higher speeds than a short boat. There are other important variables as well, such as the hull design and the weight and ability of the paddler. Unless racing is in your plans, however, don't be too caught up in the potential speed of any particular kayak.

THE IMPORTANCE OF MATERIALS

The material from which a kayak is constructed affects its weight, durability, performance, appearance, and price.

Fiberglass (composite)

Many high-quality touring kayaks are constructed from fiberglass (made by fitting cloth to a mold and applying resin). Fiberglass kayaks are prized for their performance, beauty, strength, durability, and weight. They weigh about 10–20 percent less than comparable plastic boats. In addition, their high luster and sculpted lines are difficult to replicate in less expensive materials. The most expensive fiberglass kayaks are made from Kevlar, an ultrastrong fabric. Kevlar boats are about 15–20 percent lighter than other composite kayaks and are less rigid and brittle. They are less likely to break than fiberglass boats but are more difficult to repair if damaged.

Plastic (rotomolded polyethylene)

Many touring and most recreational and sit-on-top kayaks are made of a durable and inexpensive plastic. Plastic boats are generally 25–40 percent less expensive than their fiberglass counterparts. Unlike glass boats, plastic kayaks are susceptible to heat damage and must be protected from excessive heat (such as from the sun or unvented garages). Their shapes can be permanently distorted by improper handling. Another disadvantage of a plastic kayak is its weight. When considering one of the larger and better-outfitted touring kayaks (with rudder, bulkheads, and hatches), make sure that the boat's weight is manageable for you. If you can't lift it, it won't leave your garage.

Canvas or synthetic material on a wood or aluminum frame (folding kayaks)

Folding kayaks are for paddlers who travel with their boats or have no place to store a kayak. Disassembled, the kayak fits into two or three bags. The assembled boats are roomy and stable and have proven themselves seaworthy in exotic locales across the globe. These are fine craft, but paddlers will pay handsomely for their portability. Folding kayaks tend to be among the most expensive types of kayaks.

Wood

There is no denying the outstanding aesthetics and performance of a hand-built wooden kayak. They are light and fast, but they are the most fragile of all kayaks and require a higher degree of maintenance. They are also very expensive, unless you construct the boat yourself. For a fraction of the price of a finished wooden boat, handy paddlers can purchase a boat-building kit. In general, it takes about 80–100 hours for a novice builder to construct a wooden kayak.

KAYAK FEATURES

The following three features are commonly found on touring sea kayaks and less often on recreational kayaks. Depending on your kayak's intended use, these features may be indispensable, convenient, or merely unnecessary. Before you pay handsomely to obtain these options (and add weight and complexity to your kayak), know the purposes served by the following:

Rudders and skegs

The principal purpose of *rudders and skegs* is to keep a boat on course while paddling in wind and rough seas. Rudders and skegs permit you to travel farther with less effort on windy bays and open ocean. When used properly, the slight drag they add is far outweighed by their labor-saving abilities. If you plan to tour the Massachusetts coast, rudders or skegs are advisable for coping with the ever present wind. Rudders are highly advisable on double touring kayaks.

Many purists dislike rudders because novices often rely too heavily on them and consequently never develop essential paddling skills. Kayakers must learn to maneuver their boats well without using rudders, because rudders can fail and consequently endanger ill-prepared boaters. Boats with rudders also have spongy, rather than rigid, foot pegs. This can cause some loss of power on a good paddler's forward stroke.

When not in use, rudders are lifted out of the water by cables on the kayak deck. A skeg can also be retracted into its boxed fitting in the keel of the kayak. Any boats with fixed-position rudders or skegs should be avoided, for they are easily damaged by shallow rocks and beach landings. While it is critical to learn how to handle your boat without the use of a rudder or skeg, these features can save you a great amount of energy and time in difficult conditions. Volumes have been written on the pros and cons of rudders versus skegs; it is ultimately a question of personal preference. Test paddle both.

Bulkheads

A *bulkhead* is a watertight wall within the kayak, usually placed fore and/or aft of the cockpit, dividing the kayak into sections. Touring kayaks usually have two bulkheads, but recreational kayaks may have one or none. Bulkheads provide flotation and dry storage compartments for gear. Without bulkheads, water can fill a kayak from bow to stern after a capsize. To compensate for the absence of bulkheads, paddlers must carefully and tightly position air-filled flotation bags to provide buoyancy and displace water in the event of a capsize. A boat with bulkheads is usually more convenient for learning and practicing braces and rolls.

Hatches

Hatches are resealable, watertight openings in the deck of a kayak that provide convenient access to a storage compartment. Large hatches allow for easy stowage of bulky gear but are more likely to leak. Small circular screw-on hatches are more watertight but less convenient. In a boat with bulkheads, hatches provide access to the front and rear compartments. Boats without bulkheads may lack hatches entirely. In such boats, gear is stowed via the cockpit in the areas behind the seat and in front of the foot pegs.

TEST PADDLING

It is extremely important to "try on" your boat prior to purchase. An excellent way to test a variety of boats is to attend a kayak symposium. There you can paddle a good selection of the latest-model kayaks and speak directly with the manufacturers' representatives. Symposiums are held in Massachusetts and southern Maine several times each summer (see Appendix A). Symposiums also offer a variety of workshops geared for the novice paddler. Other ways to try out boats is to take a class or tour, rent a kayak, or visit a kayak retailer that allows prospective purchasers to sample their fleet.

Boarding a kayak on the showroom floor can tell you a little, but paddling a kayak can tell you a lot. A word of caution, however: Inexperienced paddlers may be most comfortable initially in very stable kayaks and may therefore choose boats that could limit their enjoyment as their skills improve. Be aware of this pitfall, and try to choose a boat that challenges you, especially if you are a relatively athletic and adventurous person.

ESSENTIAL GEAR

tips for test paddling

1. **CHECK THE INS AND OUTS.** Test the cockpit for ease of entry and exit.

2. **ADJUST THE FOOT PEGS.** Your knees should be slightly bent and splayed as if there were a beach ball between them.

3. **CONSIDER THE FIT.** A kayak should feel snug around the hips and legs, but not so tight that it causes cramping. If the fit is close but not perfect, it's always possible to add foam for thigh padding and to change or adjust an uncomfortable seat. Don't forget to check foot space (size 13 won't fit in every boat).

4. **TAKE IT THROUGH A DRILL.** Find out how easily the boat turns, then paddle forward and backward and lean to test its stability. Check its tracking and its tendency to yaw. The boat should feel lively and responsive but not as if it has a mind of its own.

5. **SPEND TIME IN THE BOAT.** A kayak is a significant investment. Take your time.

6. **TEST SEVERAL MODELS.** Paddle kayaks of different sizes, shapes, and composition to find a boat that's right for you.

View from Boston Light on Little Brewster, Boston Harbor.

Novice kayakers are often surprised by the amount of gear necessary to outfit a sea kayak. The cost of your boat is generally only 50–75 percent of the total you'll spend to enter this sport. Don't skip any of the following *essential* gear: It is critical to your safety on the water.

Paddles

Don't underestimate the value of a good paddle. The price ranges from about $40 for a heavy aluminum shaft to more than $350 for a lightweight graphite design. While a novice need not buy the top of the line, any paddler would be well served by a light, well-designed paddle. If your budget requires you to compromise on some part of your equipment purchase, compromise on something else. One only has to paddle once with a high-quality paddle to be utterly convinced. Expect to pay at least $150.

Paddles differ from one another in configuration, weight, composition, shape, and length.

Configuration: Today's most popular paddles are *feathered*, meaning the blades are set roughly at right angles to each other. *Unfeathered* paddles have blades that lie on the same plane. Whether you want a feathered or unfeathered paddle is largely a matter of personal preference. Feathered paddles reduce wind resistance, but some claim that unfeathered paddles may reduce the likelihood of injury caused by turning the wrist.

Some paddlers compromise by purchasing a *breakdown* paddle that can be fitted together either way. These two-piece paddles also have the advantage of stowing conveniently within kayaks, car trunks, and luggage. One should not, however, frequently change the setting of an adjustable paddle because many paddling maneuvers (bracing, in particular) depend upon instinctive reaction, and a paddler needs to know instantly how the paddle is oriented. In addition, two-piece paddles require some attention to maintenance to keep the joint free from salt and grit.

Weight and composition: The weight of a paddle makes a difference. Paddles range in weight from less than 2 pounds to about 3.5 pounds. Find a paddle that weighs no more than 2.5 pounds. A paddle's weight is largely determined by the materials from which it is made. Fiberglass and wood paddles tend to fall acceptably in the midrange. If price is no object, ultralight carbon graphite paddles are terrific. Paddles to avoid have heavy aluminum shafts and plastic blades. These paddles (in a breakdown variety) may be used as a spare paddle to carry on your boat. When considering the weight of a paddle, test its swing weight by holding it horizontally and "air paddling." The paddle should feel well balanced and not excessively heavy at the blades. A light, well-designed paddle will save your arms and shoulders from unnecessary stress.

Blade shape: The choice of blade shape is mostly a matter of personal preference. Blades may be asymmetrical or symmetrical, short or long, wide or thin, flat or "spooned." Try a few different blades prior to purchase. Some general rules are that spooned blades provide more power but can increase flutter; dihedral blades help reduce flutter; asymmetrical blades improve efficiency while reducing the stress on forearms and wrist; wide blades put more pressure on arms but allow quick acceleration; and long, narrow blades do not accelerate quickly but can efficiently maintain cruising speeds and are easier on the arms. It's really not as confusing as it sounds. Most fine paddles intelligently combine the best attributes of several shapes. If your budget allows, purchase two paddles with different blade shapes (e.g., long/thin and short/wide) so you can match your paddle to touring conditions. For example, in wind or when carrying a heavy load, a long, thin paddle will be most comfortable. When racing in light wind, a shorter, wider blade is preferred.

Length: A correctly sized paddle fits both the paddler and the paddler's boat. Wider, deeper boats generally require longer paddles, while narrower boats demand shorter ones. The length of a paddle should also match one's style of paddling. Paddlers who favor slow, powerful strokes will enjoy a longer shaft. Paddlers preferring to paddle faster with less power will want a shorter shaft. Paddle length is sized in centimeters, with most paddles running from 210 to 250 centimeters and 230 centimeters an average length. The only foolproof way to choose a paddle is to test it in your own boat. Once again, it's really not as confusing as it sounds. More than 75 percent of paddlers use a 230-centimeter paddle.

Lastly, pay attention to the shape of the shaft. For comfort and a better grip, some paddlers prefer an oval shape, especially women with smaller hands.

Kayak symposia allow kayakers to test a variety of boats.

Drip rings and paddle leash: Drip rings are the indispensable plastic rings that keep water from running down the shaft. A paddle leash is a line or elastic cord attached to the paddle and also to your boat. Losing your paddle can be a matter of life or death, so it is advisable to use a leash. You can make one simply by purchasing a four- or five-foot length of 3/16" to 1/4" line. Paddle leashes are especially advisable for sit-on-tops.

Personal Flotation Devices (PFDs): Legally, you must always have a Coast Guard–approved PFD on board your kayak, and ideally you should *always wear it.* Quite simply, in the event of a capsize, it will be far too hard, time consuming, and energy draining to put on your PFD in the water. PFDs, in addition, provide additional insulation in cold Massachusetts waters. Consequently, choose this constant companion well, making sure you get the comfort and fit you need. There are racks of excellent PFDs available for kayakers, and your choice depends largely on personal preference. Kayakers usually wear a Class III Coast Guard–approved life vest. These jackets are close fitting and short enough in the back that they won't interfere with the cockpit edge or sprayskirt. Make sure that the cut allows unrestricted arm motion (to avoid chafing). Also check that the jacket does not ride up on your torso and end up near your chin. When testing the fit, look for snugness and adjustability; you may want to add a few layers beneath the jacket in inclement weather. Draining pockets are nice features, as are loops to hang whistles or lights. Sewing anything on a PFD voids its Coast Guard approval, so if you want a pocket, make sure the vest already has one. Lastly, think about increasing your visibility with a brightly colored or reflective PFD. Yellow, orange, and neon green are good choices. Red looks considerably darker when wet than on the showroom floor.

Good PFDs are expensive, so treat yours kindly. Store it out of direct sun and heat when not in use, and do not place anything on it that would compress the foam. Buoyancy is affected by age, so older PFDs must be water-tested to make sure they have sufficient buoyancy.

Sprayskirts (Spray Decks): Another essential piece of gear for most sea kayakers is a properly fitting sprayskirt. The purpose of a skirt is to keep you dry and to keep water from entering your kayak. Even if you're not planning to roll, a skirt keeps waves from swamp-

the savvy paddler:
the cost of an outfitted kayak

The following represents the approximate retail cost of an intermediate-priced touring kayak and all the essentials. Purchasers can save considerably by buying used equipment or finding items on sale. Expect to pay more for top-of-the-line quality and less for economy purchases.

Essential Items
Plastic Rotomolded Kayak with Rudder	$1,000.00
Paddle	150.00
Spare Paddle	50.00
Sprayskirt	50.00
PFD	75.00
Pump	24.00
Sponge	3.00
Paddle Float	32.00
Light or Strobe	10.00
Signaling Devices (Whistle, Mirror, and Flares)	32.00
Tow Rope and Pouch	35.00
First-Aid Kit	45.00
Chart	20.00
Total	**$1,526.00**

Optional Items
Wetsuit (full)	$130.00
Wetsuit (shortie)	65.00
Dry Suit	305.00
Dry Jacket	165.00
Neoprene Gloves	21.00
Neoprene Booties	24.00

ing your boat and paddle drips from chilling your legs. Many new kayakers fear the sprayskirt will trap them in their boats. A little experience soon dispels this fear (a correctly sized skirt removes quite easily), and kayakers are soon likely to feel more secure with their skirts firmly in place.

A sprayskirt must fit snugly around the cockpit coaming yet be easy to remove in the event of a capsize. Sprayskirts are made in several sizes, ensuring a proper fit for each boat. Skirts also come in a variety of materials, from coated nylon (the least expensive, coolest, and quickest to dry, but most apt to leak) to neoprene (the most expensive, durable, and waterproof, but warmest). Paddlers who never intend to master the Eskimo roll probably can survive quite well with a simple nylon sprayskirt. If your paddling demands mastery of the roll and frequent braces, it is best to invest in a sprayskirt that has, at the least, a neoprene spray deck and fabric upper. This is also a comfortable option, since neoprene is very warm and slow to dry. All skirts should be outfitted with a grab loop so paddlers can release the skirt quickly after capsizing.

How can you tell if your sprayskirt fits correctly? First, the skirt must fit both you and your kayak. Step into the skirt and pull it up just short of your armpits. Nylon sprayskirts have an elastic drawstring and often suspenders to keep the skirt in place. If you have a neoprene skirt, the tunnel (the upper half of a sprayskirt) should form a waterproof seal around your torso but not be uncomfortably constricting. Next, make sure the skirt opening fits the cockpit coaming. One test is to put the skirt on the cockpit coaming (without you in it), and then try to lift the boat up by the skirt. A properly fitting skirt will allow you to raise the boat for a few seconds before it slowly slips off. Too loose a skirt will slip off immediately, while one that's too tight won't quit at all. This test works well with fiberglass kayaks and less well with plastic kayaks whose coamings are thicker and more slippery. The best test is, of course, in the water. A new sprayskirt should not leak or be excessively hard to put on or remove.

Flotation (Buoyancy Bags) and Waterproof Gear Bags

If your kayak does not have bulkheads (see discussion, above), you need to outfit the kayak with a flotation system (fore and aft) in case of capsize. Without such a system, the kayak will quickly swamp and sink, or be so full of water that it's impossible to paddle. In boats without bulkheads, adequate buoyancy is achieved through the use of specially designed plastic air bags which are contoured to fit snugly in the kayaks' front and back compartments. The partially deflated bags are inserted in the boat, then inflated and wedged tightly behind the kayak's seat and in front of the paddler's legs. The bags must fill the entire area forward of the foot pegs and behind the paddler. Webbing or straps should secure the bags in place. Before any outing, the paddler must check these bags to ensure that they are properly inflated. *Never* paddle without a set of flotation bags, and check them frequently for tears and wear.

If you are carrying gear in a kayak without bulkheads, use the type of waterproof gear bags that can be loaded, sealed, and then inflated. These bags provide both displacement and flotation and fit snugly in their compartments. Look for bags that have long inflation tubes so that more air can be added after the bags are stuffed in place.

Even if your boat has bulkheads, carry flotation bags within the bulkheads in case the bulkheads or hatches leak. This backup system of flotation can be a lifesaver. The bags will ensure that your gear will stay dry while also giving the boat some buoyancy insurance. Waterproof gear bags come in a variety of sizes and styles to fit your needs. If commercially available gear bags are too pricey, stow your gear in two heavy-duty plastic garbage bags. These bags must be carefully sealed and placed within a canvas or nylon bag. Rough surfaces inside the boat quickly tear unprotected plastic bags.

Pump, Bailers, and Sponges

Every boat has to carry an effective device to rid the boat of water. Depending on your budget, this may mean a mounted electric pump or a bleach bottle with the bottom cut off. A happy medium is a plastic hand-held bilge pump, commonly available at marine and outdoor-equipment stores. It is relatively inexpensive and light and fairly efficient. Stow it next to the seat and secure it with a cord. If you carry it under the bungees on the outside of the boat, make sure it has a cord attached; rough seas or rescue attempts can dislodge it just when you need it. In addition, make sure your bilge pump has a flotation collar so that it will float if knocked overboard. Lastly, carry a large natural or synthetic sponge to soak up small amounts of water.

Spare Paddle

Don't skip this potentially lifesaving equipment. If money is an issue, pick up a used or inexpensive paddle to keep as a spare on deck.

Paddle Float

A paddle float is a rescue device that should be carried by *all* paddlers, but it is especially critical for those who paddle solo. Inexpensive, lightweight, and easy to stow, a paddle float consists of an inflatable plastic bag or foam "mitten" that slips over the blade of a paddle. If plastic, the float is then inflated and secured on the blade. When an outfitted paddle is attached to the bungees behind the cockpit (creating a stabilizing outrigger), an able paddler can climb into the boat without outside assistance. The paddle-float self-rescue is a very difficult maneuver in heavy seas but quite manageable in calm water. The technique should be learned and practiced to make this wee bit of equipment a real lifesaver.

Audible Signaling Device

Carry a device that can alert other boats to your position in the water. Lying low on the surface of the water, kayaks are not easily seen by other boats. The Coast Guard recommends a device that makes a sound audible for 0.5 nautical mile. One option is to buy a small freon-charged horn. It weighs less than an ounce, has a range up to a mile, and sounds about a hundred times before a new cartridge is needed. The horn is easily stashed in a PFD pocket, and an extra cartridge can be stowed on the boat. An alternative is to buy a simple pea-less whistle at a marine supply store and clip it on your PFD.

Visual Signaling Device/Emergency Signal Kit

Every paddler should carry an emergency signaling kit in the event that help must be summoned. It is advisable to carry more than one device, because the effectiveness of any one depends on the particular emergency conditions. Signaling devices also often fail, necessitating the use of a backup system. Suggested devices include flares, smoke, signaling mirrors, and strobe lights. Note that flares, particularly the small hand-held ones, often fail due to age, water damage, or defect. Flare guns are considerably more reliable but also more expensive and bulky. Smoke-generating devices are inexpensive and more reliable, but they may have limited effectiveness because wind dissipates smoke quickly. Signal mirrors are low-cost devices that should be carried on every kayak. Lastly, a bright, compact strobe is a light, reliable means of signaling that every paddler should attach to their PFDs.

Any signaling device is useless unless you know how to operate and maintain it. Store all devices where they may be reached in the event of an emergency. The pockets of your PFD are the best choice, as long as the devices can be kept from water damage. Do not pack them away in gear bags in the bottom of your storage compartments. They must be accessible to be useful!

Personal Tow System

All paddlers should carry a towline of at least fifty feet of 1/4" (minimum) line. If you or another paddler is incapacitated, this line will be indispensable. Personal towing systems are sold in compact, ready-made pouches that are worn around a paddler's waist, on the outside of the PFD. Inside the pouch is the towline, which should be long enough to stretch a kayak length between boats. Essential to this system is a quick release mechanism (buckle or Velcro) on the waist belt which the tower can quickly disengage if problems arise. Personal towing systems are available at marine and outdoor-supply stores. Like your PFD, the pouch should be an essential part of your kayaking wardrobe.

Rope Stirrup

All paddlers should carry a simple thirteen-foot loop of rope to use as an emergency stirrup to aid the re-entry of a paddler in the water. When the loop is hung around the cockpit coaming, it provides a foothold to help a tired paddler climb back into the cockpit. This inexpensive and simple device can be a lifesaver in cold water and can be easily stored in your tow-system pouch.

Light

According to law, kayakers paddling after dark must carry a light to prevent collision. A high-intensity diver's flashlight is a good choice. Obviously any flashlight you take on board should be waterproof. Some paddlers favor a climber's headlamp for night paddling. Disposable glow sticks are another option. They can be activated as needed and wrapped around one's hat or clothing as well as around the boat's fore and aft toggles. These do not cast light, of course, but they do increase visibility.

Secondly, kayakers must also carry a distress signal at night. Acceptable devices include either an approved distress light (such as a strobe light) or flares. (For more about flares and strobe lights, see emergency signaling, above.)

Compass

Never leave home without a compass. You can choose a marine compass that can be mounted onto the deck of your kayak or a hand-held hiker's compass, which is lighter and more economical. The mounted compass is easier to use and is much more likely to accompany you on your trips. It is easier to read and does not require you to stop paddling to adjust the setting. Deck-mounted compasses are easily damaged, however, particularly during boat transport, so you may want to consider the mounted types that are removable. Lastly, if you are purchasing a hiker's compass, choose one that is mounted on a clear plastic straight edge (to align with the bow of your boat when setting a course).

Charts

Always carry a chart (marine map) of the area in which you'll be paddling. Charts are available at marine stores or can be ordered from National Oceanic and Atmospheric Administration (NOAA) via mail or the Internet. Charts should be kept on deck under the bungees in front of the cockpit. Waterproof map holders keep charts dry, or you can buy the more expensive waterproof charts. Don't keep maps on deck in zip-lock bags, for inevitably these bags leak and tear. (See Appendix B for more information on charts.)

First-Aid Kit

Paddlers should always keep a standard first-aid kit aboard their kayaks in an easily accessible location. Waterproof kits specifically for boating are available. A few small items, such as aspirin, band-aids, and seasickness pills, should be stored in the pocket of your PFD for immediate access.

Kayak Repair Kit

Every kayak should have at least a rudimentary repair kit. At the minimum, paddlers should bring along a small roll of waterproof duct tape and a knife for emergency repairs. For extended outings a more complete kit is advisable.

Adequate Clothing

Clothing sufficient to protect you from water, wind, and sun is a critical component of your safety equipment. Dress in layers that can be shed or supplemented depending on the conditions. Always carry a second set of warm, dry clothing in a waterproof bag within your boat for emergency use.

Starting from the top, a brimmed hat is critical in all seasons to shield you from the sun and/or to keep you warm. Use cords or a hat clip to keep the hat from blowing away. Polarized sunglasses with an eyeglass cord are also a necessity for most kayakers. For upper body comfort, a polypropylene top wicks moisture away from the skin and retains warmth even when wet. Avoid cotton. Wind jackets are essential on cool days. Wetsuits, either short or long overalls, are recommended for cool weather or spring paddling on cool water.

Dry suits are the only kayaking gear that will keep a paddler from direct contact with cold water, thus offering the best protection from hypothermia. Dry suits are entirely waterproof and have snug rubber seals at the neck, wrists, and ankles. These suits are very expensive, but they are a *necessity* for early-spring and winter trips in Massachusetts. Three-season kayakers may wear a wetsuit and a dry top but must realize that this combination offers significantly less protection.

Lastly, neoprene booties offer warmth and protection for cold toes. Polypropylene or wool socks under sandals or sea shoes can also suffice. For paddlers' hands, neoprene gloves provide warmth

VHF marine radio vs. cellular phones

While a cell phone is convenient to carry aboard a kayak (and one should certainly do so), they have limitations at sea. Frequently kayakers are out of range of cell towers, and cell phones generally cannot provide ship-to-ship communications. Distress calls on a cell phone will be heard only by the party called, not by all who might respond with assistance. Lastly, a caller's location usually cannot be pinpointed by a call.

VHF marine radios, on the other hand, were designed with sea safety in mind. A distress call will be received not only by the Coast Guard, but by ships which may be in a position to give immediate assistance. By monitoring VHF channel 16, a kayaker receives the Coast Guard's storm warnings and other urgent marine information. In addition, VHF marine radios can be used anywhere in the world. If you plan to paddle far from shore or need to ensure communication with other kayakers or boaters, there is no substitute for a VHF radio.

and an adequate grip. Alternatively, "poogies" attach to the paddle and shield hands from cold spray and wind.

Food and Water

It is essential to your safety that you eat and drink well while paddling. A well-fueled body will perform better and stay warmer in times of crisis. Place high-energy snacks and sweet liquids within easy access. Don't skimp on quantities or quality; it could save your life. (See *Hypothermia*, chapter 2.)

Other Safety Equipment

Depending on your trip's duration and destination, you may want to carry additional safety equipment, such as the following:

Communication Equipment: Many paddlers carry cellular phones for emergency communication. If you own one already, carry it when paddling within range of a cell tower. (To call the Coast Guard, dial *CG.) Many kayakers also carry VHF radios for emergency signaling and to communicate with other boats or with kayaks in your own party. VHF radios have a range of five to ten miles and can be a very effective way to signal distress. Both cell phones and radios must, of course, be carried in a waterproof pouch.

Weather Radio: Weather radios are specialized radios that receive only NOAA broadcast channels and thus provide constant and up-to-the-minute information on current weather conditions and forecasts. They are available in lightweight and compact sizes and are very inexpensive. Weather radios are essential for multiday paddling trips and extremely useful for all ocean kayakers.

Emergency Position–Indicating Radio Beacons (EPIRBs): EPIRBs send distress signals which potentially can be detected over a very wide range. One type of EPIRB sends signals that are picked up by an international network of search-and-rescue satellites. These devices cost several hundred dollars and can be activated only once.

chapter
two

KAYAK SAFETY
TRIP PREPARATION AND OCEAN HAZARDS

CHAPTER 1 focused on all the "stuff" needed to start you paddling and keep you safe. Ultimately, however, sea kayaking is not about "stuff." While your equipment is your ticket and your lifeline, it's how you use it that makes all the difference. Kayaking is about skill, understanding your environment, knowing your limits, and respecting the immense power of the sea. With each stroke you become stronger and wiser. You learn to read the sea and anticipate hazards before they endanger you.

In this chapter, you'll learn how to prepare yourself for a safe paddle by arming yourself with information. You'll learn how to recognize common ocean hazards caused by Massachusetts weather, topography, tides, and current. Also included is a bit of "preventive kayaking": how to avoid, detect, and treat hypothermia, the most dangerous threat to New England kayakers.

INSTRUCTION AND PRACTICE:
The Key to Safe Paddling

A generation of inexpensive, stable boats has made kayaking instantly accessible. Without instruction, however, inexperienced kayakers

Pool sessions are a great way to learn to Eskimo Roll.

can quickly get themselves into deep trouble. On-water kayaking clinics with qualified instructors send novices paddling in the right direction, stop bad habits before they start, and teach critical safety and rescue skills. Instruction can be found in a variety of settings, from symposiums to tours, group lessons to private lessons. Informal assistance can also be gained from kayaking clubs or simply by paddling with more-experienced kayakers.

It is especially important to develop confidence and proficiency paddling in rough water. This is done most safely in the company of experienced kayakers or by attending on-water clinics. Gain as much experience as you can in wind, surf, waves, and currents. In the presence of instructors and more-experienced paddlers, ask questions, try difficult maneuvers, and attempt rescues. To find a convenient source of instruction, consult the list of kayaking clubs, outfitters and organizations found in Appendix A.

PADDLING IN WIND

The Basics

Wind is a sea kayaker's constant companion but not his best friend. Strong winds chill, exhaust, impede, and blow off course even the most proficient paddlers. Wind also generates waves that frustrate and endanger. Therefore kayakers must be constantly vigilant about wind and learn how to interpret forecasts; how to handle boats in wind; how to paddle in waves; and how to find protected places to launch, land, and paddle.

Wind direction is described by its place of origin. For example, a westerly wind blows from the west. Its speed is often expressed in knots or by its range on the Beaufort Wind Scale (see figure 2.1). From June to September in Massachusetts, the prevailing winds range from west to southwest. From midfall to midspring, these winds shift between west and north. The most mild winds occur between May and August, while the strongest blow from December to March. New England's worst weather and winds arrive with the "nor'easters" in fall and winter.

How much wind is too much for a kayaker? Most novices start to feel uncomfortable in winds above fifteen knots, nearly all kayakers are unable to make real progress against winds over thirty knots, and it is recommended that all paddlers avoid winds over thirty-five knots. Paddling into a strong headwind is dangerous because paddlers can't rest without losing ground. In questionable weather, find protected areas to paddle where waves and wind fall within your paddling abilities. Finally, learn to recognize what conditions are just too hard for you to handle.

When the winds are blowing offshore, look for sheltered places to kayak. Areas where the coast has a high and continuous line of cliffs, steep hillsides close to the shore, a tall forest bordering the beach or a continuous dune ridge provide shelter from the wind. Be particularly cautious when a break occurs in the sheltering barrier, because high and dangerous winds are likely to funnel through the break. Hazardous areas include narrow entrances to bays, harbors, and river mouths.

Kayakers should take the following precautions in offshore wind: Before launching, listen to a weather forecast. Know the wind direction and expected changes. Use common sense and caution at the launch site. Don't be fooled by the calm sea close to shore. If

The Beaufort Wind Scale (edited for kayakers)

Beaufort Force No.	Speed (mph)	Rating	Wind State	Sea Conditions
0	0	Very easy	Calm	Mirror like
1	1–3	Very easy	Light air	Ripples. Great for novices.
2	4–6	Easy	Light	Small wavelets, not breaking.
3	7–11	Fair	Gentle breeze	Few, scattered white-caps.
4	12–16	Moderate	Moderate breeze	Fairly frequent white-caps. Novices should seek protected paddling, unless onshore wind.
5	17–21	Moderately difficult	Fresh breeze	Whitecaps prevalent. Longer, moderate waves. Paddling into wind is difficult. Dangerous for novices on open water.
6	22–28	Difficult	Strong breeze	Large waves forming. Whitecaps every-where. Small-craft warnings. Rescues become difficult.
7	29–35	Very difficult	Moderate gale	Large breaking waves, foam, spray. Sea very rough. Communication difficult. Rescues very difficult.
8	36–45	Dangerous	Gale	Large waves breaking continuously. Open water extremely dangerous. Wind catches kayak and paddles. Intense foam, spray. Rescues almost impossible.

Beaufort Wind Scale reaches Force 12 (hurricane), but the upper limit for expert kayakers on open water is Force 8

The Beaufort Wind Scale.

whitecaps are visible a distance offshore, postpone your paddle or amend your route to hug the coastline. If the wind shifts while you are paddling, head toward shore *immediately*. Don't wait for conditions to deteriorate.

Onshore Wind

Onshore breezes (wind blowing from sea to shore) also create problems for kayakers. An onshore wind creates waves that make launching and landing difficult. Once past the rough surf zone, however, paddlers usually find much calmer water. Thus a route paralleling the coastline is generally the safest route for kayakers in an onshore wind. Paddlers must be particularly careful if the forecast predicts rising onshore winds, because returning to the beach will become increasingly difficult. In windy conditions, choose a protected cove for put-in and takeout to avoid dangerous wind-generated surf.

Avoiding Wind

A good strategy for novice kayakers concerned about wind and waves is avoidance. The first step is to obtain a current *marine* weather report. The easiest and quickest way is to purchase an inexpensive weather radio. These radios receive continuous marine forecasts broadcast by NOAA, updated every few hours. It is very important to consult a *marine* weather forecast and not rely simply on land forecasts. Marine forecasts deliver critical information on wind speed, wave heights, sea breezes, fog, and squalls. Especially with regard to wind speed, land forecasts can be misleading. Wind accelerates over water, and a land forecast can often underestimate wind by 50 to 100 percent. If you're caught without a weather radio, abbreviated (and not nearly as informative) marine forecasts are broadcast on commercial AM and FM stations (e.g., WBZ, 1030 AM, every ten minutes). Other stations in Massachusetts broadcasting marine forecasts are listed in *Eldridge Tide and Pilot Book*.

Alternatively, find up-to-date marine weather information on several websites (see box). Another option is to call the Coast Guard for the latest forecast. An additional resource by phone is the recorded National Weather Service forecast for Massachusetts, which includes specific coastal forecasts, available at 508-822-0634. Listen for wind velocity, wind direction, state of the seas, and anticipated changes.

obtaining a weather report on the internet

The internet is a great place to obtain quickly an up-to-date marine weather forecast. Check out the National Weather Service's Boston site at www.tgsv5.nws.noaa.gov/er/box for forecasts within Massachusetts. For the latest marine weather forecast for the northeastern states, check: www.nws.fsu.edu/buoy/ne.html. This is an interactive site with incredible specificity. If you know the *buoy number* in the area where you'll be paddling (check on your marine chart), enter that number and receive the current weather conditions and forecast at that particular buoy! Another good weather site is Intellicast, found at www.intellicast.com/weather/usa/. Most of these sites (and more) can be easily found through links on the excellent North Shore Paddlers Network site, www.nspn.org.

Next, when wind is an issue, kayakers should take out their charts and search for relatively protected areas to paddle. The key is *wind direction*. Kayakers should avoid areas where the fetch (the distance the wind travels over the water) is great. Bays and tidal rivers may offer refuge from wind and waves, but not always. If the wind is funneling right up a river or blowing directly into a bay, it will be a poor choice. On the other hand, if the wind is blowing from the southwest and the chosen route is just north of a large cape, the land mass may block the worst effects of the wind as long as kayakers stay close to shore. The more kayakers know about the topography of the coastline and the wind's predicted direction and velocity, the better they'll be able to gauge the wind's effects on their proposed course. In calculating the wind's effect, tides and currents must also be considered. (See *Understanding Tides*, page 32)

PADDLING IN WAVES

Sea kayakers must learn how to read the water and detect hazardous waves. Mastery of surf and rough water requires expertise, practice, and experience, but avoiding trouble often can be accomplished by the observant beginner. Described below are common types of dangerous waves; dumpers, boomers, and clapotis, and tips on avoiding them.

Dumpers

Dumpers are the thunderous waves that break onto a beach with explosive force. They are extremely dangerous to kayakers because of their violently falling water and strong undertows (currents that run out to sea). Dumpers occur when waves hit a beach with a steeply shelving bottom. Beaches with gradual slopes produce waves that break much more gently. Launching or landing on a beach with dumping waves should always be avoided. When choosing your route, check your chart carefully to detect beaches where dumpers are likely to form, and plan accordingly.

Boomers

A *boomer* is an offshore breaking wave created by a sudden change in water depth. Boomers are dangerous because they catch kayakers unaware and can capsize a kayak far from shore. They often occur in "rock gardens," where the bottom of the sea is strewn with boulders, reefs, or rocky pinnacles. Boomers are difficult to avoid because coastal kayakers may not always know that they are passing over submerged objects. They are also difficult to detect because they do not "boom" with every swell. In order to break, the swell must be a certain height.

To avoid boomers, check your chart carefully for rocks, especially subtidal and intertidal rocks. Intertidal rocks are marked by asterisks (*) and subtidal by plus signs (+); see *Reading Charts*, Appendix B. Once on the water, scan the rocky areas you have identified for telltale foam or breaking waves. If you spot a boomer or can locate an area where one is likely to occur, paddle around and not through it. If you don't have a detailed chart, scan the water ahead for signs of boomers. Steer clear of areas where rocks peek through the surface.

Clapotis

Kayakers must also avoid areas of *clapotis*, where irregular standing waves converge and break unpredictably. Clapotis occurs when waves hit steep barriers such as cliffs, headlands, piers, and sea walls. Waves bounce back off these surfaces and create a confused and dangerous sea. To avoid clapotis, keep a safe distance from steep-sided obstructions. Usually the area of standing waves does not extend too far out to sea, so paddlers can safely set a course that parallels the shoreline.

Tidal Races

Tidal races also produce dangerous waves. A tidal race occurs when a tidal stream accelerates due to the narrowing of a channel. The constriction and acceleration create waves that can topple a kayak. When a tidal race flows into swell, more breaking waves are created. A tidal race also refers to water that accelerates when squeezed around a headland. A related phenomenon, *overfall*, occurs when there is a reduction in water depth. When water flows over a sandbar, for example, the vertical constriction causes the water to accelerate, thus producing waves.

A very hazardous situation develops when there is a strong outflow of water at a river's mouth into ocean swell. Paddlers must be especially careful at ebb tide, when water tends to rush out faster through rivers or channels and when sandbars are exposed or closer to the surface, thus creating overfall or breaking waves. In some cases, as when the Merrimack River flows into Plum Island Sound, it may be necessary to portage to avoid trouble.

UNDERSTANDING TIDES

Sea kayakers must understand the influence of tides. Paddling *with* the tide can make a twenty-mile tour a breeze. *Against* the tide, the same distance can be a nightmare. Tides erase easy landings, uncover sand spits, produce miles of mud flats, and flood favorite picnic spots. They also produce dangerous waves and strong currents. Learn to respect the power of tides whenever you venture out onto the ocean.

The Basics

Tides are created by the gravitational influence of the moon. In Massachusetts, there are two high and two low tides every day, about six hours and twelve minutes apart. The time of the tides changes about fifty minutes each day. Thus if high tide is at 8:00 A.M. today, it will be at 8:50 A.M. tomorrow. When the tide is coming in, it is *flooding*. When it is going out, it is *ebbing*.

It is very useful for paddlers to know how fast the tide is running at any particular time. For a short duration, usually at high tide and at low tide, there is a period of *slack water*, when the movement of water is at its slowest and currents at their weakest. The "rule of twelfths," allows easy estimation of how much the tide will rise or fall (or how strong the current will be) during any hour of its six-hour cycle. The tide rises:

1/12 the first hour	3/12 the fourth hour
2/12 the second hour	2/12 the fifth hour
3/12 the third hour	1/12 the sixth hour

This pattern (1-2-3-3-2-1) indicates that the tide rises faster at the center of its cycle and tapers off at either end. Usually, tidal streams will be at their slowest at high and low tide. This general rule, however, has exceptions, and a current table, when available, must be consulted when paddling in areas of strong tidal currents.

Twice monthly, just after the full moon and new moon, there are *spring* tides, which rise higher and fall lower than average tides. Currents are stronger at these times. (Note that these tides have nothing to do with the spring season.) *Neap* tides also occur twice a month, falling between the two spring tides (halfway between the new and full moon). Neap tides are below-average tides, rising not quite as high and not quite so low as an average tide. Lastly, when the moon is closest to the earth, it is in *perigee*. When farthest away, it is in *apogee*. When perigee coincides with a spring tide (a full moon or new moon), the tides and currents will be at their most extreme.

So, how do you use all this obtuse information? Fortunately, kayakers need not memorize the phases of the moon. The trip descriptions in this book alert paddlers to general tidal influences. And before setting out on any trip, paddlers can check tide tables and, if necessary, current tables. For all outings, follow the steps below:

Consult a Tide and Current Table

A handy and vastly informative book to have on hand is *Eldridge Tide and Pilot Book*. Published yearly, *Eldridge* contains tide tables for the entire East Coast, from Maine to Florida. For each day of the year, it indicates the time of high and low tides for sixty-eight specific Massachusetts sites from Newburyport to Westport Harbor. Complete tables of daily current predictions are included for Cape Cod Canal, Pollock Rip, and Woods Hole. Eldridge also shows predictions of current change and velocity for sixty-four additional sites in Massachusetts. The uninitiated may find this encyclopedic manual daunting, but it is really quite easy to use.

Another way to obtain daily information on tides is over the Internet. Check NOAA's site for Massachusetts at www.nws.noaa.gov/er/box/matides.html. There you'll find data for forty locations, listing high and low tides for the next four days.

Daily newspapers (*Boston Globe, Boston Herald*, etc.) give the high and low tides for Boston Harbor (or other local harbors, depending on the paper's place of origin), but paddlers often need more site-specific information than newspapers routinely provide. Times of high tide can differ by more than *three* hours in certain locations in Massachusetts, so you need to check your location specifically.

Consult Your Chart

Once you know the times of high and low tide, check your chart to determine how the tides will influence your trip. Not all areas of the coast will be greatly affected by tides. In general, kayakers have little to worry about when paddling along the open coastline. Places of concern for kayakers include deep harbors with narrow entrances, estuaries where rivers drain a large amount of water, the area around a headland, and anywhere the flow of tidal water is constricted by natural landforms or artificial barriers. Remember that water can be constricted vertically as well as horizontally, so check the chart for sandbars, reefs, or other shallow areas that cause tidal currents to accelerate.

If your route is affected by tides, you may need to adjust the timing of your trip or the location of your put-in and takeout in order to use tidal flow to your advantage. Plot your journey so that you are paddling with the tide in areas where tidal influence is strong. If you can't avoid kayaking against the tide, plan to avoid such paddling late in the day when your energy is spent. If possible, do your toughest paddling first and then ride the tide home. When paddling against the current, kayakers can paddle from eddy to eddy ("eddy hop") to avoid swiftest water. In areas where the tidal current exceeds or even approaches 3 knots, do not attempt to paddle against the tide. Even with currents of 1.5 to 2 knots, an extended passage will be very difficult for a novice.

Learning to plan a trip with charts, tide tables, and current tables takes practice. Novices should take advantage of every opportunity to learn. When paddling with more-experienced kayakers, pick their brains for their trip-planning criteria. It is tempting to "show and go" and let others worry about the tides. But you'll learn more if you participate actively in trip planning and understand why a particular route is chosen. Eventually you will be making these decisions yourself.

Check for Tide–Generated Hazards

Using your chart, you may be able to predict the presence of the following tide-generated hazards. Once in the water, knowledge of the tide's strength and direction can help you avoid or anticipate these hazardous conditions.

Tidal Current and Opposing Wind. The most common tidal hazard to kayakers is fast tidal water flowing into strong wind, which causes a rapid and often dramatic increase in wave steepness. Be aware of the direction of the current in relation to the wind, and be mindful that the wind can change direction and velocity very suddenly. In contrast, when the wind blows in the same direction as the current, the wind actually smooths out the sea. This may lead an unsuspecting paddler to wander far from shore on a smooth sea, only to be caught in dangerous waves when the current inevitably reverses.

Tidal Current and Narrow Passages. When a waterway narrows, horizontally or vertically, its current speed increases. Coastal kayakers routinely wander through narrow passages, between rocks and offshore islands, between islands and the mainland, and between two offshore islands. When paddling through such passages, kayakers must be ready for sudden increases in current, perhaps with accompanying waves and overfalls. In any waterway, the fastest-flowing water will be at the center, so to avoid excessive current stick closer to the channel sides.

Tide Rips. A tide rip is an area of fast-flowing, turbulent water with steep waves that occurs whenever the smooth flow of a strong current is abruptly altered. Rips commonly occur in narrow passages, over isolated shoals well offshore, at prominent points of land along the shore, and over sand spits. The severity of a tide rip builds if the wind blows counter to the current. Prominent tide rips are often indicated on marine charts, but small rips or rips very close to land may not be shown. Kayakers must always be alert to areas of whitecaps occurring in a channel, off a point of land, or above a shoal or sandbar. Tide rips may also appear as a patch of dark water. Beware of water sounding like the rapids on a river. Give any suspicious areas wide berth.

Kayakers must watch especially for hazardous waves occurring off headlands. A headland jutting into a fast-moving tidal stream can cause water to accelerate off its end, forming a tide rip. Rough water may extend for considerable distance from the landform. In addition, headlands usually have underwater shallows extending well out to sea. Water rushing over these underwater shelves produces overfalls. The best rule of thumb is to pass a headland a sufficient distance from shore to avoid getting caught in tide rips or reflected and refracting waves.

Obstructed Currents. Another common hazard to kayakers occurs when a strong current is interrupted by a bridge support, rock, island, buoy, or similar obstruction. Waves can build on the upstream side where the current is forced to change direction abruptly. This rough water can upset an unobservant kayaker, especially if approached too quickly. Kayakers should steer well clear of any obstructions and be particularly vigilant when carried forward rapidly by a swift current.

USING MARINE CHARTS

Reading marine charts is an art that requires mastery by coastal kayakers. Hidden in their somewhat arcane iconography (and often excessively small print) is valuable information regarding marine hazards, location of navigational aids (buoys, lighthouses, etc.), condition of landing and launching sites, and more. The maps included in this book may occasionally be sufficient to guide a kayaker under ideal conditions, but a wise kayaker will *always* bring along a chart of the area. In the event of inclement weather or emergency, paddlers need to know as much as possible about the area in which they're navigating.

Appendix B describes how to obtain and read a nautical chart. It describes resources useful to the Massachusetts kayaker, but it does not delve deeply into the art of navigating. For such information and more, consult *Fundamentals of Kayak Navigation* by David Burch (Globe Pequot Press, 1993). For those overwhelmed by the detail of this treatise, I recommend *The Coastal Kayaker's Manual* by Randel Washburne (Globe Pequot Press, 1998).

Remember that a good dose of common sense can help immensely to keep kayakers on track. Simple good habits like keeping a mental list of landmarks passed, looking backward as well as forward, and keeping track of time to estimate the distance paddled will go far toward helping paddlers find their way. In the enthusiasm of a launch, many forget to look behind them to memorize the landing area, or the landmarks that identify the entrance to the harbor or beach. Practic-

SOUNDINGS IN FEET

Example of a marine chart (Manchester Harbor).

ing these good habits on every paddle makes them second nature. Add to this the following skills, and you will be far less likely to lose your way.

Charts: A series of charts (or maps) of the Massachusetts coastline is published by the National Oceanic and Atmospheric Administration (NOAA). Many private publishers re-issue these charts in various forms, but paddlers can be assured of the most up-to-date charts (and usually the least expensive) by purchasing NOAA's charts. Charts can be mail-ordered directly from NOAA or found at the seventy-seven authorized marine outlets throughout Massachusetts. Visit your local marine shop for knowledgeable sales help and valuable regional information, or order directly from NOAA by writing the Distribution Division (N/ACC 3), National Ocean Service, 6501 Lafayette Avenue, Riverdale, MD 20737-1199. You may call 800-638-8972, or fax 301-436-6837. To determine which chart you need, NOAA issues a free catalog showing all available charts. This catalog also lists the names and addresses of all authorized dealers.

Chart Scale: Often several NOAA charts cover the same area. The difference is scale, and chart scale means a great deal to a kayaker. Kayakers can find both large- and small-scale charts. *Small-scale* charts cover large areas; thus landmarks on small-scale charts appear *small*. An example is a chart where the scale is one foot to 150,000 or even 250,000 feet (written as 1:150,000 or 1:250,000). Such a chart will usually lack the detail necessary for kayak navigation. On *large-scale* charts (where, for instance, one foot represents 10,000 feet) landmarks appear *large*. Such a chart, however, covers so small an area as to necessitate carrying several charts and having to piece them together on the deck of the kayak. The solution is to find a happy medium, perhaps 1:25,000 or 1:40,000. Often charts of this scale contain inserts depicted in larger scale, particularly around harbors.

Massachusetts Charts: Two particularly useful (and economical) NOAA charts for Massachusetts kayakers are No. 13274, *Portsmouth Harbor to Boston Harbor,* and No. 13229, *South Coast of Cape Cod and Buzzards Bay.* It is unfortunate that the whole Massachusetts coast is not similarly covered. Obtaining charts in appropriate scale for the rest of the coast necessitates the purchase of at least ten additional charts, or a chartkit (a collection of charts bound together for a particular region) is a significant investment. Many experienced kayakers enjoy the convenience of using NOAA Chart No. 13268, a relatively small-scale chart (1:80,000) that covers the entire Massachusetts Bay.

To protect your substantial investment, purchase a waterproof chart holder to keep your chart dry on deck. Don't rely on zip-lock bags, as they inevitably leak. Spraying charts with fixative (available at art supply stores) protects them from wear caused by folding and refolding. Alternatively, laminate charts by purchasing sheets of peel-off/stick-on laminate, available at most office supply stores. For detailed instruction on reading and interpreting marine charts, consult Appendix B.

OCEAN TRAFFIC HAZARDS

Kayakers' small size and slow speed place them at a distinct disadvantage in ocean traffic. In busy areas, kayakers must be constantly vigilant about the movement of other boats. Regardless of the law, kayakers must always yield the right of way, simply because other boats often cannot see them, or, even if they do, may not be able to maneuver fast enough to avoid collision. The following guidelines can help prevent accidents:

Increase visibility: Kayakers should choose bright colors for their boats, clothing, PFDs, and accessories. Paddle blades should be white or bright colored so they can be used for signaling.

Assume invisibility: Paddlers must always assume that other boaters do *not* see them. Kayakers must practice defensive paddling, giving other boats wide berth and staying far outside traffic lanes. When a kayak needs to be seen, the kayaker must act aggressively. Turning broadside and waving a paddle is the most eye-catching position.

Carry visual distress signals: As a last resort, kayakers should be prepared to send up flares or smoke to alert other boaters of their presence. As added protection, paddlers should also carry horns or whistles that can be accessed and sounded immediately.

Avoid shipping lanes: Kayakers should never, never place themselves in the path of a large ship. The height of the bow prevents most ships from seeing a kayak within 1,000 feet. Even if the kayak could be seen, an emergency stop can take half a mile for a medium-size cargo ship, and its turning radius requires hundreds of yards. If kayakers must cross shipping channels, careful scouting must be done. Great care must be taken, since large ships move deceptively fast. Kayakers should cross the lane perpendicularly to minimize the time spent in the danger zone.

Safety in numbers: When a group of kayakers crosses a channel, they should first scout the traffic, then travel together across the lane. This will increase their visibility.

Show consideration for working boats: Kayakers should watch lobster and other fishing boats carefully and stay well clear. Their occupants are working and may be preoccupied. As a common cour-

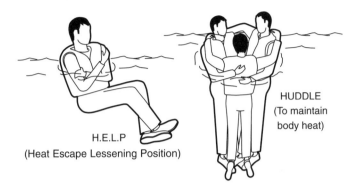

H.E.L.P
(Heat Escape Lessening Position)

HUDDLE
(To maintain
body heat)

tesy, kayakers should always avoid their path. One way kayakers can predict the path of lobster boats is to note the color and shape of the buoys on their boats and match them to the buoys in the water. Chances are the boats will be heading for the next buoy.

HYPOTHERMIA

No chapter on kayaking safety can be complete without a discussion of hypothermia. Hypothermia is a kayaker's most constant and dangerous threat. More kayaking fatalities are attributed to hypothermia than to any other cause. Hypothermia is the cooling of the body's core temperature, resulting in weakness, disorientation, unconsciousness, and sometimes death. Learning to prevent, recognize, and treat hypothermia is essential to all kayakers. General guidelines are described below, but hypothermia is so dangerous to Massachusetts paddlers that it is advisable to learn more about its prevention and treatment than can be described in this chapter. For more information on hypothermia and first aid, consult the bibliography on page 330.

Prevention

One prevents hypothermia by staying warm, hydrated, well fueled, and free from fatigue. This sounds relatively easy, until you consider that even a summer capsize in Massachusetts coastal waters can be problematic. Average water temperatures in Massachusetts Bay range from 43° F in spring, 61° F in summer, and 54° F in fall to 39° F in winter. Temperatures are similarly chilly in Nantucket Sound and just slightly warmer in Buzzards Bay. Thus an extended time in any of these waters even in July could easily bring on hypothermia.

Guard against hypothermia by practicing the following preventive measures:

Avoid Prolonged Exposure to Cold Water: Minimize exposure to cold water by acquiring the skills to get out of the water quickly after a capsize and back into your boat. Learning to Eskimo-roll saves you from uncomfortable wet exits and tedious bailing. Realistically, however, most paddlers can never claim a 100 percent reliable roll, so the mastery of other rescue skills is essential. Under controlled conditions and with the guidance of an instructor, paddling partners should practice until they can efficiently perform solo and assisted rescues in a variety of ocean conditions. In cold water, it is essential to remove yourself from the water as quickly as possible before you lose control and strength in your hands, arms, and legs. In 40° water, you'll lose function in your extremities in only a few minutes. Remember, if you can't perform an unassisted self-rescue, *never paddle alone.*

Dress for the Water: Dress for the temperature of the water, not the air. By doing so, your chances of surviving an extended period in the water improve dramatically. This may mean wearing a wetsuit, dry suit, or other insulated clothing on a summer day. Consequently, you may need to take measures to avoid overheating (or *hyperthermia*). To keep cool, douse yourself with sea water and drink plenty of fluids.

Keeping warm *in* water is very different from keeping warm on land. Layers alone are not adequate insulation against cold water. Clothing that keeps you warm on land may become nearly useless when wet. Thus the necessity for specialized clothing (i.e., neoprene wetsuits, gloves, and booties; dry suits or dry-top jackets). Dry suits, though expensive, offer the best protection, especially if a layer of warm fleece is worn underneath. For winter paddling in Massachusetts, a dry suit is a necessity.

To determine the need for protective clothing, consider the type of paddling you plan to do, the weather, and the water conditions. Dress more conservatively if you're trying an unfamiliar boat, paddling alone, attempting a difficult crossing, or fighting strong currents or waves. Taking risks means you may be taking a swim, so be prepared! Finally, remember *always* to stow a warm change of clothes in your kayak. This simple precaution may save a life.

Fuel Up: The body's ability to produce heat is enhanced when it is well fueled and well hydrated. Don't skip breakfast, and remember to include a bit of protein as well as a large portion of carbohydrates and sugar. Snack liberally on energy foods throughout the day (trail mix, energy bars, chocolate, etc.) and frequently drink water or fluid enhanced with electrolytes. Sweet drinks are especially valuable; they digest easier and more quickly than solid foods. Warm sweet drinks are the best, because they convert to energy even faster and should always be carried when paddling in the fall, winter, or spring (try warm jello). Lastly, drink before you feel thirsty. Thirst is often not a good indicator of your need for liquids.

Avoid Fatigue: Your body will be better able to ward off hypothermia if it's not fatigued. Set realistic paddling goals, and be flexible. Consult your charts before you set off, and know safe landing and resting places along your route.

Stay Warm: While hypothermia can be triggered quickly by a dunking in icy water, it can also result from a long period of mild chill. Enduring cold sea spray on your upper body for hours (or days), wearing damp clothes, or sleeping in an inadequate sleeping bag can slowly bring on hypothermia. Pay attention to keeping warm at all times, especially on multiday paddling trips. Pack your gear carefully to ensure that it remains dry and useful at takeout.

Windchill is also a common problem for ocean paddlers. To lessen its effects, wear headgear, gloves, and a wind-breaking paddling jacket. Your PFD also will provide insulation against the chilling effects of both wind and water.

Many shoulder season and winter paddlers carry a large sheet of bubble wrap to use as an insulating blanket in an emergency. It is lightweight and far more effective than a space blanket.

Conserve Your Energy—Don't Move! In most instances, do not attempt to swim in cold water. Unless you are extremely close to shore or are wearing good thermal protection, the energy required to swim will hasten the onset of hypothermia. Swimming speeds heat loss by circulating the cooled blood in your extremities to your somewhat warmer and more critical core (your heart, lungs, and brain). It is said that an average adult capsizing in 50° water has only a 50 percent chance of surviving a fifty-yard swim.

After capsizing, pull as much of your body out of the water as possible. Your body loses heat twenty-five times faster in cold water than in cold air. If you've lost your kayak, assume the "heat escape lessening position" (HELP) by crossing your arms across your chest, crossing your ankles, bending your knees to your chest, and keeping your thighs together (see figure 2.3). If others are in the water with you, huddle together to conserve body heat. Always keep your head above the cold water, because approximately 50–85 percent of heat loss is through your head. Lastly do not remove your clothes once immersed. Instead, tighten cuffs and collars, and zip and button outerwear to trap water warmed by your body and prevent colder water from flowing through.

Watch Companions for Signs of Hypothermia: Know the warning signs of hypothermia, and watch your companions carefully. They may not know that they are suffering from hypothermia. Keep an especially close watch on children, who are particularly susceptible to excessive heat loss. Others at risk include tall, thin people and paddlers of any size who lack a good layer of insulating fat. The following section describes the warning signs of hypothermia. Read it carefully.

Detection

During hypothermia the core body temperature drops from 98.6° to 90° or above (mild hypothermia) to below 90° (severe hypothermia). Warning signs of mild hypothermia include a loss of ability to reason normally and a loss of coordination. Look for the "umbles": a hypothermic paddler may fumble, mumble, grumble, bumble, and grumble. This is often accompanied by shivering, muscle weakness, ashen face, and stiffness. Be aware that victims often deny their condition.

In patients with severe hypothermia, shivering eventually stops because muscles grow too cold and the body uses up all available fuel. Muscles become so rigid that movement is impossible. The patient may suffer from hallucinations, confusion, and loss of memory. If the core body temperature continues to drop, coma, weak respiratory function, and heart arrhythmias may result. The entire body appears to shut down, and the victim in fact may appear dead.

Treatment

In many situations mild hypothermia may be effectively treated in the field, but severe hypothermia is a medical emergency and professional medical attention *must* be sought immediately. In any event, effective treatment of hypothermia requires great care and patience. Incorrect measures may seriously injure or even kill a severely hypothermic patient.

Mild Hypothermia: Early treatment of mild hypothermia is usually quite effective. Upon detection, stop paddling and get the victim to a safe, dry environment as quickly as possible. Second, prevent further heat loss by moving the victim to a warm place, removing wet clothes, and insulating the patient with dry clothes or warm human bodies (skin-to-skin contact in a sleeping bag can be effective). It is critically important to make sure the victim is *dry*. Shelter the victim from wind by erecting a tent or windbreak. If insulating material, like bubble wrap, is available, wrap the victim. Pay attention especially to warming the chest, neck, head, and torso. Third, administer warm, sweet drinks (hot jello is excellent, avoid alcohol and caffeine), offer simple sugars, and allow the patient to rest near a source of heat. Following recovery, watch the victim carefully for signs of relapse. Often the victim's internal temperature regulating mechanism is off-kilter, causing hypothermia to recur over the next few days.

Severe Hypothermia: Emergency medical attention should be sought immediately, for it is extremely difficult and risky to treat a victim in the field. The goal is to warm the injured party gently enough to avoid damage to the already weakened heart. You should prevent further heat loss by insulation, but do *not* attempt active rewarming. Keep the victim immobile in a supine position. Cover the torso, thighs, head, and neck with dry clothes or blankets. Handle the victim extremely gently. Do not stimulate, move, or try to warm the victim's extremities. If cold blood pooled in the arms and legs suddenly starts to circulate, it could cause a cold shock to the heart and lead to cardiac arrest.

If the victim appears dead, do not give up. Remember the adage, "No one is dead unless he's warm and dead." Look for a faint pulse or breathing. If none can be found after at least two minutes (heart and respiration may be extremely weak), then a qualified person may attempt cardiopulmonary resuscitation (CPR) if this can be done without delaying the arrival of expert medical attention. If a weak pulse is present do not attempt CPR, because it may cause fatal cardiac arrhythmia. In all cases of severe hypothermia, get help for the victim as quickly as possible.

COLD SHOCK

A related cold-water hazard is *cold shock*, a traumatic response to the body's sudden immersion in cold water. Cold water can trigger a reflexive gasp that draws water into the lungs, causing drowning. A PFD that keeps your head above water can prevent this aspiration of water. Also, sudden immersions can cause instant increases in heart rate and blood pressure, resulting in cardiac arrest. Lastly, immersion in very cold water can lead to loss of consciousness. Proper protective clothing reduces the risks of all of the above.

chapter
three

COASTAL ACCESS
IN
MASSACHUSETTS

A N UNFORTUNATE REALITY of Massachusetts sea kayaking is the scarcity of public access to the ocean. Today only about one-quarter of the state's coastline is publicly owned. A closer look reveals that most of the public coastline is concentrated in a small number of communities on Cape Cod. Furthermore, there is not only a shortage of statewide access points, there is also scant information on their location. Add to this a dearth of legal parking and the booming popularity of water sports, and you have a real challenge for Massachusetts paddlers. This chapter informs paddlers of their legal rights of access to the coast, describes resources that help paddlers find their way to the sea, and instructs kayakers on what they can do to protect and increase public access in Massachusetts.

UNDERSTANDING YOUR RIGHTS

The difference between coastal ownership in Massachusetts and all other coastal states (excluding Maine) is that in Massachusetts private landowners commonly own beach property down to the *low-tide* line. Thus paddlers usually *cannot* land on the wet sand for a picnic, a leg-stretching walk, or a long rest stop unless they have plotted their landing carefully to fall on a public beach or public accessway. In most other coastal states, by contrast, the public owns the land seaward of the *high-tide* line, and in some states, like California, public ownership extends even higher.

Why is Massachusetts different? According to the Massachusetts Supreme Judicial Court, the Commonwealth gave away title to the intertidal zone (the land between the mean high-tide line and low-tide line) in the 1640s to the upland owners. Forevermore, apparently, the wet-sand area, as well as the upland dry sand, became the private property of the upland owner.

Yet all was not lost, because this ownership came subject to a few very important *public* rights. The original law that granted private ownership reserved for the public the rights of "fishing, fowling, and navigation" in the intertidal zone. These reserved rights include the right to walk or otherwise pass freely within the intertidal shore in order to fish, fowl, or navigate. Courts have also held that the reserved rights include the "natural derivatives" of these activities. Thus "fishing" includes shellfishing, "fowling" probably includes bird-watching, and "navigation" allows the landing of a kayak and the carrying (or dragging) of a boat across the wet sand. The law is clear, nevertheless, that public rights do *not* include picnicking, sunbathing, or strolling in the intertidal zone.

Submerged lands, on the other hand, are almost always publicly held. Paddlers, therefore, can always walk or picnic in shallow water, as long as they are not using the intertidal zone. Exceptions do exist to the rule of private ownership to the low-tide mark, but these lands represent a small minority. One example is Provincetown, where large sections of the intertidal zone are publicly, not privately, owned.

FINDING ACCESS TO THE COAST: GUIDES AND RESOURCES

A couple of very useful resources identify some of the state's public lands and accessways. Foremost is Massachusetts Coastal Zone Management's (MCZM) *Massachusetts Coast Guide: Access to Public Open Spaces along the Shoreline, Volume I: Greater Boston Harbor and the North Shore.* Published in 1995, this volume is the bible of public accessways for the northern third of coastal Massachusetts. Included

Green crab, found off Monomoy Island, Chatham.

are twenty-four maps showing all public lands, descriptions of each public space, and information on parking and use restrictions. Copies of the guide are limited in number. Request a copy by contacting MCZM, 100 Cambridge Street, Boston, MA 02102; 617-727-9530. Internet users can find this guide on the Web at www.appgeo.com/atlas/project_source/czmat/czmat_fr.html. Paddlers can only hope that MCZM will publish additional volumes covering the remainder of the Massachusetts coast.

A second useful, but somewhat out-of-date, government publication is *Public Access to the Waters of Massachusetts*, published by the Public Access Board, a division of the Massachusetts Department of Fisheries, Wildlife & Environmental Law Enforcement. This book provides information and maps for all state-funded public landings. To receive a copy, contact the Public Access Board, 1440 Soldiers Field Road, Brighton, MA 02135; 617-727-1843.

Kayakers also can look for information on legal access in *Atlantic Coastal Kayaker*, a monthly publication dedicated to the art and enjoyment of sea-kayaking. Edited by Tamsin Venn, an Ipswich resident, this magazine includes trip descriptions as well as articles on Atlantic flora and fauna, kayaking safety, camping, and exhaustive lists of clubs, symposia, races, and other kayak happenings. To subscribe, write Atlantic Coastal Kayaker, P.O. Box 520, Ipswich, MA 01938 or log on at www.qed.com/ack/. In addition, kayakers can check out the Massachusetts trips described in Venn's *Sea Kayaking along the New England Coast* (Appalachian Mountain Club Books: Boston, 1991).

Lastly, kayakers can also find access information on the websites of two Massachusetts paddling clubs, the Boston Sea Kayakers Club (www.bskc.org) and the North Shore Paddlers Network (www.nspn.org). Since Internet resources are constantly expanding, kayakers should check the links to these sites for other new information sources.

WORKING FOR GREATER ACCESS
Historic Rights of Way to the Sea

The hidden wealth of historic rights of way is largely an untapped resource in Massachusetts coastal communities. Rediscovering and preserving a town's historic rights of way to the sea can significantly increase access for sea kayakers and the public. What are "historic rights of way to the sea"? Due to lack of funds, many coastal communities were unable to buy lengthy segments of shoreline to dedicate for public use. In lieu of large and costly segments of public land, towns provided coastal access for the local public by obtaining footpaths, landings and other rights of way between shore roads and the water's edge. Although generally of modest proportions, these historic town ways were rather numerous, as evidenced by recent inventories in Gloucester, Rockport, and Marblehead. Together these towns laid out a total of nearly 100 ways to the sea.

Over the years, many of these historic rights of way to the sea have been lost or forgotten. The circumstances of their disappearance are as varied as their modes of creation. Some ways vanished from private deeds when transfers of ownership took place, due to a lack of public vigilance and accurate record-keeping. Other access ways may still be officially "on the books" but are presently hidden and unknown as a result of concealment by abutting property owners. Many coastal landowners may be unaware that a public right of way abuts their property. A few landowners, however, are expert in the art of access intimidation. Cars parked to obstruct passage, crushed stone laid to make vehicular ways look like driveways, plantings obscuring where private lawns end and public paths begin, signs warning of fictitious hazards—the ruses are ingenious and often effective.

In the few towns where concerned citizens have worked together, much has been accomplished. The goal of historic rights of way preservation projects is to rediscover and, where possible, reassert public claims to a community's hidden and almost forgotten ways to the sea.

The preservation of historic ways to the sea cannot be achieved in Massachusetts without the involvement of citizen advocates. This is an area where diligent and civic-minded sea kayakers could really make a difference. Kayaking thrives when there is an abundance of public accessways and landings. Increase the number of access points in your own or favorite coastal community by starting or join-

Consult your tide tables! (Low tide off Monomoy Island.)

ing a preservation effort. MCZM offers a comprehensive guide to the process entitled *Preserving Historic Rights of Way to the Sea: A Practical Handbook for Reclaiming Public Access in Massachusetts* (1996). To obtain a free copy, contact MCZM 100 Cambridge Street, Boston, MA 02102; 617-727-9530.

Funding for Coastal Access Projects

Each year, two state grant programs give small citizen groups thousands of dollars to fund access-enhancing projects. Kayaking groups may apply to these grant programs to fund the preservation of historic rights of way to the sea, the clearing of a path, or the construction of a landing. Depending upon the nature of the proposed project, kayakers should consider the following programs:

1. Coastal Access Small Grants Program, Department of Environmental Management (DEM), 100 Cambridge Street, Room 1404, Boston, MA 02202; 617-727-3160.

    DEM awards small grants supporting local and regional projects that improve and enhance the general public's access to the coast. Principal categories of funding include, but are not limited to: 1) creating new coastal pathways; 2) enhancing or restoring existing coastal pathways; 3) reclaiming public accessways; and 4) developing educational initiatives around public coastal access. Maximum grant is $3,000.

2. Greenways and Trails Demonstration Grants Program, DEM, 100 Cambridge Street, Boston, MA 02202; 413-586-8706.

    DEM awards grants to support innovative greenway and trail projects throughout Massachusetts, particularly those projects which will serve as models for other greenway and trail initiatives. Possible grants include improving river access and promoting river protection. Maximum grant is $3,000.

    In addition to state grant programs, Recreation Equipment Incorporation (REI) of Seattle, Washington, and Reading, Massachusetts, offers an environmental small grants program. Grants are available to nonprofit organizations to promote "muscle-powered" outdoor sports, such as kayaking. For more information call REI at 800-999-4REI.

chapter four

ENVIRONMENTALLY SOUND KAYAKING

MASSACHUSETTS SEA KAYAKERS have terrific opportunities to view marine mammals and seabirds and to visit offshore islands and barrier beaches. If these activities are pursued
carelessly kayakers can cause unintended but serious harm to animals and the environment. The key to environmentally sound
kayaking is threefold: Ideally, all kayakers should acquire basic
knowledge about local wildlife and their habitat. Secondly, kayakers
should act as environmental stewards, taking positive steps to protect the environment and improve water quality. Third, whether
kayaking in a familiar or unfamiliar environment, paddlers can apply
a few general guidelines for kayaking without impact (KW/OI)
which will serve them well in any situation.

THE MASSACHUSETTS COASTAL ENVIRONMENT
Offshore Islands
Colonial Nesting Birds: About 100 islands off the coast of Massachusetts are used for nesting by migratory birds known as colonial
nesting seabirds and water birds. All colonial nesting birds depend
upon islands to provide safe, undisturbed, and predator-free places
for breeding, nesting, and raising their young. Any kayaker passing
one of these islands from spring to late summer can immediately

grasp why the birds are called "colonial." The birds tend to have small nesting territories, and often many pairs share an island. Certain islands attract thousands of mating pairs of various species. It is not uncommon to see cormorants and gulls crowding a rocky shoreline, with the upland accommodating herons, ibis, and egrets.

Several species of colonial nesting birds breed in Massachusetts. Some of these birds, such as herring gulls, black-backed gulls, and double-crested cormorants, are currently abundant. Less abundant but locally numerous are black guillemot, common eider, and black-crowned night-heron. A few, such as the roseate and least tern, are listed as endangered under the Endangered Species Act.

Spring and summer are the birds' most important seasons. From April through August the birds court, mate, lay and incubate their eggs, and raise their young. Disturbing nesting seabirds during this breeding and nesting time is extremely dangerous to the eggs and chicks. Repeated disturbances can threaten the health of a species, because some colonial nesting birds lay only one egg a year.

To protect these birds, kayakers should stay at least 100 yards from the islands and never land on or near a nesting colony during the critical spring and summer months. Since many seabirds build inconspicuous nests on rocky beaches or in crevices, a careless step from a kayak could destroy a nest or hatchling. Even without landing, approaching too close flushes birds from their nests, and a kayaker's lingering presence can cause permanent abandonment. Unguarded nests leave eggs vulnerable to predation and expose the eggs to fatal damage from heat, cold, and rain. At the very least, a kayaker's invasive approach forces the birds to use energy for defense instead of for incubating eggs and feeding their young.

Not every island is a nesting area for seabirds, of course. Kayakers will find that most of the documented nesting islands are identified in the trip descriptions. Some of these colonized islands are privately or federally protected sanctuaries and are so posted. Others may be obvious due to the presence of numerous gulls and cormorants. Kayakers wishing to explore offshore islands should choose the many islands where nesting does not occur. These islands are also more pleasant and safer for exploring, since gulls especially are known for their aggressive behavior toward intruders.

Seals: Some offshore islands in Massachusetts are also the winter home of harbor seals. In a few rare cases, they are the year-round home of gray seals. Harbor seals are usually seen from late fall to early spring. They winter here before returning to cooler Maine waters, where they breed and raise their pups. Like seabirds, seals breed in colonies on islands, ledges, or isolated stretches of coastline. In Massachusetts, gray seals are known to live and breed off southeastern Cape Cod (Monomoy Island National Wildlife Sanctuary) and on islands west of Nantucket. Seal pups are born in protected coves between mid-April and mid-June.

While harbor seals should never be approached or harassed, it is especially important to give wide berth to Massachusetts's resident gray seal colonies. Kayakers are more likely to encounter gray seals during vulnerable breeding and pupping periods, and human curiosity can pose a real hazard for pups. When kayaks approach colonized islands, frightened seals jump into the water to escape. Under these stressful conditions, mother seals may abandon their pups, and young seals may find it impossible to return to the safety of the ledges.

To protect seal colonies residing in Acadia National Park, the National Park Service set forth the following "boater ethics." These rules are equally applicable to seals in Massachusetts waters:

- Give seal haul-out areas the widest berth possible. Kayakers should maintain a 100-yard buffer zone from any island or ledge occupied by seals. Researchers have observed seals panicked by kayaks up to a mile away. They theorize that seals either retain genetic memories of being hunted by humans in kayaks or that a kayaker's profile and slow pace mimic those of a killer whale, one of their major predators.

- Retreat immediately if seals raise their necks or chests into the air, move toward the water, or enter the water. This behavior indicates that the seals are disturbed. Leave the area immediately because your presence prolongs their stress.

- View seals through binoculars. With glasses, kayakers can get excellent views from a safe distance.

Barrier Beach and Dunes

In several places along the Massachusetts coast, kayakers encounter barrier beaches. Barrier beaches are thin strips of sand and dunes separated from the mainland by salt marsh and tidal estuaries.

Examples include Plum Island in Newburyport, Crane Beach in Ipswich, Wingaersheek Beach in Gloucester, and Nauset Beach in Orleans. Barrier beaches are the mainland's first line of defense against the force of ocean storms. Without these beaches, productive salt marshes and the invaluable habitat they provide for shorebirds and spawning fish would cease to exist. Barrier beaches also provide habitat for several rare nesting birds, including the endangered least tern and piping plover.

The waters surrounding barrier beaches are some of the richest and most beautiful places to kayak. Paddlers must be aware, however, of the fragility of these areas. For instance, the vegetation growing on a barrier beach is the key to its survival. Without their sparse beach grass, sand dunes would quickly disappear. Dunes form when wind, carrying particles of sand, is slowed by stalks of grass. Losing momentum, the wind drops its load of sand. The grass anchors this new sand, and a dune is born. Beach grass is superbly adapted to grow in this poor soil, but it is easily destroyed by repeated trampling of its delicate stem and buds. To preserve barrier beaches, kayakers must stay off the dunes. Growing on the secondary and back dunes of a barrier beach is often a healthy crop of poison ivy. Kayakers consequently need little urging to keep out of these areas.

Kayakers must also exercise caution landing and walking along barrier beaches because the threatened piping plover builds fragile nests just above the high tide line on several barrier beaches in Massachusetts. Consequently some beaches, such as the Parker River Wildlife Refuge (compromising much of Plum Island) are closed from April to mid-August to provide undisturbed nesting habitat for the plovers. To protect the birds, read trip descriptions carefully to discover known plover habitats, look and obey signs indicating closure.

Marshes and Tidal Flats

The salt marsh and tidal flats lying behind barrier beaches provide rich feeding grounds for thousands of migratory birds. Coastal Massachusetts is part of the Atlantic flyway, one of North America's most important bird-migration routes. Thousands of Canada geese and tens of thousands of ducks refuel each year in Massachusetts marshes on their annual journey. Egrets, herons, and sandpipers, commonly seen in the fall, also feed on the mud flats.

In this scenic wonderland of bird and aquatic life, a kayak is welcome, but its movement should not interrupt the inhabitants' activities. At low tide when birds feed on the flats, kayakers should keep their distance. Approaching too close causes birds to move off, preventing them from replenishing the energy needed for their long migration. At high tide, when birds move up the beach to rest before their next feeding, kayakers should again leave them undisturbed. Birds should not waste their limited energy evading paddlers.

KAYAKERS AS ENVIRONMENTAL STEWARDS

At the very least, kayakers should "leave only footprints," as the old backpacking adage goes. Carrying out trash, leaving wildlife undisturbed, and carefully disposing of all human waste (at least 100 yards from any water source) is a good start. Being a true environmental steward, requires one to go further.

What difference could kayakers make? In Massachusetts, pollution plagues our coast and waterways. Our beaches are fouled by storm water, our harbors by boats' improper waste disposal, our coastline by inappropriate development, and our rivers by all of the above. To create a healthy environment for marine creatures and paddlers, kayakers must get informed and get involved. Appendix A lists many local groups working for environmental protection on both the state and local level. Your membership and/or active involvement is a great start. If your time is limited, your membership and financial support of these nonprofit organizations will help them do the work for you.

Environmental stewards are also good watchdogs. Keep an eye on your favorite paddling areas. Be suspicious of any development in wetlands or piped discharges to waterways, and stay alert to any changes in water quality, land use, or habitat. Changes in nesting patterns or populations of bird and marine life may indicate environmental disturbances. Report any concerns to your local conservation commission, environmental advocacy group, or Massachusetts Department of Environmental Protection.

Kayaking without Impact (K W/O I)

The following four rules of conduct will help kayakers enjoy the natural resources of the coast without disturbing its wildlife or damaging their habitat and will encourage paddlers to improve and protect their favorite waterways.

• **Keep a distance of 100 yards from wildlife:** This buffer zone is usually sufficient to allow birds and mammals to remain undisturbed by your presence. For some particularly sensitive species or individuals, even 100 yards may be too close. If an animal stops its normal activity, move away.

• **Watch from afar:** Kayakers interested in close-up views of wildlife should carry binoculars. There are many brands of waterproof binoculars available in a range of sizes, prices, and strengths. A power of at least 8 x 30 will be most satisfactory for bird-watching.

• **Obey signs:** Pay attention to posted area closings, sanctuary notices, marking of buffer zones, or warnings included in this book's trip descriptions. Posted areas include National Wildlife Refuges and Massachusetts Audubon wildlife sanctuaries.

• **Inform and Involve yourself:** Kayakers act most responsibly and respectfully when they have knowledge of the environment through which they paddle. By touring with naturalists, reading books, toting field guides, and keenly observing, kayakers *inform* themselves and learn valuable lessons. For instance, observing wildlife behavior is very important. Recognizing feeding, breeding, and resting behavior is far more useful than identifying a species. When one recognizes what a particular bird, mammal, or marine creature is doing, the creature becomes more than an object. It becomes a being with a purpose, worthy of being left to pursue its needs uninterrupted.

Kayakers interested in protecting a particular natural resource must get involved in environmental advocacy. Whether one's passion runs to preserving a watershed, a body of water, a public accessway, birds, or fish, there are advocacy groups needing help. Appendix A lists many of these local organizations, and involvement is only a phone call away.

chapter
five

KAYAKING
TRIPS

NEWBURYPORT TO IPSWICH

trip 1 PAVILION BEACH TO PLUM ISLAND SOUND

Level of Difficulty: Moderate to strenuous

Round–Trip Mileage: 8.4 miles to Sawyer's Island and 14.6 miles to Plum Island Turnpike

Attractions: Beautiful salt marsh, sandy beach at Sandy Point State Reservation, Parker River National Wildlife Refuge, picnicking at Sawyer's Island, superb bird-watching

Precautions: Biting greenhead flies from mid-July to mid-August. Deer ticks present spring through fall. Bring bug repellent in any season. Watch for strong current at the entrance to Plum Island Sound (opposite Pavilion Beach) and under the Plum Island Turnpike Bridge at midtide. Avoid low tide in the Plum Island River due to mud flats. Throughout the sound, paddle defensively, because motorboat traffic is very heavy in summer. To protect nesting birds and wildlife habitat, observe beach closings and refuge restrictions. Plum Island beach is closed April to mid-August to protect piping plover.

Charts: NOAA 13282 (1:20,000), or NOAA 13274 (1:40,000)

Tidal Information: Use the tide tables for Portland. High tide at Plum Island Sound is 12 minutes later; low tide is 37 minutes later. At low tide the sound has extensive mud flats and Plum Island River is impassable in spots. The river is passable three hours on either side of high tide.

Launch Site: Pavilion Beach, Ipswich; free parking.

THE AGAWAM INDIANS called it heaven. In spring and early fall, kayakers will agree. A trip up Plum Island Sound provides access to a world of shore and sea birds, shimmering salt marsh, towering dunes, narrow passages, and abundant beauty. With Plum Island as its centerpiece, the 4,662-acre Parker River National Wildlife Refuge provides rich exploring opportunities. A haven for bird-watchers, the refuge is a major feeding ground for migrating waterfowl of Canada's Maritime Provinces and northern New England. Peak numbers appear in the fall and early spring, when paddling is at its best in the quiet marshes.

Launch your kayak at the north end of Pavilion Beach. This trip is best begun about two hours before high tide (Pavilion Beach has extensive mud flats at low tide). Ride into Plum Island Sound on the incoming tide, play in the Plum Island River when it's full of water (it drains almost to mud at low tide), and paddle back to Pavilion Beach with the ebb tide. This timing assumes minimal rest stops. If you plan to picnic at Sandy Point State Reservation, visit Sawyer's Island, or add some exploratory paddling, adjust your departure time accordingly. The route described below is a full-day trip. For shorter paddles, consult the map and choose just a portion. Unfortunately, launching options in this area are limited. Pavilion Beach, the Essex County Greenbelt Association's property on Sawyer's Island (requiring prior permission or a 0.9-mile walk to parking), and the muddy landings beside the Plum Island Turnpike are the alternatives. If two cars are available, a one-way trip is a good option.

From Pavilion Beach, turn left to paddle north up Plum Island Sound past the beach community of Great Neck. Across the mouth of the sound to the east is Sandy Point State Reservation, a state-run beach. It's the only place kayakers can land on the southern half of Plum Island. Three-quarters of the eight-mile-long "island" (actually a barrier beach) and much of the adjacent salt marsh are contained within the Parker River National Wildlife Refuge.

The refuge is protected habitat for nesting shorebirds and other wildlife. More than 6,000 geese and 25,000 ducks stop here on their annual migration to rest and refuel. Common in the sound are Canada geese, scoter, and old-squaw ducks. Other seasoned visitors include loons, black ducks, phoebes, warblers, vireos, dowitchers, willets, yellowlegs, sandpipers, egrets, and heron. The refuge beach provides nesting areas for threatened piping plovers and least terns. Aerial hunters, such as red-tailed hawks, kestrels, osprey, and northern harriers, cross its skies searching for the mice, snakes, and rabbits that populate the marsh and barrier beach. All in all, more than 200 species of birds frequent the refuge.

Bird life is only part of the wonder of the Plum Island estuary. The salt-marsh environment has been called the most important single habitat in New England for the production and maintenance of marine life. Two-thirds of all marine fish and shellfish depend on salt marshes during some portion of their lives. This marsh is part of the 17,000-acre Great Marsh extending from Cape Ann to New Hampshire. It is a nursery for numerous fish, including bass, flounder, mackerel, and smelt. Tasty Ipswich and Essex clams also live and breed here.

Paddle north up Plum Island Sound. After Sandy Point State Reservation at the southern tip of Plum Island, pass Grape Island to your right, about 1.1 mile from Pavilion Beach. This small, thicketed island (about 0.5 mile long) once hosted a summer hotel and year round community. The remnants of a wooden wharf can still be detected at its shore. Stay left (west) of Grape Island and continue in a northerly direction. As you pass the island, look for bank swallows darting in and out of their burrows in the eroding cliff. Do not disembark on Grape Island; it is part of the wildlife refuge.

West of Grape Island is the elusive, low-lying Middle Ground. At low tide, Middle Ground is an island of waving marsh grass, but at high tide water nearly submerges the small island. Although most of Middle Ground lies within the refuge, federal officials allow "no impact" picnicking on the island.

If you are paddling at low tide, swing west of Middle Ground to find water deep enough to paddle. Hugging the north shore of Great Neck and following navigational buoys north is one way to keep afloat at low tide. (This advice becomes clear after one examines the chart for Plum Island Sound—the only foolproof route north at low tide is a serpentine course from buoy to buoy.)

As you paddle, look for landmarks to guide your return. Because Plum Island Sound changes dramatically with the rise and fall of the tides, it is easy to become disoriented. Numerous narrow channels divert, delight, but confuse even observant kayakers. Explore, but make sure you have a compass and a detailed chart on deck (preferably NOAA No. 13282). To help you navigate, take note of the buoys marking the channel as you pass them. Another obvious landmark is the water tower atop Great Neck, which is visible from quite a distance.

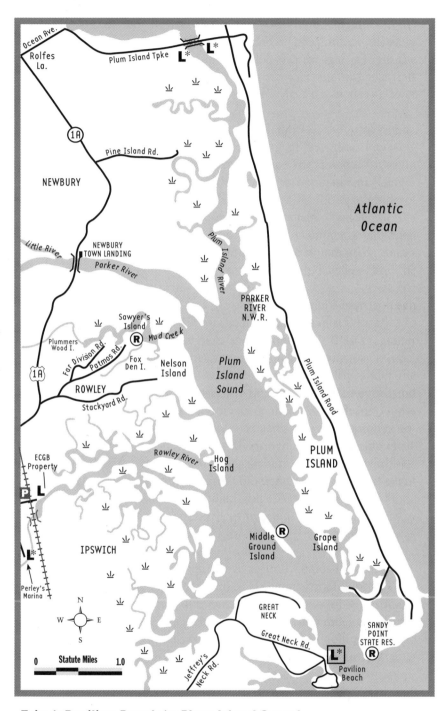

Trip 1: Pavilion Beach to Plum Island Sound

Just past Grape Island, the Rowley River enters the sound to the west (approximately 1.3 miles from Pavilion Beach). Its entrance is marked by a green can buoy numbered 19. The Rowley River salt marsh is incredibly beautiful and can be explored from Plum Island Sound or from a landing upriver on the Rowley (see Trip 2). If time allows, consider a paddle upriver for magnificent open vistas of sky and marsh.

Proceeding north from the mouth of the Rowley River, pass on your left (west) privately owned Hog Island named for the pigs which once grazed and rooted there. A few houses distinguish this low-lying island. The next island north of Hog is Nelson Island, about 1.8 miles from the Rowley River mouth. Nelson Island is a tidal island connected by a 350-year-old causeway to Route 1A. The island is difficult to find by water, but at high tide one should be able to pick out its thin cluster of trees rising above the marsh grass to the west. Kayakers cannot land on the island because it is part of the wildlife refuge. A lovely island for picnicking is just a mile farther.

The best option for a rest stop is Sawyer's Island, owned in part by the Essex County Greenbelt Association (ECGA). The island is tucked away in a secluded corner of the marsh, just off Mud Creek. To reach Sawyer's Island, find Mud Creek, 0.7 mile north of the Rowley River mouth and 0.4 mile south of the mouth of the Parker River. (If you reach a wide river entering from the west with homes along the banks, you have overshot Mud Creek and reached the Parker River. Backtrack 0.4 mile to find Mud Creek.) Seasonally the creek is easy to find, because the owners of Hog Island mark its junction. Watch for poles adorned with white plastic bottles and red reflectors.

At the marked poles, turn west (left) up Mud Creek. After about 0.4 to 0.5 mile, reach the creek's intersections with smaller Carlton and Sawyer's Creeks. At the junction, paddlers can look west and clearly see their destination, the oak-shaded island with a cedar-shingle house and flagpole. Stay right on Mud Creek, and after another 0.5 mile reach the north bank of Sawyer's Island. (The island is the first oak knoll (clump of trees) you meet after leaving the sound.) Land on its north shore, ECGA invites no-impact use by kayakers and other nature lovers. Up the beach, kayakers can picnic in an open field or under the shade of oaks. Marvelous views of the marsh can be enjoyed from this quiet spot. Visit at high tide because Mud Creek narrows to a thread at low tide.

Little River, Newbury.

Follow Mud Creek east to return to the sound. Those returning to Pavilion Beach (approximately 8.4 miles round-trip) should retrace their course. Kayakers proceeding north reach the Parker River on the left in about 0.4 mile. A short paddle up the Parker River is a nice diversion, especially when the tide is low and the water level prevents passage north on the Plum Island River. To explore the Parker River, turn left and paddle 1.4 miles west to the Route 1A bridge. Pass under the bridge and delve into more marshland by heading northwest on the Little River, the first creek that joins the Parker on the right, just 0.15 mile after the bridge. Turn right up the Little River and enjoy the quiet, meandering creek. This river is spectacular in fall when the Newbury foliage is bright. At high tide, paddlers can stop for a shady picnic on the riverbank where the creek narrows between rock outcroppings just after leaving the Parker River.

Within a few hours of high tide, kayakers can continue paddling north from the mouth of the Parker River up the Plum Island River. When traveling upriver, kayakers will note several creeks heading west (left off the main channel). To avoid getting lost, stay

plum island: an embattled barrier beach

The importance of Plum Island to the salt-marsh ecosystem cannot be overestimated. The marsh would be rapidly destroyed if the barrier beach did not shield it from wind, storms, and waves. Since the early 1600s, the barrier beach itself has narrowly survived several environmental assaults. In the days of the Agawam, Plum Island was covered in a climax forest of white pine. After discovery by Europeans, these highly prized trees (read: ships' masts) quickly disappeared to outfit the king's navy. The next assault came from the settlers' cattle. In a short time, beasts overgrazed the island, stripping it of the vegetation that held its soil. In only fifty years a productive, stable, forested "heaven" became an eroded and endangered beach. Fortunately, early Ipswich residents recognized its value and took steps to prohibit grazing. Although the white pine never returned, today beach plum, cherry, black oak, and black pine, as well as beach grasses and shrubs, anchor its shifting sands.

Still threats to the beach persist. Development on northern Plum Island destroys protective sand dunes, replaces natural vegetation, and greatly accelerates erosion. Numerous measures to save cottages and commercial establishments has only increased the erosion rate. Despite $4 million spent by the Army Corps of Engineers to build jetties, dredge the harbor, and replenish the beach, the northern end of the island continues to erode at a dramatic pace.

Development on barrier beaches is always risky business. This has been proven in countless instances on barrier beaches from Massachusetts to Florida. Public funds may be better spent to relocate ill-placed development than to undertake expensive and environmentally damaging measures to preserve the status quo. In any event, Massachusetts is terrifically fortunate to have the majority of this invaluable barrier beach protected within the Parker River National Wildlife Refuge.

right at most intersections. The best bet is to choose the main channel (containing the most water and flow) closest to Plum Island. It is, however, also possible to paddle too *far* east. A handy navigational tip is to follow the small refuge Hunting Area signs. A line of these signs marks the main channel of the Plum Island River all the way to the turnpike bridge.

Those with a keen sense of direction can try exploring the creeks running west. Pine Island Creek is nice, leading to tiny Pine Island and beyond to more salt marsh. Little Pine Island Creek, about 0.5 mile north of Pine Island Creek, is exceedingly narrow and winding. Be aware that land flanking these creeks is either privately owned or part of the national wildlife refuge. Consequently, landing is prohibited.

About 7.3 miles from Pavilion Beach, arrive at a bridge over Plum Island River (the Plum Island Turnpike). Watch for swift current under the bridge. This is a good turnaround point. To return, head in a southerly direction back to Pavilion Beach, this time staying left at most junctions. (Again, follow those little signs!)

For additional paddling in Plum Island Sound, see Trips 2 and 3.

Directions to Launch Site: From Route 128: Take Route 128 to Exit 20 (Route 1A). Drive north on Route 1A for 8.0 miles, noting the point where Route 133 joins Route 1A. Continue north on Route 1A/133 just 0.6 mile to a bend in the road where Route 1A north and Route 133 west head to the left to travel (as South Main Street) through the center of Ipswich. At this turn, continue *straight* on County Road. After 0.9 mile on County Road, bear left onto Jeffreys Neck Road (a sign indicates Pavilion Beach). Proceed 1.7 miles to another fork and bear right onto Little Neck Road. Continue on Little Neck Road 1.4 miles to its end at Pavilion Beach, where there is a large parking area. Launching is permitted at the beach's north end.

Alternate Launch Sites: (1) Plum Island Turnpike Bridge. Drive I-95 to Exit 57 (Route 113) in Newburyport. Drive 3.7 miles on Route 113 east to the traffic light at Rolfes Lane in Newbury. Turn left on Rolfes Lane and proceed 0.6 mile to the Plum Island Turnpike at its end. Turn right on the turnpike and drive 1.4 miles to the bridge over the Plum Island River. Just before the bridge is a pullout on the right leading to a parking lot. Across the bridge is another pullout and parking with access to the west bank of the river. Access is easier on the east side, but both are muddy at low water. (2) Sawyer's Island, Rowley. Take Route 128 to Route 1A north (Exit 20). Drive Route 1A north 14.8 miles to Stackyard Road in Rowley, about 2 miles from the traffic light in the center of Rowley. (Alternatively, take I-95 to exit (Route 133). Drive Route 133 west to Route 1A north in Ipswich. Turn left and take Route 1A north to Stackyard Road.) Turn on Stackyard Road and proceed 0.2 mile to Patmos Road. Turn left and proceed another 0.2 mile to a fork and bear right. Drive 0.9 mile farther to a small parking area marked with a small ECGA sign. To use this lot, kayakers must call ahead to get the combination to the padlock on the gate. Those who do not call ahead can unload their boats and drive back to the mailboxes (0.9 mile), park beside the road, then walk back and launch left of the cedar-shingle house near the wooden dock. Do not park in the driveway of the private home! To obtain parking permission, call 978-768-7241. (3) Perley's Marina, Rowley; see Trip 2. (4) Batchelder's Landing, Rowley; see Trip 2.

Camping: Several private islands in Plum Island Sound are open to low-impact camping. *With prior permission from the Essex County Greenbelt Association*, kayakers can camp on Sawyer's Island. This property is adjacent to a private residence, so campers must be respectful of neighbors. Since Sawyer's Island is accessible by land, provisions may be dropped off by car. More-remote camping is available on Fox Den and Plummers Wood Islands, two privately owned islands. Neither island is accessible by land. Fox Den Island is located just 0.2 mile southwest of Sawyer's Island, off Sawyer's Creek. It is the second wooded island reached by turning southwest off Mud Creek. Find Plummers Wood Island by continuing 0.8 mile west on Mud Creek from Sawyer's Island. The generous owner of the islands welcomes campers, but he expects visitors to respect the land as he does and to leave it in the same condition as it was found. Exercise extreme care when building fires and extinguish them completely.

trip 2 ROWLEY RIVER AND SALT MARSH

Level of Difficulty: Easy to Rowley River, moderate to Plum Island Sound destinations

Round-Trip Mileage: 5.8 miles to Rowley River mouth, 10.5 miles to Sawyer's Island or Sandy Point State Reservation (add 2.2 miles for Egypt River exploration)

Attractions: Beautiful salt marsh, Parker River Wildlife Refuge, great bird-watching

Precautions: Watch for strong winds and current as Rowley River enters Plum Island Sound. Southeast winds can churn up three to four foot waves at the mouth. Motorboat traffic is very heavy in summer. Exercise great care at low tide, because low water significantly narrows the navigable channel, increasing traffic congestion. Mosquitoes are a problem through August, greenheads persist from mid-July to mid-August, and ticks pose hazards spring through fall. Bring bug repellent. Avoid low tide in the sound as mud flats impede passage.

Charts: NOAA 13282 (1:20,000), or NOAA 13274 (1:40,000)

Tidal Information: Mean tidal range eight feet. Use the tide tables for Portland. High tide at Plum Island Sound is 12 minutes later; low tide is 37 minutes later. The Rowley River is navigable at low tide, but paddle near high tide if possible, especially if exploring the Egypt River. Plum Island Sound has extensive areas of mud flats at low tide. Plum Island River is not passable three hours on either side of high tide.

Launch Site: Perley's Marina, Warehouse Road, Rowley; $10 charge for parking and launching.

A **PADDLE DOWN THE ROWLEY RIVER** is a trip to a paradisiacal expanse of sky and salt marsh. The marsh is green in summer but splendidly gold and russet in fall. Visit late in the season to catch the bird migration and miss the insatiable mosquitoes and greenhead flies of midsummer. Perfect for lazy exploration, this trip sends paddlers first up the Egypt River, a narrow and winding inlet, then down the wider Rowley River to Plum Island Sound. Wonderful for bird-watchers and those who enjoy the scenic splendor of the salt marsh.

Attention to the tide tables is a must for this paddle. The Rowley River falls approximately eight feet to reveal mud flats and shallow water which is difficult or even impossible to paddle in places. At low tide, kayakers must paddle in a narrow channel that, in summer, is often crowded with powerboats. Consequently, avoid the river two hours on either side of low tide.

From the boat launch turn southeast (right) to enter the Egypt River. Paddle briefly through the marina's floating parking lot of boats, then along a narrow channel through the marsh. After 0.6 mile the river forks. Take the west (right) branch, which is the tiny Egypt River. The river becomes increasingly narrow and winding as it reaches southward through the marsh. The relative remoteness of this little tributary makes it a great place to watch birds, enjoy the scenery, or just slice quietly through dark-green water. When the river's tight turns become too tedious (about a half-mile from the fork), turn around and head back to the marina and the wider waters of the Rowley.

Pass again the marina and boat ramp, and then head north. In just over 0.1 mile, paddle under a railroad bridge. For the next 2.0 miles the river heads northeast, winding its way to Plum Island Sound. A few houses along the left bank look lonely in this vast marsh. Fortunately, residential development is scant, and a set of significant parcels north of the river are preserved as open space by the Essex County Greenbelt Association (ECGB). Note the dark-brown, glass-walled "pedestal house" on the left bank. The house is owned by the ECGB and houses the Marine Biological Laboratory. With prior permission, the ECGB allows kayakers to put in at the beach next to the house (see alternate launch sites, below).

Channel markers keep paddlers in sufficiently deep water and prevent wandering off the main channel. Numerous creeks flow into

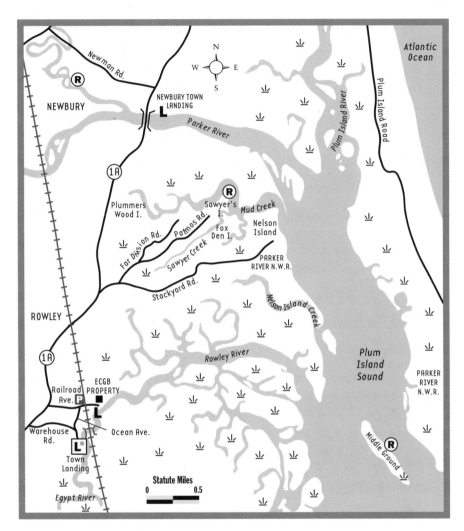

Trip 2: Rowley River and Salt Marsh

the Rowley, and if time (and tide) permit, exploring is recommended. To do so, however, one must have excellent navigational skills, for it is very easy to become turned around in the narrow, grass-rimmed passages.

Depending on the height of the tide, kayakers might encounter sandy islands in the middle of the river. A prominent sand spit, about 1.7 miles from the boat ramp, makes a nice picnic spot. Lie back to enjoy the endless sky and watch for red-tailed hawks,

anatomy of a salt marsh

When you paddle through a salt marsh, you are not only paddling through one of New England's most beautiful environments, you are enjoying one of the most important habitat in New England for the production and maintenance of life. Most people are surprisingly ignorant about the ecology of a salt marsh. Kayakers should not be. Here is a brief primer:

What grows in a salt marsh? Although the marsh may stretch miles before your bow, the ecosystem is dominated by only *two* species of grass, saltwater cordgrass (*Spartina alterniflora*) and salt-meadow grass (*S. patens*). Saltwater cordgrass is the tall grass at the water's edge. Salt-meadow grass is the lower grass growing on the high marsh, usually swirled like giant cowlicks along the ground.

Why so little diversity? The salt marsh is an extremely hostile environment for plants. Twice daily, tides flood the grass, drowning roots and radically changing the salinity of the water. In between, hot sun scorches the plants dry. Only a handful of plant species can survive this extreme vacillation.

Why is this expanse of grass and mud so important? Number one: *shelter*. Two-thirds of all commercially valuable fish and shellfish spend some portion of their lives

kestrels, and northern harriers. Earthward, picnickers can easily spy bright white egrets, radiant against the dark mud of the riverbank. Great blue herons are also often seen feeding along the bank.

Resuming your paddle, the Rowley bends southeast to meet Plum Island Sound, 2.9 miles from the boat ramp. Watch for increased current and wind at the river's mouth. The mouth is a good turnaround point for those out for only a short paddle.

Kayakers who want to further explore Plum Island Sound have several attractive options. Those who enjoy the quiet confines of the

here. The marsh is birthplace, nursery, or habitat to blue-fish, flounder, striped bass, oyster, clam, shrimp, and scallop, among others.

Number two: *food*. Although less than 10 percent of the marsh grass is eaten directly, the rest decomposes in water and is spread by tides throughout the area, indirectly feeding a multitude of marsh creatures. A salt marsh is two and a half times as productive as a cultivated field for producing food, all without the intervention of chemicals, man, or machinery.

Number three: *pollution control*. Salt-marsh grasses play a critical role in breaking down pollutants and in capturing many of the toxins that flow into the marsh from rivers and ground water. Although scientists cannot fully explain why, chlorinated hydrocarbons and heavy metals are selectively removed by the vegetation and sediments of a marsh.

All three of these critical roles are lost, of course, when marshes are filled for development. Ignorance of the role of salt marshes caused New England to lose the *majority* of its coastal wetlands over the last century. Preservation of the remainder, as well as reclamation projects to rehabilitate wetlands damaged by development, is the challenge for Massachusetts in the twenty-first century.

narrow tributaries of the salt marsh can picnic at Sawyer's Island (about 5.5 miles from the put-in). This option is described in Trip 1 and requires paddling north 2.1 miles up Plum Island Sound to Mud Creek, then paddling west about three-quarters of a mile to Sawyer's Island. A second option, if the tide is high, is to paddle north up Plum Island Sound to reach Plum Island River, also described in Trip 1 (minimum one-way distance from the put-in is more than six miles). Kayakers looking for more-open water can venture south to Sandy Point State Reservation, a public beach at the southern end of

Plum Island (about 5.0 miles from the put-in). Though some kayakers may gravitate to the easily accessible beach, more boat traffic and less scenic vistas lie to the south.

To reach Sandy Point State Reservation, turn right (south) from the mouth of the Rowley into Plum Island Sound (consult map for Trip 1). At high tide the sound is more than a mile wide at this point. In lower tides, the grassy island of Middle Ground sits in the center of the sound. Forested Grape Island lies to the east and the northern end of Great Neck sits to the south (marked by densely set houses and crowned by a blue water tank). As you paddle south toward Great Neck, you'll pass numerous creeks reaching into the vast marsh to the east. To reach Sandy Point, set your sights on Great Neck and paddle south, eventually passing Great Neck's Ipswich Yacht Club. The sound narrows as you approach Ipswich Bay, and consequently the current increases. Find Sandy Point State Reservation at the southernmost end of Plum Island, usually marked by a sizable group of powerboaters enjoying the public beach. Though less scenic and more crowded than other locations in the sound, the state reservation offers the only legal opportunity to enjoy the Plum Island beach on this side of the sound. To avoid waves and current, land on the west-facing beach. When exploring the reservation, watch for poison ivy, use paths, and stay off the fragile dune grass.

Directions to Launch Site: Take I-95 or Route 1 to Route 133 east. Drive Route 133 east to Route 1A north. Turn left and drive Route 1A north 1.9 miles to Warehouse Road in Rowley. Turn right on Warehouse and follow it 0.5 mile to its end at Perley's Marina.

Alternate Launch Sites: (1) Batchelder's Landing, Rowley. Follow above directions to Warehouse Road on Route 1A. Proceed north on Route 1A just 0.3 mile to Railroad Avenue (watch for sign for commuter rail station). Turn right on Railroad Avenue and find parking for train station after 0.3 mile. Continue over tracks and onto narrow road which leads after 0.2 mile to Essex County Greenbelt property. The put-in is to the right of the first house on the river. Drop off boat and park in train station lot. Do not launch within one hour of low tide due to mud. (2) Pavilion Beach, Ipswich; see Trip 1. (3) Sawyer's Island, Rowley; see Trip 1.

Camping: Off Mud Creek; see Trip 1 for details.

trip 3

PAVILION BEACH TO ESSEX BAY
(Circumnavigation of Castle Neck)

Level of Difficulty: Strenuous; protected and open water

Round-Trip Mileage: 9.0 miles

Attractions: Beautiful salt marshes, Crane Beach, Hog (Choate) Island, superb bird-watching

Precautions: Biting greenhead flies from mid-July to mid-August. Ticks present spring through fall. In any season, bring bug repellent. Watch for large surf off the sandbars at Crane Beach and swift current at the entrance to Essex Bay. Heavy motorboat traffic in summer. Observe beach closings and refuge restrictions to protect nesting shorebirds and wildlife habitat.

Charts: NOAA 13282 (1:20,000), NOAA 13279 (1:20,000), or NOAA 13274 (1:40,000)

Tidal Information: Use tide tables for Portland. High tide at Plum Island Sound is 12 minutes later; low tide is 37 minutes later. Mean tidal range around eight feet. Avoid paddling at low tide due to extensive mud flats. Fox Creek is passable two hours on either side of high tide.

Launch Site: Pavilion Beach, Ipswich; free parking.

THIS FABULOUS TRIP CIRCUMNAVIGATES beautiful Castle Neck and combines exciting open-water paddling with intimate salt-marsh gunkholing, all in one of the most scenic spots in coastal Massachusetts. Bird life is magnificent in the spring and fall, and the unspoiled scenery is spectacular year-round. Because this trip requires paddling in unprotected Ipswich Bay, it is not recommended for novice paddlers. The fetch is huge at Crane Beach, and waves can build to considerable heights at the sandbar in front of the beach. In addition, tidal currents can create steep waves at the entrance to Essex Bay. For a safe and enjoyable trip, spend some quality time with your tide tables and weather radio. This is a marvelous trip with challenging passages—it requires kayaking with care and forethought!

Launch from the north side of Pavilion Beach. At low tide, kayakers must carry the boat a considerable distance across the mud flats. The best time to launch for a circumnavigation is two hours before high tide. This timing assumes minimal rest stops and completion of the trip in about three hours. If long rest stops or excursions on Crane Beach or Hog Island are planned, leave a little earlier. This timing will allow kayakers to paddle out at slack tide to the mouth of Essex Bay, enter with the incoming current, ride the tidal current up Castle Neck River, and paddle through Fox Creek and Hay Canal while they're filled with water. (To paddle this trip in the reverse direction, start at high tide or slightly after from Pavilion Beach, and follow the trip description in reverse order.)

Alternatively, paddlers with all day to play can leave Pavilion Beach 1-2 hours before low tide. This timing allows kayakers to ride the falling tide to the sand bar off Crane Beach where a few delightful, lazy hours can be spent. The bar, found just 150 yards off the beach, uncovers at low tide and provides a couple of sandy, secluded acres for superb sunbathing and picnicking. In July, this may be the only stretch of sand within miles without a greenhead fly. To while away some time (you have to wait for the flooding tide to complete this circumnavigation), play in the swells on the far side of the bar. Another attractive, time-consuming option is to paddle to Hog Island for a leisurely hike while waiting for Fox Creek to fill.

From Pavilion Beach, paddle southeast toward Castle Neck and Crane Beach. Kayakers will feel the pull of the current as they exit Plum Island Sound and may encounter current-generated waves. Barely visible atop wooded Castle Hill is the Crane Estate built in 1927 by plumbing fixture magnate Richard Crane. A hundred years before the mansion was completed, the watch fires of the Agawam Indians could be viewed there each summer. By any measure in any culture, it is a magnificent site, with views to the estuary and the 4.2-mile-long sandy beach below.

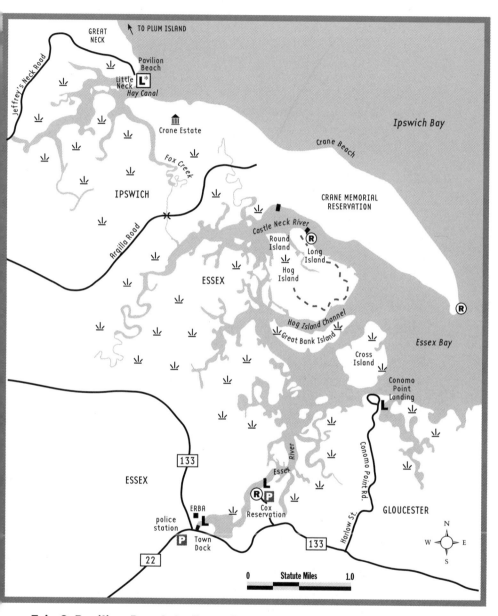

Trip 3: Pavilion Beach to Essex Bay

Continue southeast, paddling parallel to the beach. On a misty morning, the few strollers along the dunes resemble Giacometti sculptures, stick figures dwarfed by the expanse of sand. Directly east, the coast of Cape Ann defines the horizon five miles away. Depending upon conditions, it may be necessary to keep a fair distance from shore to avoid breaking surf. Even when there is no swell, the shoals off the beach can generate breakers. Take care if strong offshore (southwest) winds kick up. In that event stay as close as possible to the shoreline.

After approximately four miles, reach the mouth of Essex Bay. With care, round the end of Castle Neck (keeping an eye out for tidal current). A scenic punch confronts paddlers as the green wooded islands of Cross and Hog rise majestically out of the gracefully curving bay, surrounded by golden salt marsh and green hills. Turn right to paddle northwest up the Castle Neck River, which runs right up the backside of Crane. To the right are inviting sand beaches with dunes above. In spring and fall, migrating shorebirds are abundant. To the left, about 1.75 miles from the mouth of the bay, is the equally inviting boat landing on Long Island which beckons Hog Island hikers. (See Hog Island description in Trip 4.)

Follow the Castle Neck River around the northern tip of Long Island and Round Island (really part of Hog Island), then enter the beautiful salt marsh created by the barrier beach. Here bird life is abundant, especially in spring and fall. At low tide sandpipers, plovers, egrets, and herons feed on the mud flats. At high tide, birds rest along the bank or in the salt-marsh grass. To see the greatest number of birds, plan your paddle for the first falling tide of the day. At that time, birds come out to feed on the mud flats after their night's rest.

After passing Hog Island, navigating the next part of the marsh is a bit tricky. The goal is to find Fox Creek and follow it under the Fox Creek Bridge at Argilla Road. The complication is that numerous channels heading west have no outlets. In addition, this portion of Fox Creek is not shown on the marine charts. Kayakers should paddle west along what looks most like the main channel, looking northwest until the concrete bridge over Fox Creek is visible. Signs leading to the bridge read *No Wake Strictly Enforced*. (Do not head northwest on the first narrow channel that flows off Castle Neck River; this winding channel is a dead-end, albeit scenic, tour through the marsh, finally ending at Argilla Road at the bottom of the Crane Estate.)

a woman's touch

In the late 1800s, women's millinery was for the birds. Feathers were the rule, and sometimes whole birds sat atop hats. Most in demand were the long white plumes of egrets and herons, but no bird was immune. Gulls, sparrows, pigeons, blue jays, and even crows were sacrificed. Feather-covered fans, capes, muffs, and coats added to the toll. It is estimated that in the late nineteenth century, well over 5 million birds a year were killed for use on hats and clothing. The result was the decimation of sea and shore birds, in some cases almost to extinction.

To the rescue came an unlikely ally. In 1896, a Boston blue blood, Harriet Hemenway, was repulsed by a newspaper account of the bloody slaughter of herons. Using her considerable wealth and influence, Ms. Hemenway launched a personal campaign to convince her similarly situated friends to stop buying feather products. Fortunately, Harriet carried her persuasive fervor far beyond her social circle. She convened a meeting of Boston's scientific and political leaders, and the group immediately formed the Massachusetts Audubon Society, whose purpose was "to discourage buying and wearing for ornamental purposes the feathers of any wild bird" and "to otherwise further the protection of our native birds." In 1897, the society successfully lobbied the Massachusetts Legislature to pass protective legislation. Other states soon followed suit. Finally in 1913, Congress enacted a bill protecting migratory birds, followed by the 1916 Migratory Bird Treaty with Great Britain.

The rest is familiar history to bird lovers. The Massachusetts Audubon Society continues to wield great influence on state and national conservation issues. Harriet Hemenway died at the age of 102 in 1960. She lived long enough to tackle other important social issues (including championing the rights of working women), long enough to realize the impressive organization she inspired, and long enough to enjoy the resurgence of several species of nearly extinct sea and shorebirds. So doff your unfeathered caps, kayakers, to the memory of this marvelous crusader!

Assuming success in finding Fox Creek, paddle under the bridge and continue to follow the narrow creek as it twists and turns through the marsh. The guardhouse of the Crane Estate is visible to the northeast, and to the northwest one can see the water tower atop Great Neck. After passing on the left of the wooden remains of docks, reach the channel on the right that flows between Little Neck and Castle Neck (Hay Canal). Turn right to paddle through Hay Canal (named when the area produced prodigious amounts of salt-marsh hay for the Boston Haymarket). At the east end of Little Neck, turn north (left) to return to Pavilion Beach. Beware of submerged rocks at the eastern edge of Little Neck.

A slightly longer circumnavigation includes paddling around the south end of Hog Island. The longer route adds about two miles to the route and allows exploration of the beautiful Essex River salt marsh. To travel around Hog Island, simply head south along the east shore of the island instead of proceeding directly northwest on Castle Neck River. Once the island is cleared, paddle west, then turn north to travel up the west side of the island. Note, however, that this circumnavigation is possible *only* within an hour or two of high tide because of mud flats immediately west of the island. (See Trip 4 for more information on paddling in the Essex River Estuary.)

Directions to Launch Site: See Trip 1.

Alternate Launch Sites: (1) If surf prevents launching at Pavilion Beach, launching at high tide is possible across the street from the beach into the Ipswich River. A small parking lot marks the launch site. (2) Essex Town Boat Ramp, Essex; see Trip 4. Starting at the boat ramp adds approximately four miles to the round-trip distance.

trip 4

ESSEX RIVER TO HOG (CHOATE) ISLAND

Level of Difficulty: Moderate; protected water

Round-Trip Mileage: 8.0 miles

Attractions: Thousands of acres of beautiful salt marsh; scenic island with hiking trails; sandy beach for picnicking; extensive bird life, especially in late summer and fall

Precautions: Greenhead flies persistent from mid-July through mid-August. Bring bug repellent for mosquitoes spring through fall.

Charts: NOAA 13282 (1:20,000), or NOAA 13274 (1:40,000)

Tidal Information: Extensive mud flats at low tide; mean tidal range about 9.0 feet.

Launch Site: Essex Town Boat Ramp, Essex.

THE ESSEX RIVER BASIN is one of the most exquisite place to paddle north of Boston. Paddlers can lose themselves (quite literally) in the beautiful and intimate reaches of its tidal marsh. Kayakers also can visit the 680-acre Crane Wildlife Refuge and hike on the scenic trails of Hog Island. For picnicking kayakers, Crane Beach is only a few strokes away, and lunch is superb beneath the dunes. Paddlers, especially in late summer and fall, enjoy easy viewing of snowy egrets, great egrets, sandpipers, terns, and great blue herons, with the occasional dramatic flight of a hawk or harrier overhead. With changing seasons, skies, and tides, the beautiful Essex River Basin is never the same twice.

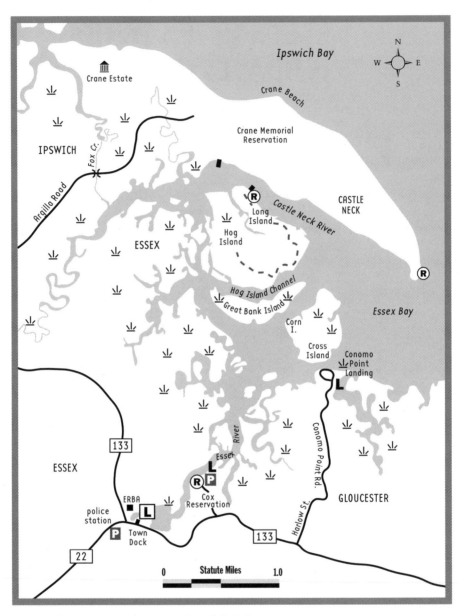

Trip 4: Essex River to Hog Island

This trip is substantially easier if you ride with the tides and paddle when the estuary has ample water. The tide rises and falls nine feet, exposing extensive mud flats at low tide and cutting off entry into much of the marsh. While it is possible to paddle at low tide, kayaking then is restricted to the main channels and circumnavigation of Hog Island is impossible. (Keep an eye on the tide's movement to avoid getting stranded.)

To take the greatest advantage of high water in Essex Bay, leave the landing about an hour or two before high tide. With this timing, kayakers will have a few hours to explore the bay with maximum water. The timing will also necessitate paddling against the current to return, but it is manageable for most paddlers if the winds are not strong. High southwest winds (common in summer) will impede progress back to the landing, and strong northeast winds will steepen the waves of an incoming tide. Bring a weather radio, especially for all-day outings to monitor wind speed and direction. If you want to spend a full day in the bay with a few hours to explore Crane and Hog Islands by foot, sit down with the tide tables and plan your trip carefully to avoid a low tide paddle.

The exact paddling route around Hog Island changes from year to year due to shifting sandbars and channels. It is therefore impossible to describe the best route with accuracy. The following information will be helpful but cannot guarantee that you won't paddle down a few dead ends or end up in inch-deep water. For up-to-date advice, check with the knowledgeable staff at Essex River Basin Adventures (ERBA), adjacent to the boat landing, prior to departing (see below).

From the Essex Town Boat Ramp, the route to Essex Bay is fairly clear. Follow the channel (and perhaps the line of boat traffic, especially in summer) as it meanders generally in a northerly direction. Channel markers lead to the entrance of the bay, about two miles from the landing. Look for landmarks to guide your return. With the rise and fall of the tide, the marsh's appearance changes dramatically, and it is surprisingly easy to make a wrong turn.

Once at the mouth of the Essex River, look north to a view dominated by Hog Island, a high, wooded drumlin whose steep western slope rises 177 feet above the marsh. Hog Island is part of the Crane Wildlife Refuge, which also includes portions of Castle Neck, four other islands, and the salt marsh along the Castle Neck

River. More than 180 species of birds visit the refuge, including red-throated loons, osprey, and (very rarely) bald eagles. Its islands provide homes to otter, mink, and deer, and the surrounding water feeds flounder, striped bass, and mackerel.

To make the highly recommended visit to Hog Island, kayakers must make their way to the northeast side of Long Island, where there is a boat dock. One way is to paddle toward the highest point on Hog Island, on the island's west side. Bear northwest; even at low tide a channel will bring you to the southwest side of the island. Before reaching the island, arrive at the Hog Island Channel. If you left the landing at or before high tide, there will be enough water to paddle up the western side of Hog Island. It is possible to paddle up the west side only for about an hour or so on either side of high tide. At all other times, mud flats block the narrow channels. Try to time your paddle so you can take the west route because it is especially quiet and beautiful.

If there is not sufficient water to the west, turn right (east) and follow the channel along the south edge of Hog Island. At the east end of Hog Island Channel, turn northeast and paddle along the east shore

Launching off Crane Beach's south side with Hog Island in the distance.

of the island; then turn northwest up the Castle Neck River to the boat dock on the northeast side of Long Island. Long Island is open to visitors from 9:00 A.M. to 3:30 P.M., from Memorial Day through Columbus Day. There is no charge for members of The Trustees of Reservations (TTOR), but nonmembers must pay a small fee.

To hike Hog Island, leave your boat at the beach by the dock. (Long Island is connected to Hog Island by a ridge at its eastern end.) Just upland from the boat dock, a gravel road heads southeast, passing a late-eighteenth-century barn and then the historic Choate House, built in 1725. Rufus Choate, born in this house in 1799, succeeded Daniel Webster to the U.S. Senate and was considered the greatest trial lawyer of his day. In fact, in 1999 Hog Island was officially renamed Choate Island in memory of this famous family. Beyond the 250-year-old Choate House, hikers can continue on the road to reach the top of the Hog Island drumlin for breathtaking views north to Plum Island, Plum Island Sound, and the Ipswich River. Watch for deer and fox living on the island, as well as sheep, goats, and llamas. Use bug repellent to ward off ticks. As of this writing, a house constructed for the movie set of *The Crucible* still stood on the island and looked convincingly like a relic of the early eighteenth century. It's easily spotted, and worth a visit if it's still standing.

Just across Castle Island River from Long Island is Castle Neck and Crane Beach. Crane Beach is a four-mile-long barrier beach protecting the Essex River estuary from storms. For centuries, the Agawam Indians used the estuary to harvest finfish and shellfish, building summer encampments atop Castle and Wigwam Hills. (Today the grand Crane Estate sits atop Castle Hill, visible to the northwest). After the arrival of the Europeans in 1600, the area was used for harvesting salt hay until the early 1900s. The beach today is a wonderful place to land, rest, and explore. Stay off the fragile sand dunes, however, and do not trample the deceptively delicate grass that stabilizes the dunes.

On your return, if there is ample water, paddle around the west side of Hog Island or head back along the east side to the mouth of the Essex River. When paddling down the east side of Hog Island, check the tall trees of the southeast corner of the island for hawks. The branches give a variety of raptors an excellent perch from which to search for prey. From the southeast edge of Hog, if water is low, kayakers can paddle northwest up the Hog Island Channel to find the deepest route in which to return to the mouth of the Essex River.

After passing the northwest edge of Grand Bank Island, kayakers can turn south toward the mouth. When the tide is in, kayakers can head directly south from Hog Island over Great Bank Island, and continue south (staying west of Corn Island) to reach the Essex River. From the Essex River, kayakers can pick up the numbered channel markers and follow them back to the boat ramp.

For additional exploration of this beautiful estuary, check Trips 3 and 5. For a bit of history, visit the Essex Shipbuilding Museum, located next to the town landing. For more than 300 years, Essex shipbuilders built world-renowned ships at this location. If you need refreshment, Essex is famous for seafood restaurants offering fresh fried clams (they were invented here!). Finally, check out the abundance of high-quality antique shops also along Main Street. Like the estuary, the town of Essex is worth a return trip.

Directions to Launch Site: From Route 128: Take Route 128 to Exit 14. Drive west on Route 133 4.1 miles to the public boat launch, located just after the parking lot for Periwinkles Restaurant. Look for the triangular Essex River Basin Adventures (ERBA) sign.

Leave the boat at the launch and park free behind the Essex Fire/Police Station just 0.15 mile up Route 22, a short walk to the right (stay left at the fork).

From Route 95: Take Route 95 to Exit 54 (Georgetown/Route 133). Follow Route 133 toward Rowley to the intersection of Route 1A and Route 133. Turn right and follow Route 1A several miles through Ipswich. At the Route 1A/Route 133 split, bear left and follow Route 133 into Essex. Just after Route 133's intersection with Route 22, bear left on Route 133 and turn immediately left to reach the public boat ramp, as described above.

Alternate Launch Sites: (1) Clamhouse Landing at Cox Reservation, Essex County Greenbelt Association, 82 Eastern Avenue, Essex. From Exit 14 (see above), drive 2.3 miles west on Route 133. Turn at the first driveway on the north (right) side of Route 133, west of Farnum's Restaurant and two driveways east of the Essex Towers. Arrive soon at a barnlike building and parking lot. Check out the map on the side of the barn which indicates the road to the put-in. Drive to the put-in and drop off the boat. Then drive back 0.25 mile to the barn to park your car. Call ahead for permission to launch and park; 978-768-7241. (2) Conomo Point Town Landing. From Exit 14 (see above), drive about one mile west on Route 133 to Summer Street. Turn right on Summer Street, then left on Concord Street. Bear right at a fork onto Conomo Point Road. Follow Conomo Point Road to a town landing on the right. Limited on-street parking for non-residents near the landing. This landing can be used only within hours of high tide.

trip 5 LOWER IPSWICH RIVER, IPSWICH

Level of Difficulty: Easy; protected water

Round-Trip Mileage: 4–6 miles

Attractions: Beautiful salt marsh; extensive bird life, especially in fall

Precautions: If paddling to the mouth of the Ipswich River, watch for tide rips between Little Neck and Castle Neck as the river enters Plum Island Sound. Ipswich River has mud flats at low water. Strong southwest winds can create waves and impede passage up the Ipswich River.

Charts: NOAA 13282 (1:20,000), or NOAA 13274 (1:40,000)

Tidal Information: Mean tidal range, 8.7 feet. Avoid paddling at low tide due to extensive mud flats.

Launch Site: Ipswich Town Wharf. Launching fee from Memorial Day to Labor Day.

PADDLING THE IPSWICH RIVER can be a strenuous adventure or a gentle meander though beautiful salt marsh. Kayakers seeking an easy trip can explore the *very* narrow Labor in Vain Creek and paddle just short of Plum Island Sound to explore more salt marshes north and south of the river. Stronger kayakers can ply the reaches of Plum Island Sound, paddling north to Plum Island or south to Crane Beach. In any direction, this is marvelous territory to explore by kayak. Two salt-marsh conservation areas, lovely Greenwood Farm owned by The Trustees of Reservations and Sally

Weatherall Memorial Reservation owned by the Essex County Greenbelt Association, add beauty and additional paddling options.

Launch at the Ipswich Town Wharf. Do not launch at low tide because of extensive mud flats. Paddle down the river (generally northeast) past banks crowded with riverside houses. About 0.6 mile from the launch, notice a split in the river, with one fork heading under a bridge in a southerly direction. This is Labor in Vain Creek. At 2 hours before and after high tide, kayakers can paddle down this quiet, winding, and very beautiful creek. Houses disappear, and paddlers can enjoy birds, marsh, and in fall blazing color from trees on the horizon. Watch for dark clouds of tree swallows chasing insects above the marsh. Look also for red-tailed hawks riding thermals and surveying the high ground for rodents. After about 1.5 miles the creek becomes too narrow for paddling, so kayakers must turn around and return to the Ipswich River.

Upon returning to the Ipswich River, turn right and continue paddling toward Plum Island Sound. The river winds its way east. Narrow channels head off to the left, but kayakers should generally stay right. For those who enjoy marsh paddling, a worthwhile side trip follows one channel left (west) into the property known as Greenwood Farm. Made up of farmland, marsh, and islands, this property was once home to Agawam Indians. Its rich natural resources drew white settlers as well, who farmed the land for more than 300 years. Now owned by The Trustees of Reservations, this beautiful parcel is fortunately preserved. Explore the marsh for sign of great blue herons or snowy and American egrets. At dawn or dusk, paddlers may be treated to the hooting of a great horned, snowy, or short-eared owl. To find the right channel, paddle past a grassy island in the center of the river (about 1.2 miles from the put-in), then take the next major waterway heading west. Look for landmarks to guide your return, for it is easy to become disoriented in the marsh.

Another protected marsh to explore is the Sally Weatherall Memorial Reservation, just south of Great Neck. To visit the reservation, paddle toward the light-blue water tank atop Great Neck, then turn left (west) to follow the south edge of Great Neck. Exploration is possible at high tide only, and paddlers will find this end of the marsh exposed to more development and road noise than Greenwood Farm.

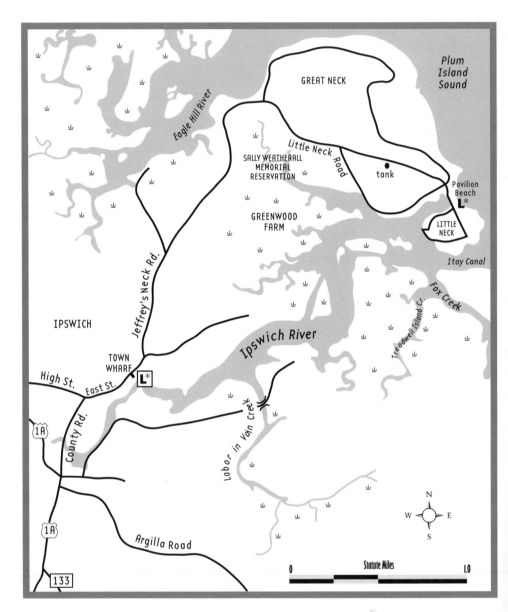

Trip 5: Lower Ipswich River

Additional protected paddling awaits kayakers at the base of the Ipswich River. Paddlers can proceed down the backside of Castle Neck by following Fox Creek, or head south on Treadwell Island Creek. Both wind gently through the marsh. At high tide motorboats use Fox Creek to circumnavigate Castle Neck, so kayakers will encounter more traffic on this small waterway. To avoid other boaters, head south on Treadwell Island Creek or veer north off Fox Creek into the marsh below Castle Hill. (See Trip 3 and accompanying map for more information on paddling Fox Creek.)

Kayaking challenges increase significantly for those who wish to explore Plum Island Sound. Access to the sound is most direct via Hay Canal, the channel between Little Neck and Castle Hill. Watch for tide rips at the ends of the channel. Approximate one-way distances from the Ipswich Town Wharf to popular Plum Island Sound destinations include 1.75 miles to Sandy Point State Reservation at the southern tip of Plum Island, 2.2 miles to Crane Beach, 4.5 miles to the mouth of the Essex Bay (eastern end of Crane Beach), and 3.6 miles to the mouth of the Rowley River. For information on paddling areas in the sound and Essex Bay, consult Trips 1 through 4.

Directions to Launch Site: Take Route 128 to Exit 20 (Route 1A). Drive north on Route 1A for 8 miles, noting the point where Route 133 joins Route 1A. Continue north on Route 1A/133 just 0.6 mile past this junction to a bend in the road where Route 1A north and Route 133 west head left to travel through the center of Ipswich. At this turn, continue *straight* on County Road. After 0.7 mile on County Road, turn right into the parking area for the Ipswich Town Wharf and boat ramp.

Alternate Launch Site: Pavilion Beach (marsh side). Launching is possible at high tide into the marsh behind Pavilion Beach. The pull-out for cars is just south of the beach parking lot on the right (west) side of the road (see Trip 1).

CAPE ANN AND THE NORTH SHORE

trip 6 ANNISQUAM RIVER EXPLORATION

Level of Difficulty: Easy; protected water

Round–Trip Mileage: 4.2 miles

Attractions: Scenic salt marsh; bird-watching; picnicking at Goose Cove Reservation and Wingaersheek Beach

Precautions: Heavy boat traffic in Annisquam River can generate dangerous wakes. Watch for strong current at midtide at the mouth of the river at Ipswich Bay. Entry into Goose Cove possible only at slack tide. Constricted current under the bridge generates large breaking waves.

Charts: NOAA 13279 (1:20,000), and NOAA 13282 (1:10,000), or NOAA 13274 (1:40,000).

Tidal Information: Mean tidal range, 8.7 feet. Use high tide for Boston. Marsh exploration best within 2 hours of high tide.

Launch Site: Long Wharf Landing, Gloucester.

THE ANNISQUAM RIVER offers pretty, protected paddling and acres of marshland to explore at high tide. Novices can find scenic and quiet paddling on the Jones River and in Lobster Cove. More adventurous kayakers can paddle into Ipswich Bay to visit sandy

Wingaersheek Beach or the many rocky coves along Gloucester's northern coast. Paddlers of all skill levels can enjoy this diverse and interesting area.

The Annisquam River is not really a river but a tidal inlet. Sea water flows in and out at each end. The tides meet where the Little River joins the Annisquam, but the river is so wide at this point that the two tidal currents mingle almost imperceptibly. Closer to the river mouths, tidal currents can be very strong, particularly in the center of the river's channel near the outlets at Ipswich Bay and Gloucester Harbor.

The Annisquam's unusual name comes from the Scottish *annis*, meaning "island," and *squam*, signifying "peaceful harbor." This salt water estuary is nearly a mile wide in places and indeed has many islands, as well as marshes, sandbars, and inlets running in many directions. Today, however, it is far from peaceful. In 1642, colonists dug the Blynman Canal which connected the Annisquam River estuary to Gloucester Harbor. Thus a great many commercial and pleasure boats ride the Annisquam River back and forth from Gloucester to Ipswich Bay. Fortunately, kayakers can sample the river's quiet beauty in the narrow and shallow places the big boats must avoid.

For the best paddle and greatest paddling options, visit the Annisquam near high tide. The river falls eight to twelve feet with the tide, exposing tiring expanses of mud flats to trap unsuspecting kayakers. Time your trip to coincide with tidal currents. It is recommended that kayakers begin about two hours before high tide for a 4-hour outing.

Launch from the landing at Long Wharf. This is a scenic place to begin your trip, but there are several other convenient options as well. (See the map on page 94 and *Alternate Launch Sites* on page 98.) From Long Wharf Landing, if the tide is in, paddle south on the Jones River. This "river" is just a small inlet, but at high tide kayakers can follow it southwest to the inner reaches of the marsh. The rich marsh is a sanctuary for water fowl and a nursery for the sea life of Ipswich Bay. Its sand flats have historically produced an abundance of clams, harvested first by the Native Americans who lived on these shores. With ample water, paddle south about 0.7 mile, then east around the south end of Pearce Island. (At low tide it's not possible to paddle on the south side of Pearce.) Be forewarned that navigating the inlets of the marsh can be tricky, and you should be prepared for the inevitable false channel and necessary backtrack-

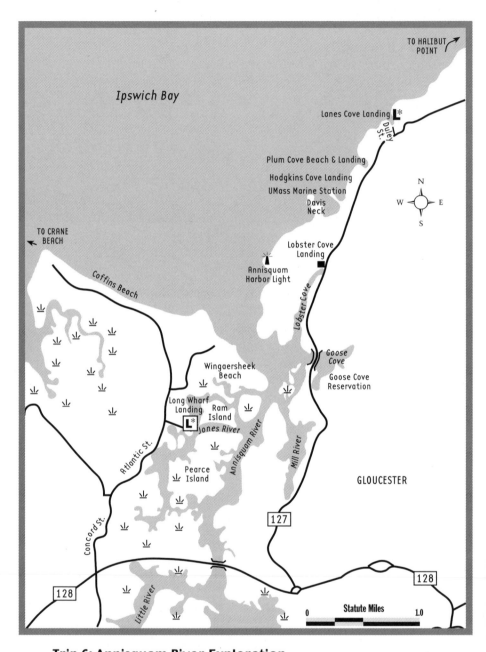

Trip 6: Annisquam River Exploration
Trip 7: Annisquam River to Lanes Cove and Crane Beach

ing. Passing Pearce moving east, meet the main channel of the Annisquam River, marked by buoys and a plethora of pleasure boats, 1.0 mile from the landing. Turn left (north) and ride up the channel. Stay well to the side to avoid the wave-generating boat traffic. The strength of the current will also be less closer to the river banks.

For a more direct route to the main channel of the Annisquam, or if launching within two to three hours of low tide, kayakers should paddle east from the launching ramp. The island of trees on high ground just to the east-northeast of the ramp is Ram Island. Paddling east, the Jones River takes kayakers by the south side of Ram Island, past a wooden dock, to the main channel of the Annisquam 0.7 mile from the landing. After gaining the channel, note to the right the tall, lighted piling with the square green marker numbered 19. Recognizing this marker will help kayakers find the Jones River on their return.

From Pearce Island, it is a 1.5-mile paddle northeast to reach the entrance to Goose Cove. From marker 19, it is just 0.9 mile. To enter the cove, kayakers must pass under Route 127. (Passage under the narrow bridge should be attempted *only* during slack tide, because at all other times the current runs very swiftly under the bridge.) For a tranquil picnic, paddle a quarter-mile to the south end of the cove to reach Essex County Greenbelt Association's Goose Cove Reservation, occupying twenty-six acres of a rocky promontory at the cove's southeast end. Visit in spring for the flowering cherry and shadbush and the plentiful flycatchers, vireos, and warblers. At the water's edge, watch for great blue and black-crowned night herons, black ducks, and ring-billed gulls. Paddlers can land along the rocky shore and stretch their legs by sampling one of the reservation's short trails. Keep track of the tide, however, to ensure safe passage out of the cove under the bridge.

Paddle north out of Goose Cove to find quaint Lobster Cove, just 0.25 north of the highway bridge. At the mouth of Lobster Cove sits the Annisquam Yacht Club and the quaint town of Annisquam. Kayaking Lobster Cove is a pleasant detour, about a mile round-trip. Pass lovely summer homes with lawns and gardens rolling down to private docks. The water is usually filled with activity from a great variety of pleasure boats. A footbridge spans the narrow cove, popular with young fishermen (watch their lines!). This wooden bridge, built in 1847, once carried vehicular traffic and opened like a draw-

Annisquam Harbor Light.

bridge for coasting schooners. Most of Lobster Cove is private, but kayakers can take a break at two public landings, Lobster Cove Landing, and Head of Lobster Cove Landing. (See map.)

Continuing up the Annisquam River toward Ipswich Bay, kayakers pass Wingaersheek Beach to the west. At low tide, the beach is enormous, feeling spacious on even the hottest summer day. At high tide, however, the surf shrinks the beach to stingy proportions, crowding the sunbathers blanket to blanket, Coney Island-style.

If conditions permit, paddle into the bay. Consider current and wind direction, however, before leaving the river. Currents are strong at the mouth, and opposing wind can generate steep waves. Rewards are high, nevertheless, for those who venture out. Beautiful Annisquam Harbor Light overlooks Ipswich Bay from the eastern shore and is certainly worth a closer look. Its whitewashed walls and red-roofed keeper's house are classic New England. The light sits on Wigwam Point, a popular summer camping spot for Native Americans until the early 1800s. Wigwam Point is about 0.4 mile from the mouth of the Annisquam.

The lighthouse is a good turnaround point. Kayakers seeking a longer trip can paddle northeast up the coast of Gloucester to visit a

essex county greenbelt association

The Essex County Greenbelt Association is a nonprofit land trust dedicated to preserving open space in Essex County. Its programs help local communities and landowners preserve ecosystems, foster agricultural usage, and protect scenic vistas and special natural features. Some of the beautiful coastal sites owned and maintained by the ECGA include the Goose Cove Reservation in Gloucester (Trip 6), the Cox Reservation in Essex (Trip 4), and the incredibly beautiful Rowley Marsh in Rowley (Trip 2). Become a member of the ECGA to help preserve more of beautiful Essex County, a true haven for Massachusetts kayakers. Members receive a guidebook describing their most spectacular properties, a newsletter, and invitations to many special events. To join, call 978-768-7241 or write the Essex County Greenbelt Association, Inc., 82 Eastern Avenue, Essex, MA 01929; www.ecga.org.

series of scenic coves, or venture west to the mouth of Essex Bay. (See Trip 7.)

Directions to Launch Site: Take Route 128 to Exit 13, Concord Street, in Gloucester. At the end of the ramp, turn left on Concord Street, and drive 0.8 mile (pass under Route 128) to Atlantic Street. Turn right on Atlantic Street (signed for Wingaersheek Beach) and drive 0.8 mile to the Long Wharf Town Landing on the right. Free parking available at landing.

Alternate Launch Sites: (1) Dunfudgin Landing, Gloucester High School. Take Route 128 to Exit 14 in Gloucester. Turn right onto Route 133 East. Drive 2.9 miles on Route 133 to Route 127. Turn left onto Route 127 and drive over the Blynman Canal Bridge; then turn left at the traffic light (Centennial Avenue). Gloucester High School is just 0.15 mile farther on the left. The landing is behind the school; fee for launching. Launching at Dunfudgin Landing adds about three miles round-trip to this paddle. (2) Lanes Cove: Take Route 128 to Exit 11 in Gloucester. Drive three-quarters of the way around the Grant Circle rotary to pick up Route 127 north. Follow Route 127 for 4.5 miles to Duley Street (at the Lane's Cove Market). Turn left and follow Duley Street 0.1 mile to the cove. Park along the side of the road. For other put-ins, consult map.

trip 7 ANNISQUAM RIVER TO LANES COVE AND CRANE BEACH

Level of Difficulty: Moderate to strenuous; open water

Round–Trip Mileage: 7.0 miles to Lanes Cove, 10.6 miles to Halibut Point, 8.4 miles to Crane Beach

Attractions: Beautiful lighthouse; scenic rocky coast; long sandy beach and dunes; great bird-watching

Precautions: Watch for strong current at midtide at the mouths of both the Annisquam and Essex Rivers. Rough water may be encountered in open water along the coast of Cape Ann and Crane Beach. Boat traffic can be heavy at the mouth of the Annisquam. Paddlers to Halibut Point must watch for refracting waves and rips at the point. Watch the weather and winds on this open-water paddle.

Charts: NOAA 13279 (1:20,000), and NOAA 13282 (1:10,000), or NOAA 13274 (1:40,000)

Tidal Information: Mean tidal range, 8.7 feet. Use high tide for Boston.

Launch Site: Long Wharf Landing, Gloucester.

CAPE ANN IS A KAYAKER'S PARADISE, offering gorgeous, rocky coastline; challenging open water; marvelous bird life; and quaint, weather-hardened towns. Kayakers return again and again to Cape Ann, for the ocean's moods are infinite. There's a quality to the light and color of the water—an alluring harshness and wildness that is particular to Cape Ann. Think of a painting by Winslow Homer or Fitz Hugh Lane. Kayakers are drawn to Cape Ann's elemental seriousness, to the gravity of its beauty, its challenges, and the freshness of its wind. For the best trip, paddle Cape Ann in the off-season. Harbor seals, shorebirds, and solitude then add to the area's considerable charm.

The suggested put-in for this trip is Long Wharf Landing on the Annisquam River, but one can use Lanes Cove, another convenient launch site. If launching from Long Wharf, consult Trip 6 to reach the Annisquam Harbor Lighthouse. If leaving from Lanes Cove, 1.7 miles northeast of the lighthouse, the round-trip distances are 3.4 miles to Annisquam Harbor Light, 7.0 miles to Halibut Point, and 7.4 miles to the eastern tip of Crane Beach (Castle Neck) and the mouth of the Essex River.

From the Annisquam Harbor Lighthouse, kayakers have two choices: tour the rocky shore and coves of Cape Ann to the north or head west to explore a magnificent barrier beach (Crane Beach) and the marshy inlets of the Essex River. Before choosing your route, consider tides and wind. A trip into the Essex River basin is not recommended within two hours of low tide due to shallow water and extensive mud flats. If winds are blowing from the northeast, a trip on the sheltered (lee) side of Cape Ann, hugging the shoreline, is the better choice. On the other hand, strong west or southwest winds can generate rough water off Cape Ann's west shore. The following trip description first details the trip to Halibut Point and then describes the route to Essex Bay.

Lanes Cove, Gloucester.

THE TRIP NORTH TO HALIBUT POINT

Several scenic coves can be reached by paddling north along the coast from the mouth of the Annisquam. Aim your kayak and slalom gracefully through a colorful course of brightly painted lobster buoys along a shore still rich with crustaceans. Approximately 0.8 mile from Annisquam Harbor Light pass Davis Neck. At high tide the end of the neck looks like a rocky island. Just offshore to the northwest is a red bell buoy labeled AR. The cove after Davis Neck is Hodgkins Cove, where the University of Massachusetts Marine Station occupies a homely blue building on a narrow spit of land. Scientists there conduct "food science" research, currently investigating the edible potential of pelagic fish. Hodgkins Cove Landing, a small public boat ramp with on-street parking, is at the north end of the basin. North of Hodgkins Cove, watch for rocks and small islands that uncover at low tide.

After Hodgkins Cove, paddle north about 0.4 mile to Plum Cove, where a fine sandy beach awaits. (In summer, disembarking kayakers may find an ice cream truck in the parking lot.) Paddling north another 0.5 mile brings paddlers to the granite walls of Lanes Cove. The high, weathered walls give the small harbor a medieval feel and provide protected water in which to play, launch, and land. (Lanes Cove is an excellent put-in with free on-street parking. If provisions are needed, Lanes Cove Market is a short 0.1-mile walk up Duley St.) Continuing north, paddlers reach lovely Folly Cove about 1.3 miles farther (3.0 miles from the lighthouse). There paddlers can picnic on the rocky but scenic shore in a deep cove protected from all but the north wind. Finally, kayakers can venture 0.6 miles farther and reach the dramatic rocky headland of Halibut Point. Watch for hazardous waves and rips at the point. (For more information on paddling east of Halibut Point into Rockport, see Trip 8.)

THE TRIP SOUTHWEST TO CRANE BEACH AND ESSEX BAY

Kayakers paddling south from Annisquam Harbor Light must first carefully cross the busy boat channel marked by red and green buoys. Paddle west past Wingaersheek Beach, which, depending on the tide, may extend far into the mouth of the harbor. At higher tides, kayakers can play among the rocks that stand in the shallow water just off the beach. West of Wingaersheek Beach, kayakers pass

true confession:
how i learned to love
the shorebirds

I wasn't a bird-watcher until I took up sea kayaking. I considered bird-watching the business of little old ladies with Monty Python—sounding lists. For me, the larger, the hairier—the *better*. Grizzly, wolf, moose, and bison, preferably at close range, got my heart pounding.

But I have seen the light. I am now moved not only by the sight of a great blue heron (most of us are) but by the delicate scampering of sandpipers on wet sand. Perhaps it is their Quixotic quest, their seemingly impossible flight from South America to the Arctic Circle to mate and breed, that moves my soul. Maybe it's their Patton-like determination in such a fragile body. Or perhaps it's how they make a lonely, empty seascape come alive. Their single-minded intensity, their rhythmic feeding, even their very presence, reassures me that something is still going right in the natural world.

Kayakers who can't tell the difference between an egret and a yellowleg are missing out tremendously. The best way to learn about these incredible migratory shorebirds is to take a bird-watching paddle with Massachusetts Audubon. The enthusiasm of their naturalists is infectious. It won't be long till you stop midstroke for a ruddy turnstone or search the Internet for a short-billed dowitcher—or was that a common snipe? Like *Monty Python,* it's a heck of a lot of fun.

For information on upcoming programs, call Massachusetts Audubon's Joppa Flats Education Center (978-462-9998), Wellfleet Bay (508-349-2615), or Ipswich River Wildlife Sanctuary (978-887-9264).

a 1.4-mile, privately owned stretch of sand known as Coffin Beach. At the rocky west end of Coffin Beach is the mouth of Essex Bay, and directly across the mouth is the sandy tip of Crane Beach.

Kayakers can either enter Essex Bay or continue northwest along the outer shore of Crane Beach. If you're traveling up the beach, watch for breakers in the shallow water close to shore. Unless you're interested in surfing, don't paddle too close to the shoreline, and watch for sandbars that create breaking waves just offshore. Beautiful Crane Beach extends northwest for more than three miles, reaching into the mouth of Plum Island Sound (see Trip 3). Because Crane Beach is a successful nesting ground for the threatened piping plover, kayakers must heed signs prohibiting entry on certain parts of the beach. One misstep can crush the plovers' nearly invisible eggs and tiny hatchlings.

The backside of Crane Beach is an excellent spot for a picnic. Enter Essex Bay and paddle northwest (right) up the Castle Neck River to find a spot on the beach. This location is particularly fine in spring and fall, when boat traffic drops dramatically. With your back to the dunes, enjoy views of unspoiled Essex Bay, including Hog Island and Cross Island. In late summer and fall, an abundance of small shorebirds frantically search the wet sand for food. To the untrained eye they may all look alike, but a closer look reveals birds of different sizes, shapes, and beaks. Commonly seen are semi-palmated plovers, semi-palmated sandpipers, black-bellied plovers, killdeer, ruddy turnstones, sanderlings, and tiny least sandpipers. Many of these birds comb the same patch of sand for food, but because different species hunt for different prey, they do not compete. A field guide (see Bibliography) and binoculars are recommended.

If there is sufficient water, a trip into beautiful Essex Bay is hard to resist. (See Trips 3 and 4 for details.) Those heading back to the Annisquam can retrace their path out the mouth of the bay (watching for rips) and paddle southeast to their put-in.

Directions to Launch Site: See Trip 6.

Alternate Launch Site: Lanes Cove, Gloucester. Take Route 128 to Exit 11 in Gloucester (Grant Circle rotary). Drive three-quarters of the way around the rotary to pick up Route 127 north. Follow Route 127 for 4.5 miles to Duley Street. (Look for the Lanes Cove Market.) Turn left and follow Duley Street 0.1 mile to the cove. Park along the side of the road. For other alternate put-ins, consult map.

trip 8 ROCKPORT TO THATCHER AND MILK ISLANDS

Level of Difficulty: Moderate to strenuous; open water

Round-Trip Mileage: 9.0 miles from Granite Pier; 6.6 miles from Old Garden Landing

Attractions: Three scenic islands; historic lighthouses; Rockport Harbor

Precautions: Refracting waves may be dangerous in Straitsmouth Channel.

Charts: NOAA 13279 (1:20,000), or NOAA 13274 (1:40,000)

Tidal Information: Mean tidal range, 8.6 feet. High tide 5 minutes after Boston high tide.

Launch Site: Granite Pier, Rockport (parking fee in season).

FROM QUAINT ROCKPORT HARBOR to rocky, wind-blasted islands, this trip explores the diversity and rugged beauty of Cape Ann. The moderately challenging route includes paddling across Sandy Bay in Rockport to visit Thatcher and Milk islands. Unfortunately, in 1995 a storm destroyed the landing ramp on Thatcher Island, so until repairs are completed, an easy landing is possible only on Milk. Once Thatcher's ramp is rebuilt, kayakers will again have the opportunity to easily explore and camp on this fascinating island, whose twin towers have been a Cape Ann landmark for more than 200 years. Since this paddle is entirely in open water, monitor wind, weather and sea conditions carefully before departing.

Rockport is especially nice in the off-season, when the crowds diminish (and parking spaces appear). More important, in the spring and fall the bird migration is at its peak. Cape Ann is a major flyway through which birds, particularly seabirds, migrate. Bird-watchers will recognize rafts of common eider and ducks, including goldeneyes, browns, mallards, scoters, and mergansers. Very common are double-crested cormorants, herring gulls, and black-backed gulls, which nest on the offshore islands. In fact, kayakers have to be cautious from July to mid-August, when gulls aggressively defend their nesting sites. Landing on the islands, including Thatcher Island, during this time may earn you a peck on the head! For the birds' well-being as well as your own, avoid the islands in midsummer. If you must land, carry a raised paddle.

Kayakers may depart from the public boat landing at Granite Pier or from Old Garden Landing. Old Garden Landing should be used only in the off-season, because it is not legal in Rockport to launch a boat from a public beach (except Front Beach, where the only nonresident parking is metered). This prohibition, however, is not likely to be enforced in spring and fall. To be absolutely sure, check with the Rockport Harbormaster at 978-546-9589.

From the boat ramp at Granite Pier, paddle south toward Rockport Harbor. In the 1800s, thousands of tons of granite were shipped from Granite Pier to Europe and the eastern seaboard. A large quarry is located just west of the pier (visible from Route 127). Granite from Rockport built landmarks such as Boston's Customs House and the Brooklyn Bridge and paved streets from Philadelphia to London.

Paddle south to Bearskin Neck, the northern arm of Rockport Harbor. Once a shipbuilding center, Bearskin Neck is now a tourist mecca, housing art galleries, gift shops, and restaurants. Its colorful name comes from a day in 1710 when John Babson killed a bear there, skinned it, and laid it on a rock to dry. Curious kayakers may take a short detour into the harbor to view the yachts, fishing boats, and "Motif #1," an oft-painted and-photographed fishing shack standing on the neck. Kayakers will see artists with easels on the Old Stone Fort at the end of Bearskin Neck and on the high rocky headlands on the south side of Rockport Harbor. Both command breathtaking panoramic views of Rockport and Sandy Bay.

From the headlands, paddle southeast along the coast. Directly east, note the long ledge of rock. In 1885 the federal government initiated the dumping of granite blocks about a mile offshore to build

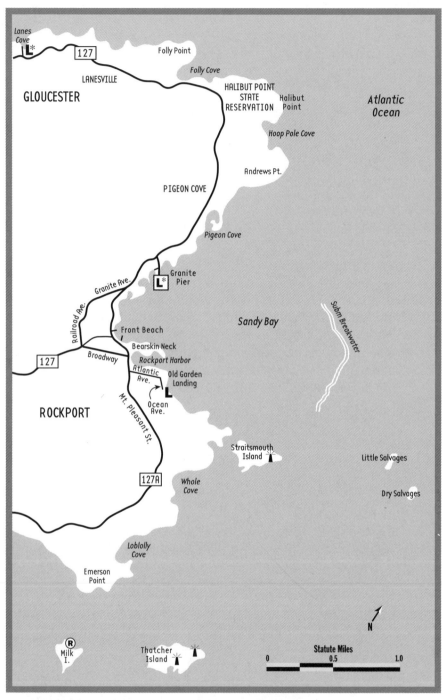

Trip 8: Rockport to Thatcher and Milk Islands

a 9,000-foot breakwater. Granite from Pigeon Cove supplied 6,000 feet of the base before appropriations were halted. The never completed breakwater now presents a serious navigation hazard and a puzzlement to ocean-gazers.

Approximately 1.2 miles south of Granite Pier is Old Garden Landing, the alternate launching site. This sheltered beach is a popular spot for scuba divers. Divers flock to Rockport for its clear water, shipwrecks, and healthy marine life. Off Old Garden Beach divers see an abundance of lobster as well as some hefty ocean scallops, conger eels, and wolffish. At the sandy beach, Granite Pier kayakers can take a break (off-season) or continue paddling east-southeast along the shoreline to Straitsmouth Island.

The grassy island soon comes into view with its prominent white lighthouse. The Straitsmouth Island lighthouse, built in 1896, as well as the light on Thatcher Island, warn mariners of the numerous hazards lying outside Sandy Bay. For example, the Dry Salvages, a cluster of low-lying rocks about a mile east, were the site of many wrecks over the last 400 years. Weather and sea conditions permitting, kayakers may paddle out to these rocks, noted not for their beauty but for their popularity with harbor seals in spring and fall. Their strange name is a result of the Yankee corruption of the French *Les Trois Sauvages*, coined by explorer Samuel de Champlain in the early 1600s to describe these treacherous rocks. Well-read kayakers may remember the haunting T. S. Eliot poem of the same name:

> ...It tosses up our losses, the torn seine,
> The shattered lobsterpot, the broken oar
> And the gear of foreign dead men...

> ...We cannot think of a time that is oceanless
> Or of an ocean not littered with wastage
> Or of a future that is not liable
> Like the past, to have no destination...

Those continuing on to Thatcher Island should pass through the Straitsmouth Channel. Watch for dangerous waves developing there. The channel is only fifty yards wide, and refracting waves bouncing off the island and the opposing shore can be a problem for kayakers. If the channel is torn up, paddle around Straitsmouth Island to the east. In late fall, seals can be found on the island.

From Straitsmouth Island it is 1.3 miles directly south-south-east to Thatcher Island. Paddle directly to the island or hug the shoreline along Whale and Loblolly Coves. Whale Cove was named for a seventy-six-foot whale that grounded there in 1798. Although rarely viewed by kayak, humpback whales cruise the waters off Cape Ann from April to November, accompanied occasionally by right and finback whales.

Thatcher Island is easily recognized by its twin stone lighthouses. These were built in 1861, replacing the lights the British erected in 1771. The story behind the island's name is a sad one. In 1635 a small boat was shipwrecked on a submerged reef near the island. Two of the passengers, Anthony Thatcher and his wife, survived by washing up on the island, but twenty-one drowned in the devastating wreck. Most tragically, the Thatchers watched helplessly as their four children were swept to their deaths. Mr. Thatcher's eloquent account of the wreck, expressed in a letter after the incident, speaks heartbreakingly about their loss.

Thatcher Island is a wonderful place to visit. Listed on the National Register of Historic Places, it is a unique historic site as well as a natural haven for seabirds, seals (late fall to early spring), and those seeking ocean solitude. When the landing was intact, hospitable lighthouse keepers maintained the trails on the island and oversaw a guest house and camping area. These facilities will reopen when the landing is rebuilt. For information on Thatcher Island offerings, contact the Thatcher Island Association, P.O. Box 73, Rockport, MA 01966; 978-546-7697. Membership in the association helps to maintain the island's structures, preserve its natural attributes, and promote educational programs on the island. For island landing conditions, call 978-546-2326.

Just 0.5 mile from Thatcher Island lies Milk Island, a rocky, low-lying island, now owned by the state and operated as a wildlife refuge. A century ago the island was used as summer pasture for sheep; today it is a nesting area for thousands of herring gulls, black-backed gulls, cormorants, and black-crowned night herons, each species occupying a different part of the island. Night herons build their nests in the scrubby bushes located at the island's center. On the northeastern shore, cormorants make nests of sticks (sometimes a foot tall) along the beach, just out of reach of the waves. Black-backed gulls occupy much of the western end, and herring gulls nest on what's left. In recent years, the population of double-crested cor-

Straitsmouth Island, Rockport.

morants has exploded in Massachusetts, more than quadrupling since 1977. In 1996, on Milk Island alone, more than 1,000 nesting pairs were counted! To land on the island, find the gravel beach on its northwest shore. When exploring the refuge, step carefully to avoid crushing expertly camouflaged eggs or chicks lying in crudely formed nests. For the protection of the nesting birds, avoid landing from July through mid-August.

After visiting Milk Island, retrace your paddle to your launching site. Further explorations of Cape Ann are described in Trips 6–9.

Trip Tip: Kayakers can paddle north from Granite Pier for another scenic open-water excursion. From the pier, turn north (left) and paddle about 2.3 miles along the rocky coast to view the dramatic headlands of Halibut Point. Along the way, kayakers pass Pigeon Cove and the headlands of Andrew's Point. This makes a nice 4.6-mile round-trip tour of the Rockport coast, but be forewarned that the water around Halibut Point is frequently rough and landing is nearly impossible at the point's rocky shore.

Another fine open-water adventure is to paddle 2.3 miles out of Sandy Bay to the Dry Salvages (just a mile from the tip of Straitsmouth Island). In calm water, landing is fairly easy on the barren rock outcropping; but be extremely careful in surf. If the sea is not too rough, you can reach a sheltered landing area by paddling into a cove on the island's south side. A pleasantly desolate picnic can be had among the seaweed, seals, sky, and seabirds. To reach the Dry Salvages, simply paddle east from Sandy Bay, crossing the breakwater about 1.2 miles from shore. Continue east to reach Little Salvages after 0.7 mile and Dry Salvages just 0.3 mile farther west.

Directions to Launch Site: Take Route 128 to Exit 11 (Route 127 north). In one mile, arrive at the junction with Route 127A. Bear left to continue to follow Route 127 north another 3.1 miles to Granite Pier on the right. (Route 127 becomes Granite Street.) Drop off boat at landing and park on pier.

Alternate Launch Site: Old Garden Landing, Rockport (spring and fall only). Take Route 128 to Exit 11 (Route 127 north), as described above. At the junction of Route 127 and Route 127A, turn right onto Route 127A and drive to Atlantic Avenue. Turn left on Atlantic and drive to its termination at Ocean Avenue and turn right onto Ocean. Old Garden Landing is the small park on the left. On-street parking is available on Highland Avenue, one block south.

trip 9 GLOUCESTER HARBOR

Level of Difficulty: Easy to moderate; protected water

Round-Trip Mileage: 5.7 miles to Norman's Woe; 8.1 miles to Magnolia Harbor; 3.0 miles to Eastern Point; 11.7 miles to Norman's Woe and Eastern Point

Attractions: Historic Gloucester Harbor; Hammond Castle; Stage Fort Park; Eastern Point Lighthouse

Precautions: Heavy boat traffic in Gloucester Harbor can generate dangerous wakes. Watch for large ships and working boats. Avoid Blynman Canal when current is strong and boat traffic heavy.

Charts: NOAA 13279 (1:20,000), or NOAA 13274 (1:40,000)

Tidal Information: Mean tidal range, 8.7 feet. Use high tide for Boston.

Launch Site: Pavilion Beach County Boat Landing, Gloucester (known locally as the "Greasy Pole" or fisherman's statue beach). Free parking.

THE WEST SIDE OF GLOUCESTER HARBOR is surprisingly beautiful. Steep, forested cliffs rise from the water, and lovely parks preserve graceful beaches and rocky shores. This trip explores the northern reaches of Massachusetts Bay and traverses one of the most important and historic fishing ports in the United States. The scenic paddle is most enjoyable in the off-season when boat traffic is light and harbor seals are frolicking.

Begin at the boat landing on the east end of Pavilion Beach. Above you stands the heroic *Man at the Wheel*, a statue depicting an

top ten list
tips for circumnavigating cape ann

Most Massachusetts kayakers are drawn, if only once, to attempt the grueling 22-mile circumnavigation of Cape Ann. While a trip of that length and difficulty is beyond the scope of this book, I include the following tips for a safe circumnavigation. For a description of the entire course, consult Tamsin Venn's *Sea Kayaking Along the New England Coast*, and for detailed descriptions of several sections of the route read Trips 6-9.

TIP 10. *Take Me to the River.* Choose a hassle-free put-in. Convenient launch sites are Pavilion Beach (the Greasy Pole) or Dunfudgin Landing behind Gloucester High School (see Trip 9 for driving directions).

TIP 9. *Slip Sliding Away.* Paddling against the current through the narrow Blynman canal is difficult and dangerous. The current is strong and traffic is heavy. Time your trip to paddle at slack tide or with the current. Alternatively, you can avoid the canal entirely by ending your trip at nearby Pavilion Beach (a short walk from your car if you launched at Dunfudgin).

TIP 8. *Time Is On Your Side.* Get an early start (7:00-8:00 A.M. is good). Early morning paddlers have a better chance of avoiding the prevailing southwesterly winds. Expect to paddle the 22 miles in about 6-8 hours.

TIP 7. *I Know it's Only Rock and Roll.* Avoid a roll in the drink by keeping a safe distance from refracting waves. After turning northeast from the Annisquam River toward Halibut Point, kayakers face a very rocky shoreline. Consequently, in windy and wavy conditions, paddle far enough from the shore to avoid refracting seas and boomers.

TIP 6. *Gimme Shelter.* After passing Straitsmouth Island (Rockport), pull-out spots are scarce. Long Beach and Good Harbor

Beach can be used in an emergency, but both present tricky landings in surf. Straitsmouth Island is the circumnavigation's midpoint, so evaluate your condition and that of the sea and weather. If need be, Rockport Harbor is an easy bail-out point.

TIP 5. *Don't Fall into the Gap.* Straitsmouth Gap, that is. This narrow passage can get rough when there is sizable swell. Tough waves can be avoided by going around Straitsmouth Island.

TIP 4. *Get Milk.* Milk Island, just southwest of Thatcher Island is a good place to stop for lunch (until they fix the ramp on Thatcher). The beach on its northwest side provides a good landing area. Avoid the island, however, when birds are nesting (see Trip 8).

TIP 3. *Bad to the Bone.* Just when you're really exhausted and most vulnerable, Dogbar Jetty at the eastern entrance to Gloucester Harbor can throw you for a loop. Make a fairly tight turn around the jetty to stay clear of the fast-moving traffic flying in and out of the harbor. Don't paddle too close to the jetty in rough water, however, or boat wakes and refracting waves may dash you onto the rocks.

TIP 2. *Nothing but Blue Skies.* Bad weather can make this trip a bear. Listen carefully to weather conditions and predictions. Err on the side of safety. There is *always* another day.

TIP 1. *A Little Help from Your Friends.* Do not paddle solo. While a large group is not recommended, paddling with three or four experienced kayakers greatly increases your safety. Kayakers can find partners through the North Shore Paddlers Network (nspn.org) or join a guided trip with an outfitter, such as Charles River Canoe and Kayak.

This list was compiled with the invaluable help of veteran Cape Ann paddlers, Leon Granowitz, John Leonard, and Bryan Mitchell.

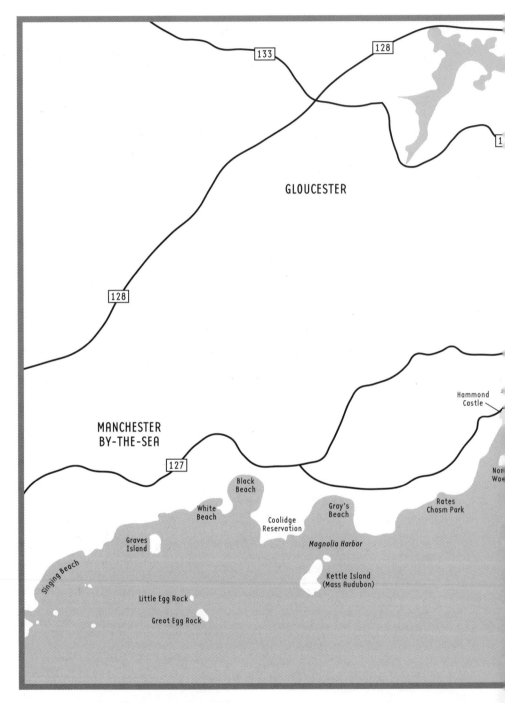

Trip 9: Gloucester Harbor

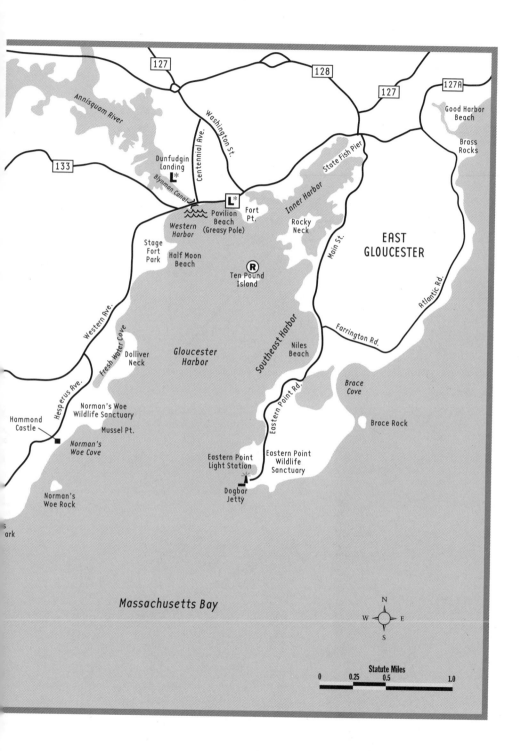

oilskin-clad fisherman which commemorates Gloucester's 300th anniversary. The statue memorializes the large number of Gloucester fishermen who have lost their lives at sea. Between 1880 and 1897 alone, 264 Gloucester fishing vessels vanished, taking with them 1,614 men. Since 1623, more than 10,000 Gloucester fishermen gave their lives to this dangerous pursuit.

From Pavilion Beach, paddle southeast toward Stage Fort Park, a public park occupying a large portion of the west side of Gloucester Harbor. Along the way, pass Blynman Canal where the Annisquam River meets the harbor. Colonists dug this canal in 1642 so vessels did not have to sail the dangerous route around Cape Ann. (Stay away from the canal entrance, as the tidal current averages more than three knots.) Stage Fort Park occupies the spot where in 1623 the Dorchester Bay Company set up both its first fish-drying platforms, or "stages,"and its first cannon. It was the site of an actual battle during the Revolutionary War when the British attempted to burn both the stages and the town. Today it is the site of a wonderful park, encompassing lovely Half Moon Beach, an ice-cream stand,

The Greasy Pole at Pavilion Beach, Gloucester Harbor.

are cod dead?

For 500 years, Europeans and their descendants fished for cod off the coast of North America. Cod fishing built New England. Abundant cod brought settlers to its shore, fed and enriched its colonies, and helped establish thriving seaports. Its golden likeness hangs prominently in the Massachusetts State House and decorates colonial manors from Newport to Marblehead. For centuries, cod supported fishing communities throughout New England and Canada.

In 1895, New England fishermen caught a total of 60,000 tons of cod. Only seventy-five years later, factory ships off the coast of Canada hauled in more than 100 tons of cod *an hour*. In that hour, one ship could catch as much cod as a sixteenth-century fishing boat could catch in a season. By 1968 the ships were pulling in three times more fish than were ever caught in a single year before 1954. That was the beginning of the end.

Since the late 1980s, the Atlantic cod population fell by two-thirds, accompanied by even more precipitous drops in populations of yellowtail flounder and the almost extinct haddock. In Canada, where overfishing by factory trawlers nearly destroyed the cod population, fishing was banned in 1992. Refusing to learn a lesson, New England fishermen continued to overfish their own fishing grounds at Georges Bank. In 1994 the National Marine Fisheries Service closed thousands of square miles of the bank. When the fish failed to return, the New England Fishery Management Council voted in 1999 to reduce further by 50 percent the daily allowable catch of cod and to ban fishing for ground fish within thirty miles of shore from Maine to the top of Cape Cod Bay.

But the story is not yet over. Whether groundfish rebound is still to be determined. Cod are not dead, but its survival depends on shared beliefs and goals. Politicians, fishermen, corporate interests, and scientists must work together to determine the best interests of the fish. This, in turn, will be in the best interest of us all.

a bandstand, a historic fort, ample parking, and Gloucester's Visitor Welcoming Center.

Leaving the park, paddle southwest along Gloucester's forested shoreline. Looking east, the island with the lighthouse is Ten Pound Island. Reportedly this island was purchased from Native Americans for ten pounds, hence its name. Although this story may be fanciful, it is documented that in 1700, colonists paid a mere seven pounds for title to all of Cape Ann. Ten Pound Island is known for its most famous guest, Winslow Homer, who lived on the island in 1880 and there completed more than 100 paintings! Presently owned by the city of Gloucester, the island offers picnic tables for public use. Kayakers can land on a gravelly beach on its northeast side.

Continuing southwest along the shore, kayakers enter Freshwater Cove on the south side of Stage Fort Park. At high tide, this cove provides some quiet exploring in the marsh at its southwestern reaches. Above the cove, a majestic "cottage" built in the 1840s overlooks the water. Leave the cove and paddle south. As you pass the rocks around Dolliver Neck, look for harbor seals in spring and fall.

About 0.7 mile from Dolliver Neck, arrive at Mussel Point. Across the harbor, the white lighthouse of Eastern Point Light can easily be seen, 1.0 mile east-southeast. Continuing south-southwest along the shoreline, about 0.7 mile from Mussel Point, arrive at the scenic western tip of the harbor mouth. On the right, as you continue to head south-southwest, is the rocky headland named Norman's Woe, the south-facing Norman's Woe Cove, and Norman's Woe Rock about 0.1 mile offshore. Norman's Woe was made famous by Longfellow's *Wreck of the Hesperus*, a dramatic but fictitious ballad about a shipwreck on these rocks. About 0.3 mile past Norman's Woe Rock, look for Rafe's Chasm, a split in the granite headland 200 feet long and 60 feet deep. During storms, waves roar into this chasm with thunderous effect. (Stay clear of the chasm's entrance.) Seaward, lobster boats work the hundreds of traps set along this stretch of coast.

A conspicuous landmark above Norman's Woe Cove is Hammond Castle, a re-creation of a medieval castle, completed in 1928. The castle opens for highly recommended tours mid-June through mid-September (and once again around Halloween). Its treasures include a Gothic hall (100 feet long and 60 feet high), a colossal pipe organ, a Roman bath within diving distance from a second-floor balcony, medieval art and artifacts, secret passageways, peepholes, and

Harbor seal.

more. The brilliant inventor who built the castle, Dr. John Hays Hammond Jr., held more U.S. patents than any other single American and is considered America's second greatest inventor, after Thomas Edison.

Norman's Woe is a good turnaround point. Depending on the wind, the water may be substantially rougher outside the harbor. If a longer trip is desired in protected water, novices can explore the east side of Gloucester Harbor, described below. Those wishing to reach Magnolia Harbor, about 1.2 miles to the west, should continue southwest along the shoreline.

Magnolia Harbor has been the site of tony summer homes since the late 1800s. Magnolia's heyday was the period from 1890 to World War II, when it was the swinging social center of the North Shore, offering in 1906 the largest hotel in New England. According to one historian, "Ambassadors, royalty, multimillionaires, presidential confidants, the great and the aspiring from the world over flocked to the...hotels of Magnolia to be seen, to play, to dance at the extravagant balls, to watch the horse shows and the gymkhanas on

Crescent Beach, to athleticize, to romance, to conspire and to eye the next rung on the ladder of Society."

Today the glamour is gone. The two largest hotels burned down forty years ago. Horses no longer race the hard sand beach, and no one gambles at garish casinos. Although the curve of the beach is still lovely, it is marred by ugly *Private Beach* signs painted on the sea wall. Despite its fall from grace, Magnolia makes a nice rest stop. Note, however, that the beach is private except for the public landing at its eastern end.

On your return, take note of Kettle Island, just south of Magnolia at the mouth of the harbor. Recently acquired by the Massachusetts Audubon Society, this island is an important nesting ground for long-legged wading birds, such as herons, egrets, and glossy ibis. In fact, in 1996 more than 200 nesting pairs of snowy egrets were found on Kettle Island and six pairs of the rare little blue heron. This colony is considered the most important heron and egret colony in Massachusetts. To protect the nesting birds and their young, do not land on the island from May through mid-July. Later in the season, kayakers can land carefully on a beach at the island's northwest end. For a truly phenomenal experience, return to Kettle Island at the dusk of a full moon to watch moonlit herons and egrets return to their nests as night falls. Each summer, Massachusetts Audubon runs a highly recommended, naturalist-guided moonlight paddle to the island. Call their Ipswich River Wildlife Sanctuary for details (978-887-9264).

To explore the eastern side of Gloucester Harbor, paddle east (left from Pavilion Beach). Eastern Point Light lies about 2.35 miles from the put-in. Use care crossing the shipping channel into Gloucester's inner harbor, for it is extremely busy with commercial traffic. Kayakers can carefully enter the inner harbor for an interesting side trip. The busy working harbor is full of pleasure and commercial boats of every size and sort. About a half-mile from the inner harbor entrance is the State Fish Pier. Across the narrow mouth lies the artist colony of Rocky Neck, worth a visit later by foot.

After crossing the boat channel to reach Rocky Neck, head south 0.7 mile to public Niles Beach (where kayakers can land easily and rest on the sandy beach). Then continue south past the mansions of Eastern Point to the Eastern Point Yacht Club and Eastern Point Lighthouse. For a good look at the lighthouse, paddle around the breakwater (Dogbar Jetty), usually lined with local fishermen. The point is a notoriously busy spot. Watch for fishing lines, fast-moving powerboats, and refracting waves off the jetty. After viewing the lighthouse, kayakers can explore the outside of Eastern Point. Follow the coastline northeast for about a mile to reach the shelter of Brace Cove, guarded by Brace Rock on its southern edge. Those looking to log miles can proceed down the rocky coast two more miles to the sandy stretches of Good Harbor. Beach or paddle three miles to Gloucester's Long Beach.

Directions to Launch Site: Take Route 128 north to Exit 14 in Gloucester. At the end of the ramp, turn right onto Route 133 east. Drive 2.9 miles on Route 133. Turn left onto Route 127 and drive 0.4 mile to the public landing on the right. There is a small parking lot at the landing and street parking along the beach. The "greasy pole" sits in the water just offshore.

Alternate Launch Site: Dunfudgin Landing, Gloucester High School; see Trip 7. This launch site requires passage through Blynman Canal and thus is not recommended because of the swift current and heavy traffic. Novices can, nevertheless, drop the boat at the public landing, then park at the high school and make the short walk each way.

trip 10 — MANCHESTER HARBOR TO GREAT MISERY ISLAND

Level of Difficulty: Easy to Misery Islands, moderate to Singing Beach, strenuous to Magnolia Harbor; all open water

Round–Trip Mileage: 3.2 miles to Misery Island; 7.2 miles to Singing Beach; 11.0 miles to Magnolia Harbor

Attractions: Large island for picnicking and hiking; scenic harbor; protected launching and landing sites

Precautions: Heavy summer boat traffic in Manchester Harbor and Salem Sound. Exercise caution in the area between House Island and Ram Rocks at the mouth of Manchester Harbor; swells can break there unexpectedly. In high southwest winds, waters outside Manchester Harbor can be quite rough. Large waves can develop in the channel between Big and Little Misery Islands at the east entry.

Charts: NOAA 13275 (1:25,000), or NOAA 13274 (1:40,000)

Tidal Information: Mean tidal range, 8.8 feet. Use Boston high tide.

Launch Site: Masconomo Park, Manchester Harbor; limited parking for nonresidents.

THIS TRIP IS BEST on weekdays or during the off-season due to the chronic shortage of nonresident parking in Manchester. Manchester-by-the-Sea sits on a lovely stretch of coastline, but the town does its best to reserve this treasure for those lucky enough to live there. Determined kayakers can, nevertheless, arrive at Manchester Harbor early enough to nab one of the twenty or so nonresident parking places at Masconomo Park. Off-season kayaking is also recommended for the unusual serenity you'll find at this normally busy harbor.

From the landing at Masconomo Park, paddlers must wind their way to the mouth of the harbor, passing Tucks Point on the right. Often a gaggle of geese or a raft of ducks is scattered along the way. Masconomo Park takes its name from the Agawam chief who welcomed the colonists landing on these shores in 1630. A few years later, most of his tribe died from the diseases they introduced. From Tucks Point, the Misery Islands Reservation can be clearly seen just 1.25 miles from the mouth of Manchester Harbor. Recognize Tucks Point by the red-roofed, white-columned Rotunda built over the water, providing views of the harbor and Gales Point since 1896. Adjacent to the quaint pavilion is the Manchester Yacht Club.

From the mouth of the harbor, it is possible to paddle directly southwest to Misery Island, but a more interesting and conservative route is to hug the Manchester shore to West Beach, then cross the 0.5-mile distance from West Beach to the island. Paddling southwest along the rugged coastline, enjoy views of the gracious homes that sit comfortably atop the steep shore. After Tucks Point, the first small cove you pass is Black Cove. Continuing southwest, the larger and more interesting bay at Chubb Creek appears after about 0.7 mile. At low tide, this is barely a bay, but at high tide it's a great place to play. If the tide is high and slack, you can even paddle under the railroad bridge and explore narrow Chubb Creek for a short distance. Exercise caution when the tide is running, however, because the current can be swift under the bridge.

From the cove, continue southwest along the shore to West Beach, a mile-long stretch of very sandy, very private beach. Landing here is unfortunately forbidden, and parking in the private lot will earn your car a quick and expensive tow to the nearest locked garage. From West Beach head across the bay to Great and Little Misery Islands. The best spot to land on Great Misery Island (the larger island) is South Beach, on the island's south side, just opposite Little Misery Island. Paddle around Great Misery's rocky west shore to find the beach.

The Misery Islands received their name in the 1600s when an unfortunate cod fisherman wrecked his boat upon their shores one cold December. After three days, nearly frozen, he was rescued. From that day on, the islands were known as Moulton's Misery,

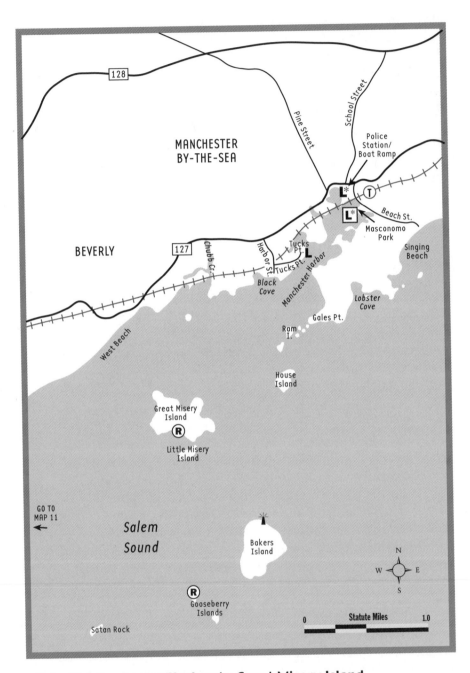

Trip 10: Manchester Harbor to Great Misery Island

memorializing the fisherman's misfortune. When the islands became a summer resort, promoters tried to change their name to "Mystery" Islands, but the new name never caught on. Rich in history and lore, the Misery Islands are a pleasure to visit.

Stretch your legs by hiking the trails of the eighty-four-acre Misery Islands Reservation. Owned by The Trustees of Reservations (TTOR), these islands are the only dedicated conservation land in Salem Sound. Nonmembers must pay a small fee to help maintain the islands and support the good works of the TTOR. On Great Misery, trails meander past remnants of buildings from the summer colony that thrived on the island in the early 1900s. Magnificent oak and maple trees, hundreds of years old, are found along the way. The tales these trees could tell about cod fisherman, winter gales, summer parties, and devastating fire! In 1926, fire nearly destroyed the entire summer colony. Bring a picnic and enjoy the shade of one of these spreading trees.

Before you head back to Manchester Harbor, investigate the remnants of an old steamer in the channel between Great and Little Misery Islands. At low tide, the wooden ribs of the *City of Rockland* are visible above the waves. The steamer wrecked off the coast of Maine and was towed here and burned after being stripped of its valuable hardware.

For a secluded picnic spot with superlative views, visit Little Misery Island after inspecting the wreck. Land on the island's north side (opposite the beach on Great Misery) and climb past Japanese black pines to the top of the small knoll. From this perch, picnickers gain exquisite views south to Baker Island (the large island with lighthouse and summer homes) and the Gooseberries (uninhabited rock outcroppings). To the southwest Marblehead is visible, as well as the small islands of Salem Sound. Those who enjoy open-water paddling can consider a four-mile circumnavigation of Baker Island and the Gooseberries from the Misery Islands. Although landing is prohibited on private Baker Island, the desolate, stony beaches on the Gooseberries are very inviting. (See Trip 13).

Trip Tips: For additional scenic paddling closer to shore, explore the coast north of Manchester Harbor. From Tucks Point, it is about 2.9 miles (one way) north-northeast to Lobster Cove and Singing Beach (paddling around the seaward side of House Island). A stop at Singing Beach is highly recommended off-season. From Memorial

Day through Labor Day, this popular swimming beach is closed to kayakers. Especially lovely in the off-season, Singing Beach lives up to its unusual name. When one walks on the sand, it squeals like a sneaker on a gymnasium floor! Fine paddling continues to the northeast as one passes private Graves Beach and Graves Island just 0.5 mile north of Singing Beach. Another recommended destination to the north is the breathtaking Coolidge Reservation, about 4.5 miles from Tucks Point. Although the reservation (owned by TTOR) is inaccessible by water, it is lovely from the sea. The topography of the site is beautiful, encompassing high bluffs and sweeping lawns—

the trustees of reservations' legacy

The Trustees of Reservations (TTOR) protects seventy-eight reservations across Massachusetts comprising more than 20,400 acres of land. All the reservations are open to the public and are enjoyed by more than 1 million visitors annually. TTOR has preserved some of the most breathtaking sites on the Massachusetts coast, including the Crane Wildlife Refuge in Ipswich, Halibut Point in Rockport, World's End in Hingham, and Cape Poge Wildlife Refuge on Chappaquiddick Island. Many of their reservations can be used and enjoyed by kayakers for picnicking, camping, and hiking.

The Trustees of Reservations is not a state-funded organization, and therefore relies for support entirely upon membership dues, contributions, grants, admission receipts, and endowments. Kayakers can help support TTOR by becoming members. In return, they'll receive a very useful guidebook to the reservations, free or reduced admission, and events information. For membership information, contact the Membership Department, TTOR, Long Hill, 572 Essex Street, Beverly, MA 01915-1530; 978-524-1858.

in total nearly fifty-eight acres of forest, wetlands, beach, and headlands. The Coolidge Reservation is open to the public Saturdays through Mondays (accessible off Route 127). For trips north of Manchester Harbor, carry NOAA Chart No. 13279, Ipswich Bay to Gloucester Harbor, or NOAA Chart No. 13274 and consult Map 9.

Directions to Launch Site: From Route 128: Take Route 128 to Exit 16 (Pine Street) in Manchester. At the end of the ramp, turn left (southeast) and drive 1.4 miles to Route 127. Turn left onto Route 127 and drive 0.3 mile to the intersection of Summer and Beach Streets. Continue straight on Beach Street 0.1 mile to Masconomo Park. Nonresidents can park in the middle of the lot (around twenty spaces are allotted). Parking is legal, but no signs indicate nonresident parking. Arrive early on summer weekends to secure a spot. If no parking is available, drop the boat off and park in the lot at the commuter train station ($15 on summer weekends) or launch at the alternate site (see below).

From Route 127: Drive scenic Route 127 north from Beverly 6.9 miles to the intersection of Route 127 (Summer Street) with Beach Street. Continue straight on Beach Street 0.1 mile to Masconomo Park.

Alternate Launch Sites: (1) Tucks Point, Manchester Harbor. Tucks Point was formerly an excellent launch site for kayakers, but nonresident parking was banned there in the summer of 1999. To determine the current policy, call the Manchester Police. It is likely that the parking ban will not be enforced before Memorial Day and after Labor Day. To find Tucks Point, follow the directions above to the intersection of Route 127 and Pine Street in Manchester. Turn right onto Route 127 and drive 0.7 mile to Harbor Street. Turn left and drive 0.2 mile to its intersection with Tucks Point Road. Turn left and follow Tucks Point Road 0.25 mile to a large unpaved lot. Launch from the beach between the Rotunda and the Manchester Yacht Club. (2) Boat ramp behind Manchester Police Station, 10 Central Street (Route 127), Manchester. Before Memorial Day and after Labor Day, kayakers can usually park behind the station. Obtain prior permission from an officer at the station. Find the station (connected to the Manchester Town Hall) by following the above directions to Route 127 and Pine Street. The police station is on the right, immediately after the Pine Street/Route 127 intersection.

trip 11   SALEM SOUND (Salem and Beverly Harbors)

Level of Difficulty: Easy to moderate; open water

Round-Trip Mileage: 3.2 miles within Salem Harbor; 6.0 miles to Lynch Park, Beverly; 12.0 miles to Misery Island

Attractions: Public parks; picnic areas; and beaches; Rockmore Restaurant (floating restaurant in season); camping on Winter Island

Precautions: Traffic is extremely heavy in summer. Use caution when crossing Salem and Beverly Channels. Watch for submerged rocks and breaking waves along edge of Winter Island.

Charts: NOAA 13275 (1:20,000), or NOAA 13274 (1:40,000)

Tidal Information: Mean tidal range, 9.0 feet. Use the tide tables for Boston. Large areas of mud flats along Forest River in Salem Harbor, Collins Cove, and along Beverly shoreline.

Launch Site: Winter Island, Salem; parking fee ($5) for nonresidents, May through October.

THIS IS A THOROUGHLY ENJOYABLE, albeit primarily urban, paddle through an interesting and bustling sound. The densely settled shoreline is dotted with beaches and parks, and maritime activity is everywhere. For inexperienced paddlers, the abundance of fellow boaters, shore fishermen, and beach picnickers is reassuring. On summer weekends, however, the hectic traffic can unnerve and even endanger novices. For safe and hassle-free paddling, kayak early or late in the day and cross boat channels with care.

The options are rich for Salem Sound paddlers. There are three principal choices: paddling south into Salem Harbor, paddling north into Beverly Harbor, or venturing farther north along Beverly's handsome coast to Misery Island and/or Manchester Harbor. Before choosing your route, consider the wind, tide, weather, and length of time you want to paddle.

The shortest route explores Salem Harbor. Paddling south from the put-in, kayakers can tour Salem Harbor and Marblehead's west shore in a brief 3.2-mile round trip (see map 12). From Winter Island, paddle 0.4 mile across the mouth of the harbor to the Marblehead shore, exercising care when crossing the Salem Channel, marked by green and red buoys. Then turn south to follow the scenic Marblehead shore and explore the reaches of the Forest River. For the best tour paddle at high tide, because the southern half-mile of the harbor turns to mud at low tide. Kayakers should avoid the Salem side of the harbor where two huge industrial complexes are located, the South Essex Sewage Treatment Plant and the Salem Harbor Power Plant. Paddlers adept at entering and exiting their boats from a high dock can stop for unique refreshment at the Rockmore Restaurant, a floating barge anchored in the harbor from Memorial Day through Labor Day. Kayakers seeking a longer tour along the Marblehead shore should consult Trips 12 and 13.

A second option takes paddlers north from Winter Island, around Salem Neck, then across Beverly Harbor to explore Beverly's scenic Gold Coast. This paddle is approximately 3.0 miles one way, with Lynch Park as a turnaround point. For this trip, head left (northeast) from the Winter Island boat ramp and paddle around Fort Pickering Light. Pass Winter Island's sandy "Waikiki Beach." Watch along the shoreline at both ends of the beach for submerged rocks and breaking waves. Next pass little Juniper Cove, which dries to mud at low tide. Continuing north, round Salem Neck and pass the Willows, a public park complete with spacious picnic areas, sandy beach, ball fields, arcade, and pier. It's a nice urban park, but launching and landing is permitted only in the off-season.

As you round the neck, Beverly Harbor comes into view. Its most prominent landmarks include the Route 1A bridge, a gas tank, and the plentiful marinas and yacht clubs at Beverly's Tuck Point. At high tide, Collins Cove to the left (southwest) provides a nice paddle, but at low tide it dries mostly to sand. Along the way to the cove, the west shore of Salem Neck offers pleasant green slopes and

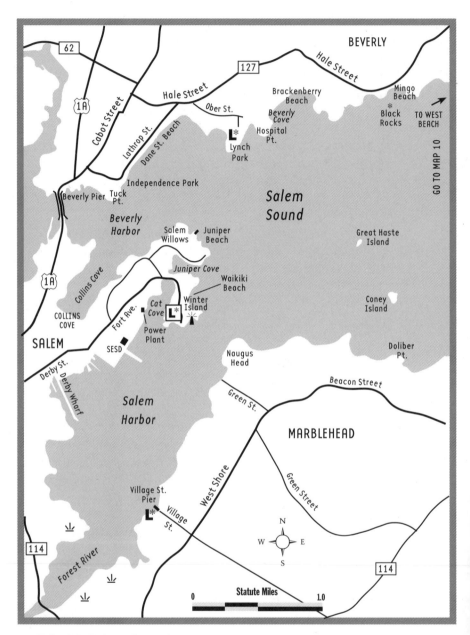

Trip 11: Salem Sound

small rocky coves. Exiting Collins Cove, carefully cross the Beverly Channel to reach Tuck Point on the opposite side of the harbor. (The channel is marked by green buoys on the south side and red buoys on the north.)

Beverly claims to be the birthplace of the American Navy and for good reason. From Tuck Point, the first American naval vessel, *The Hannah*, set sail in 1775. In July of 1776 at Independence Park (the beach just north of Tuck Point), Colonel John Glover read the Declaration of Independence to the citizens of Beverly. Colonel Glover's regiment spent a year on that beach during the Revolutionary War, protecting Beverly's valuable fleet of privateering schooners. The same regiment gained fame late in 1776 by ferrying General Washington across the Delaware.

Proceed north along the Beverly shoreline, enjoying a series of parks and sandy beaches easy on the eyes. The outgoing portion of this trip is especially scenic. Paddlers are spared the backdrop of the Salem Harbor Power Plant and instead view the numerous sandy beaches dotting the coast, as well as the many small islands punctuating the horizon of the sound.

A good turnaround for a short outing is Beverly's lovely Lynch Park (6.0 miles round-trip). The park sits on a tree-covered promontory just after Dane Street Beach (recognized by its prominent bathhouse). Approaching from the west, paddlers arrive first at the park's sandy beach, which usually provides a protected landing area. At low tide, however, extensive mud flats reach from Independence Park to Lynch Park. In summer the mud may be worth the walk, because paddlers can refresh themselves at the park's seasonal refreshment stand and enjoy shade in its gracious picnic areas. Once a privately owned estate, President William Taft used this beautiful property for his summer whitehouse from 1909–10. The actual house he used is no longer standing, but one can view its former location by finding the park's charming rose garden. Kayakers also can explore the beach at the opposite side of the park for some tide-pooling, or reboard their boats and head back across the harbor to Salem Neck.

A third paddling option is to continue north up Beverly's attractive shoreline to Manchester Harbor or cross over to Misery Island (7.2 miles and 6.0 miles one way, respectively, from Winter Island according to the above-described route; paddling directly northeast from Winter Island shortens the trip to 4.75 and 3.4 miles one way,

coastal waters and non-point pollution

❖ Fact: Every year do-it-yourself oil changers dump onto the ground or into storm drains *three times* the amount of oil spilled by the Exxon *Valdez*. This oil ends up in the ocean.

❖ Fact: One-third of Massachusetts' shellfish beds are closed due to excess levels of fecal coliform bacteria from sewage.

❖ Fact: Every American improperly disposes of 50 pounds of household toxins each year. Many of these toxins end up in coastal waters.

❖ Fact: Many laundry detergents contain phosphates that lead to algal blooms which block sunlight and use up excessive amounts of oxygen, sometimes resulting in major fish kills. These phosphates pass through municipal treatment plants untreated.

Non-point pollution is a concept that's hard to grasp for many Americans. It's not sexy, easy to fix, or cheaply resolved. Yet, non-point pollution, defined as contaminated runoff from a multitude of sources, makes up a full 60 percent of the pollution that fouls coastal waters. Many of the contaminants (soot, dust, oil, animal waste, litter, salt, and chemicals) come from everyday activities like fertilizing lawns, walking pets, changing motor oil, doing laundry, and driving. With each rainfall, pollutants from these activities are washed from lawns and streets into stormwater drains and into the ocean.

What can you do? Start spreading the news. Make "non-point pollution" as much a household word as "acid rain." Educate yourself and your neighbors about how (seemingly) innocuous practices like buying laundry detergent, neglecting animal waste, and using lawn fertilizer harm the ocean. Lastly, support broader solutions on the state or regional level, such as implementing stormwater control technology, instituting land use practices to reduce runoff, establishing buffer zones near water bodies, and tightening controls on the use of harmful fertilizers and pesticides on agricultural and recreational land (i.e., golf courses).

respectively). Continuing northeast along the shore after Lynch Park brings one immediately to Hospital Point, graced by a white lighthouse. The house on the point is the official residence for the Commandant of the First Coast Guard District. Paddlers next pass Beverly Cove, uncovered at low tide but a nice paddle at high. This beach is private, save a fifty-foot right of way at the end of Brackenberry Lane. The small public portion can be recognized by a road's-width break in the sea wall, visible from the water. Paddlers are free to land and picnic here but cannot stroll onto private property. North of the right of way is an estate originally owned by Henry Cabot Lodge, the powerful senator who in the early 1900s is credited dubiously with keeping the United States out of the League of Nations.

Next, kayakers round a small promontory (watch for submerged rocks at the point), then pass between the shore and Black Rock (an island loved by cormorants at low tide but awash at high). Use caution in this area when Black Rock is not visible, for barely submerged rocks can be hard to detect. Across from Black Rock is Mingo Beach Landing. Named for the former slave, Robin Mingo, this beach can be recognized from the water by the small Endicott College sign visible near the road, several white benches, a stone sea wall, its location on Route 127, and college buildings visible across the highway. The beach is sand at low tide and has a small public landing. The story of Robin Mingo is heart-breaking. His owner, Nicholas Thorndike, promised Mr. Mingo freedom if the tide ever got low enough for him to walk to Aunt Becky's Ledge. One day the ebbing tide finally allowed Mr. Mingo to walk to the ledge, but he died that same year. Aunt Becky's Ledge is no longer on the charts, but one can guess it's one of the submerged rocks offshore. Mr. Mingo died in 1773. In 1754, there were 28 slaves in Beverly.

Continuing northeast along the shoreline, arrive at sandy West Beach. Although the beach looks inviting, West Beach Club members are serious about their privacy and landing is therefore discouraged. Just 0.5 mile from West Beach to the southeast are Great and Little Misery Islands. A short paddle 0.5 mile southeast brings you to these interesting islands, described in detail in Trips 10 and 13. To land on Great Misery, find the sand beach on the island's south side. A trip to Misery Island from Winter Island is approximately eight miles round-trip, assuming a route that runs parallel to the coastline.

Paddlers wishing to stay close to shore can continue up the mansion-bedecked coast to Manchester Harbor. A nice picnicking destination in calm seas and low tide is the cluster of rocky islands, just outside the harbor. For a more sheltered spot, try Tucks Point. Shade, a small sandy beach, and a gazebo overlooking the harbor mark this scenic point. To find Tucks Point, turn into the harbor and paddle about 0.3 mile to the beach on your left, just past the dock of the Manchester Yacht Club. The paddling distance from Winter Island to Manchester Harbor is approximately 11.2 miles round-trip. For more information on paddling in and around Manchester Harbor, see Trip 10.

Directions to Launch Site: Take Route 128 to Exit 25 (Route 114 East) for Salem. Drive Route 114 to its intersection with Derby Street in Salem. At this intersection Route 114 turns right. Continue *straight* on Derby Street (Route 1A) following signs to Salem Willows and waterfront. At the next intersection with Hawthorne Street, Route 1A turns left; continue straight on Fort Avenue. Pass Pickering Wharf and the House of Seven Gables. Take Fort Avenue to its split at Winter Island Road and turn right. Follow signs 0.4 mile to Winter Island Park. The boat ramp is located at the park's south end. Launching is also possible from the beach adjacent to the Fort Pickering Lighthouse. Campgrounds, restrooms, showers, and a camp store are open seasonally. If traveling to Salem on Route 1A north, drive into Salem, then follow signs to Salem Willows/Winter Island (as described above). If traveling from the east on Route 114, follow Route 114 into Salem, then take Route 1A north to Fort Avenue and follow above directions.

Alternate Launch Sites: (1) Lynch Park, Beverly. Take Route 128 to Route 1A in Beverly. Drive 1A south to Dane Street. Turn left on Dane Street and drive to its end at Route 127. Turn left (north) on Route 127 and drive to Ober Street on the right. Turn right and follow signs for Lynch Park. Parking fee in summer. Long carry at low tide. (2) Village Street Pier, Village Street, Marblehead; free parking; see Trip 13.

Camping: From May through October, camping is permitted on Winter Island. Tent sites available for $15 a night. For information, call Winter Island Marine Park; 978-745-9430.

MARBLEHEAD HARBOR, BROWN'S ISLAND, AND MARBLEHEAD NECK

trip 12

Level of Difficulty: Easy; protected/open water

Round-Trip Mileage: 3.5 miles, or 5.1 miles including Marblehead Neck

Attractions: Sandy beach; island for picnicking; protected launching and landing sites; historic Old Town Marblehead

Precautions: Extremely heavy summer boat traffic in Marblehead Harbor; confused waves due to wakes, current, and refracting waves at the mouth of Marblehead Harbor; refracting waves off the north side of Tinkers Island

Charts: NOAA 13275 (1:25,000), or NOAA 13274 (1:40,000)

Launch Site: Riverhead Beach Boat Landing, Marblehead. Parking fee for nonresidents.

Tidal Information: Mean tidal range, 9.1 feet. High tide is 5 minutes before Boston high tide. Water is very shallow at dead low tide in Dolliber's Cove and Little Harbor. Leaving within an hour or so of high tide from Riverhead Beach takes advantage of the tidal current and avoids low tide at the cove and harbor. Low tide at Riverhead Beach necessitates crossing unpleasant mud flats.

PICNIC ON AN OFFSHORE ISLAND, paddle through historic Marblehead Harbor, and tour via seaside the mansions and yacht clubs of Marblehead Neck. This trip is best enjoyed during the off-season when boat traffic dips from its frenetic summer peak. Absent nerve-wracking congestion, this is an excellent novice trip.

Launching and landing at protected Riverhead or Grace Oliver Beach is usually a breeze, and if ocean swells are threatening, novices can play in Marblehead Harbor or Dolliber's Cove, where the water is often shielded from wind and waves.

Launch from the boat ramp at Riverhead Beach. The paddle from Riverhead Beach northeast to the narrow mouth of Marblehead Harbor is approximately 1.2 miles. In summer, it is necessary to weave through more than 2,000 moorings sporting a rich variety of elegant sailboats and yachts. The town center of Marblehead, dubbed the "yachting capital of the world," lies to your left. The distinctive brick clock tower of Abbot Hall is a prominent landmark. To your right, the gracious mansions and lavish yacht clubs of Marblehead Neck line the shore.

About 0.75 mile from the launch, paddle past the dock at State Street Landing on the left (look for a large crane and a building marked Doyle Sailmakers). Lucky paddlers may spot a lobster boat unloading its catch, but the dock is most often occupied by pleasure boats. The once productive waters of Salem Sound now support relatively few commercial fishermen, due to a precipitous drop in the population of cod and lobster (see sidebar).

Paddle carefully, watching for boat traffic, to the mouth of the harbor. Atop the rocky promontory on your left sits Fort Sewell, a stone fort erected in 1644 to defend the harbor against England's enemies, marauding pirates, and hostile Indians. The structure still stands within a picturesque park on the headlands. It now serves as a dramatic backdrop for summer Shakespeare productions. For a good view, one must visit the park on foot, for the fort is built into the high, grassy knoll.

Turn left around the headland to explore Little Harbor and Dolliber's Cove. If the tide is in, pass on either side of Gerry Island. At dead low tide, paddle to the outside. The first cove is Little Harbor, where the first settlers of Marblehead began their village. Within this tiny protected cove is Gerry Island, once used for drying fish and grazing cattle. Paddle north out of Little Harbor into Dolliber's Cove toward Brown's (or Crowninshield) Island, today owned by The Trustees of Reservations. Kayakers may land easily on the sandy beach on the island's west side. This is a terrific picnic spot, especially in the fall when the island is deliciously deserted. Directly west of Brown's Island lies Grace Oliver Beach, an alternative launching and landing site.

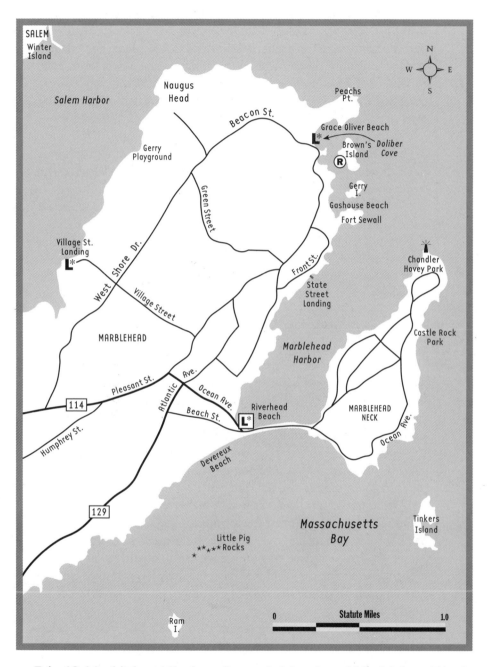

Trip 12: Marblehead Harbor, Brown's Island, and Marblehead Neck

Continue on, leaving Brown's Island to paddle southeast back toward the harbor entrance. Those wishing to call it a day can enter the harbor and paddle the 1.2 miles back to Riverhead Beach. Kayakers up for a longer trip can circumnavigate Marblehead Neck to land at Devereux Beach, a 2.8-mile paddle (one way). Those choosing the longer route must cross the 700-yard entrance (watching for boat traffic and confused waves due to wakes, tidal current, and refracting waves off the headlands). Seas are also likely to be considerably rougher in the open water around the outside of the neck. Exercise caution in strong wind, and give wide berth to the many rocks along the shoreline.

Once across the harbor mouth, pass Chandler Hovey Park and Marblehead Light on the harbor's eastern headland, Point O'Neck. The light stands on a strangely unromantic, 105-foot-tall steel structure (circa 1895). Near the lighthouse, Eugene O'Neill spent his last days enjoying this view. Paddle around the northernmost tip of Marblehead Neck and then head south along its rocky coast. Magnificent houses, most perched high above the beach, adorn its shore. The high, bare rock 500 yards east of the shore is Marblehead Rock, home to scores of seabirds.

Marblehead Neck's steep, rocky coastline affords few opportunities to land, especially at high tide. Also, with the exception of a few narrow rights of way, most of the beach on Marblehead Neck is privately owned. At the south end of the neck, paddle by Tinkers Island, watching for dangerous waves bouncing off the north side of the island.

Tinkers Island is named for the abundance of tinker mackerel that ran by its shores. In 1817 and 1819, the island acquired some local notoriety from the sighting of a monstrous sea serpent near its shore. The serpent's surfacing was said to leave a greasy film on the water off the island. Descriptions of the serpent indicated a dark-brown creature 130 feet long with a white throat and fourteen scales along its back. Tinkers is now home to a handful of summer cottages nestled amid fragrant wild rose. Common terns also nest on the island.

Past Tinkers Island, the distant Boston skyline and the sandy reach of Devereux Beach soon come into view, just 1.0 mile west. Devereux Beach was the site of a large encampment of the Nanepashemet tribe prior to European settlement of the area in the 1600s. Indians hunted in the woods behind the beach and searched

saving salem sound

In the early 1700s, 120 fishing schooners sailed out of Marblehead Harbor, employing more than 1,000 fishermen. More than 200 acres of the young town were covered with drying fish pulled from a sound once teeming with life. Today less than 20 boats fish commercially out of Marblehead Harbor. The cod and flounder are gone, as well as the once abundant lobster. Mussels and clams remain, but harvesting is illegal because of poor water quality. Whether these waters return to their former health and productivity is up to you. Salem Sound 2000 (SS 2000) works to improve and protect the waters and watershed of Salem Sound through water-quality monitoring, beach and stream cleanups, research, environmental advocacy, and public education. This small but effective nonprofit invites your help and active participation. To become a member or learn more, contact SS 2000, 201 Washington Street, Salem, MA 01970; 978-741-7900.

Marblehead Neck for stones to use as tools and weapons. The beach today is a popular spot for fishing, sunbathing, and enjoying the surprisingly fine offerings of Flynnie's, the beach snack bar. The best landing area (beware of dumping waves) is near the west end of the causeway where the beach levels a bit. Land on the beach, then carry your boat across the street to your car at the Riverhead Beach Boat Landing. On busy summer days, lifeguards may object to kayaks landing on the beach. In that event, paddle north or south of the swimming area to land.

Before returning home, take time to visit the sights of Marblehead's historic downtown. Marblehead is a charming town whose narrow streets are flanked by lovingly preserved eighteenth-century homes. Reported in 1660 to be "the greatest Towne for fishing in New England," its streets have maintained much of their historical flavor. A stroll along Washington, State, and Front Streets takes visitors past quaint colonial homes, colorful gardens, and unique shops and restaurants. First-time visitors to Marblehead should stop in at Abbot Hall to view the famous painting *Spirit of '76* and drop by King Hooper's Mansion or the Lee Mansion for a tour of a historic colonial home. For a self-guided walking tour, pick up the excellent booklet *The Lure of Marblehead* by Virginia Gamage, available at area bookstores and shops.

Directions to Launch Site: From Route 128: Take Route 128 to Exit 25 (Route 114 east). Follow Route 114 east through Peabody and Salem to its intersection with Ocean Avenue in Marblehead. Turn right onto Ocean Avenue and drive 0.5 mile to the Riverhead Beach Boat Landing on the left. (Summer parking fees for nonresidents.) Overflow parking is available across the street at Devereux Beach. If parking is unavailable, use alternative launch site below. From Route 1A: Take Route 1A north from Logan Airport 11.1 miles to its junction with Route 129 in Swampscott. Take Route 129 north 6.2 miles north to the traffic light at Ocean Avenue in Marblehead. Turn right onto Ocean Avenue and drive 0.4 mile to the Riverhead Beach Boat Landing on the left.

Alternate Launch Sites: (1) Grace Oliver Beach, Beacon Street, Marblehead. From Route 128: Exit Route 128 at Exit 25 and follow Route 114 east through Peabody and Salem to Marblehead. Turn left at the first traffic light in Marblehead onto West Shore Drive. Follow West Shore Drive 2.5 miles (it turns into Beacon Street after 1.7 miles) to Grace Oliver Beach. Free roadside parking. From Route 1A: Follow Route 1A north from Logan Airport 11.1 miles to its junction with Route 129 in Swampscott. Follow Route 129 north (Atlantic Avenue) through Swampscott 6.2 miles to the traffic light at Ocean Avenue in Marblehead. Turn left onto Ocean Avenue and drive 0.1 mile to its intersection with Route 114. Turn left onto MA 114 and drive 0.7 mile to West Shore Drive Turn right onto West Shore Drive and drive 2.5 miles to Grace Oliver Beach. (2) Village Street Pier, Village Street, Marblehead. Follow above directions to West Shore Drive. Drive 0.9 mile on West Shore Drive to Village Street. Turn left on Village Street and drive to the landing and pier at its end. Drop boats off on the beach and park in the lot just up the street. Free parking.

trip 13
GREAT MISERY ISLAND FROM MARBLEHEAD HARBOR

Level of Difficulty: Strenuous; open water

Round-Trip Mileage: 13.9 miles

Attractions: Historic Marblehead Harbor; Great Misery Island for picnicking and hiking; scenic Salem Sound and islands

Precautions: Heavy summer boat traffic in Marblehead Harbor and Salem Sound. Large waves can develop in the channel between Great and Little Misery Islands at its east end. Watch for refracting waves off the north side of Tinkers Island.

Charts: NOAA 13275 (1:25,000), or NOAA 13274 (1:40,000)

Tidal Information: Mean tidal range, 9.1 feet. High tide in Marblehead is 5 minutes before Boston high tide.

Launch Site: Riverhead Beach Boat Landing, Marblehead.

THIS CHALLENGING PADDLE takes kayakers across busy Salem Sound to an island offering pleasant picnicking and exploring. Great Misery Island was once the site of an elaborate summer colony whose ruins can be rediscovered along the hiking trails that cross the island. Now owned by The Trustees of Reservations, the island is open to the public for a small fee. On the way to Great Misery, kayakers pass a variety of small islands, most home only to seabirds. This is an interesting and rigorous trip. Kayakers will not be disappointed with the scenery, history, or challenge of the paddle.

Launch your kayak at Riverhead Beach and paddle to the entrance of Marblehead Harbor, as described in Trip 12. At the harbor entrance you'll see Cat (Children's) Island just 0.8 mile ahead to the northeast. Nearly half a mile long, Children's Island was the site of a hospital for smallpox victims in the late 1700s and the site of a children's sanatorium until 1900. Today it is home to a YMCA summer camp and hundreds of gulls.

Keep Children's Island on your right and paddle toward little Eagle Island about 0.75 mile north-northeast. About 200 yards long, Eagle Island is high rock covered in shrubbery. The island is a nesting ground for several colonial nesting seabirds. Snowy egret, cattle egret, black-crowned night heron, and glossy ibis use the tiny island. Pass to the left.

Sixty-acre Bakers Island lies about a mile northeast of Eagle Island. Numerous summer cottages cover this private island, where uninvited landings are strictly discouraged. The white Bakers Island Lighthouse rises 111 feet above the water on the island's north shore. Just south of Bakers Island lie the tiny Gooseberry Islands. These rocky islets played an important role during Salem's China Trade. Salem schooners bound for the Orient stopped first at the Gooseberries to load boulders onto the ship for ballast. Today their deserted stony beaches provide scenic rest stops for passing paddlers. Circumnavigation of Bakers and North Gooseberry Islands adds about 1.5 miles to the round-trip distance.

For those taking the most direct route to the Misery Islands, continue paddling northeast past Hardy Shoal, where Hardy Rock breaks the surface at low water. Then turn directly north to reach Great and Little Misery Islands, just 0.6 mile north-northwest of Bakers Island. The best place to land is the sandy beach on the south side of Great Misery, off the channel between the two islands.

Upon landing, look above the beach for a sign displaying a trail map. The island's grassy pastures make wonderful picnic areas, its spreading oaks providing welcome shade on sunny days. Explore the island to find the remains of the extensive summer community that once graced the island. Among the ruins are the foundations of a swimming pool, landing strip, casino, and many homes. On a hilltop to the northwest, find the stone foundations of an old clubhouse. In spring wildflowers grace the hillside. In autumn, the hilltop is an excellent place to watch migrating hawks hunt the fields below.

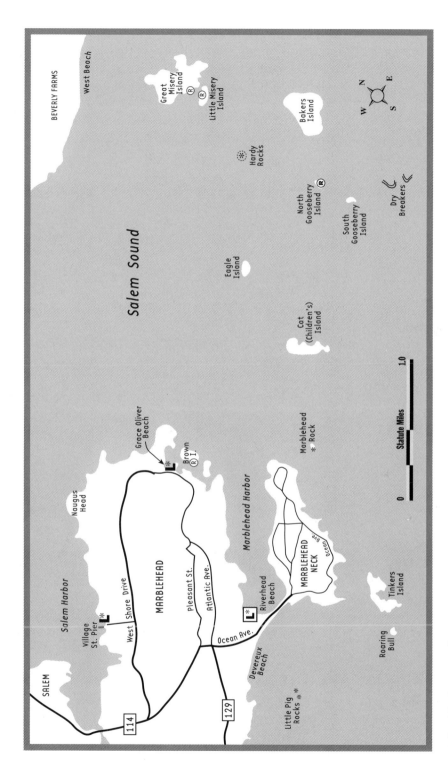

Trip 13: Great Misery Island from Marblehead Harbor

The views from Misery Island are varied, and each direction is worth the hike. To the north, one sees private West Beach of Beverly, only 0.5 mile away. To the northeast is a view of Manchester Harbor (see Trip 10). The large island to the northwest is House Island. Looking south past Bakers Island, one can see the Boston skyline. East is Salem Harbor, above which loom the smokestacks of the Salem Harbor power plant. For more information on exploring the Misery Islands, see Trip 10.

After enjoying the island, retrace your paddle back to Riverhead Beach, or tour Marblehead Neck and land on Devereux Beach, across from the put-in at Riverhead Beach (adding about 1.6 miles to the trip; see Trip 12).

Trip Tip: For a much shorter trip to Misery Islands (3.2 miles round-trip), see Trip 10.

Directions to Launch Site: See Trip 12.

Alternate Launch Site: See Trip 12.

BOSTON HARBOR

trip 14   WINTHROP AND BELLE ISLE MARSH

Level of Difficulty: Easy; protected water

Round–Trip Mileage: 3.5 miles

Attractions: Snake Island bird refuge, Belle Isle Marsh Reservation, bird-watching, Logan Airport

Precautions: Heavy traffic out of Winthrop Harbor in summer; bring bug repellent for biting flies and mosquitoes in marsh

Charts: NOAA 13272 (1:10,000), NOAA 13270 (1:25,000), or NOAA 13274 (1:40,000)

Tidal Information: Mean tidal range, 9.3 feet. Use Boston high tide. Paddle in Belle Isle Marsh only 1.5 hours either side of high tide.

Launch Site: Winthrop Harbor Boat Ramp, Shirley Street, Winthrop, free parking.

GREAT BLUE HERONS and great big planes. Paddling out of Winthrop is a unique experience. Jumbo jets rip the sky, twanging eardrums like tuning forks and sending vibrations through the floor of your boat. Yet, viewed with the proper attitude, the incessant takeoffs and landings actually provide spice and excitement to this unusual paddle. This trip's noisy course parallels Logan's northbound runway (just yards away), then swings into the protected sanctuary of the 240-acre Belle Isle Marsh, the largest remaining salt marsh in Boston. In the sanctuary, among an impressive number of herons, egrets, and waterfowl, kayakers regain a measure of sanity. The tour then swings back toward the airport, in time to see landing gear 1,000 feet above your head gobbled up at 200 miles per hour by retracting steel doors. *Vroooomm*. This paddle brings out the kindergartner in all of us. Don't forget to feed that inner child; Belle Isle Marsh Reservation offers fine areas for picnicking as well as short hiking trails.

Begin the paddle at the Winthrop Town Boat Ramp. Water quality in Winthrop Harbor could use a boost, though the landing, ironically, is only a mile north of the Deer Island Sewage Treatment Plant. Looking west, grassy Snake Island is just 0.5 mile away, in the center of Winthrop's small protected harbor. Beyond the island lies Logan Airport, and running southeast from Logan into the water are lines of lights guiding planes to the runways.

Proceed north, then west, passing Snake Island on its north side, paddling along the south-facing coast of Winthrop. Pass yacht clubs and marinas clogged with pleasure craft and a shoreline crowded with clapboard houses. About a mile from the landing, turn north up the narrow channel between Winthrop and the airport. For about 0.5 mile, paddle parallel to the runway on your left. Floating below the taxiing jets makes one feel terrifically small.

At the end of the riprapped edge of the runway, continue north toward a homely bridge. To your left, about 0.5 mile northwest, lies East Boston's Constitution Beach, with the Tobin Bridge rising in the distance behind it. One can paddle to the beach and then southwest to explore the backside of Logan. Salt marsh and grasslands bordering the airport actually provide excellent habitat for snowy owls, short-eared owls, kestrels, northern harriers, and falcons. The birds become habituated to the noise of the airport and are largely left alone. Unless kayaking in late fall to early spring, however, paddlers are unlikely to see the magnificent six-foot white owl. A better bet is to paddle north into Belle Isle Marsh if the tide permits. Proceed under the bridge, watching (and avoiding) fishermen's lines. Pass some broken pilings, then enter a whole new world.

Paddlers can thank Logan Airport for the existence of the Belle Isle Marsh Reservation. This largest remaining wetland in a city once surrounded by thousands of acres of marsh was preserved both to facilitate breeding birds and to provide an open approach for take-offs and landings. Regardless, it is a lovely refuge. At high tide,

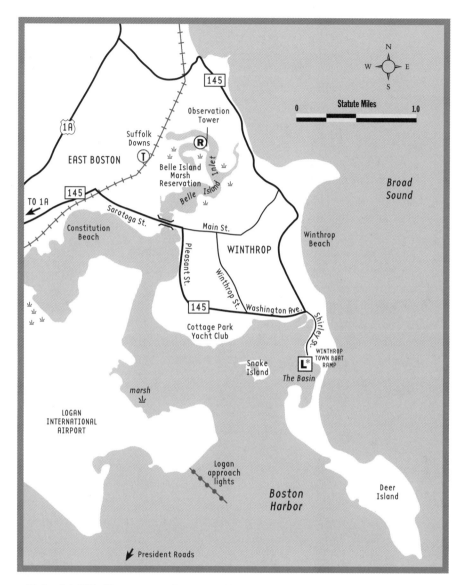

Trip 14: Winthrop and Belle Isle Marsh

kayakers can poke around its channels and even paddle a small loop around the observation tower (see map). The tower makes a good lunch stop. Nearby, paddlers can find grassy areas, benches, and walking trails. Within the marsh, southwest of the tower, sits Rosie's Pond, a favorite place for bird-watchers. Best times of year to visit are

the truth about
deer island

This island never seemed to have much luck. Originally a true island, it was so named because deer would escape to its densely forested slopes to avoid preying wolves. The hurricane of 1938 ended its island status by filling in Shirley Gut with storm-driven sand.

But this was far from the worst insult to the island. Its sad history began during the Indian uprising known as King Philip's War. More than 500 Native Americans were captured and held there in the winter of 1675 in deplorable conditions. Most died of disease, starvation, and exposure. Survivors were sold into slavery. After the rebellion was quelled, the island continued briefly to serve as a prison for Native Americans.

A few centuries later, Irish immigrants, fleeing starvation during the potato famine, were detained on Deer Island before gaining admittance into the port of Boston. Of the 4,800 Irish men, women, and children admitted to a hospital on the island between 1847 and 1849, more than 800 were buried on the island.

Nearly a century later, local police and federal agents rounded up more than 400 men and women, mostly Eastern European emigrants, who were suspected of left-wing sympathies and held them on Deer Island to await deportation. Fortunately a federal judge acknowledged the violation of Constitutional rights and released the prisoners from what the warden called his "Soviet Republic of Deer Island."

Last, but not least, Deer Island now serves as host to the country's second largest sewage treatment plant. Serving forty-three communities and more than 2.5 million people, the island has been sacrificed so that the harbor's waters can be clean. It is a more than fair trade when one considers the widespread environmental disaster that was once Boston Harbor. Although a visit to one of Deer Island's 170-foot-high digesters may not be on the top of anyone's list, a three-mile, handicapped-accessible walkway on the water's edge will open soon. The walkway promises impressive views to the city and harbor islands. An island visitor center will remind us how far we have come.

the third week of May and the months of August and September. On summer days at dawn, hundreds of herons and egrets assemble at the pond to decide which of the neighboring marshes they'll visit for the day. On cloudy days the birds don't rush off, lingering deliciously and indecisively at Rosie's. The record is a dawn count of 600 birds! Yes, this *is* East Boston.

Paddling out of Belle Isle Marsh, kayakers pass again under the small bridge. On the way back, enjoy superb views of the Boston skyline. Back at Winthrop Harbor, before reaching the landing, circle Snake Island. In years past this island acted as a bird sanctuary and was home to a significant population of threatened common terns and oystercatchers, as well as the more common egrets and herons. In fact, Snake Island is one of the few places oystercatchers breed north of Cape Cod. Unfortunately, human disturbance in their nesting area (the lagoon in the center of the island) dramatically reduced the breeding populations. For this reason, stay out of the lagoon from May to mid-July. Instead, plan to paddle *around* the island when the tide starts to fall. It is one of the best places to observe godwits, dowagers, sandpipers, and oystercatchers. At high tide, the birds sleep out of sight at the lagoon, but when the tide falls they wake up to feed at the island's edge. Viewing is excellent from mid-July through late September.

After Snake Island, paddlers can head back to the landing. Those wishing to paddle farther could venture south along the edge of Deer Island. Home to a mammoth new waste-water treatment plant (whose tanks resemble a carton of giant white eggs), the island is far from scenic. Nevertheless, the views west to Boston and southeast to the harbor islands are inspiring. Also exciting is the traffic of huge container ships passing daily through President Roads, the major shipping channel into Boston Harbor which lies directly south of Deer Island. Kayakers should approach the channel only with the utmost caution. Safer routes to the Boston Harbor Islands or Boston's Inner Harbor are described in Trips 17–20.

Directions to Launch Site: Take Route 1A north from Logan Airport about 1.5 miles to Route 145 (just south of Suffolk Downs). Turn right on Route 145 (which becomes Saratoga Street) and drive to Pleasant Street. Turn right on Pleasant Street, following signs for Route 145. At the intersection of Route 145 and Shirley Street, turn right and follow Shirley Street 0.4 mile to the Winthrop Harbor Boat Ramp on the right. Free parking.

trip 15 CHARLES RIVER AND BOSTON WATERFRONT

Level of Difficulty: Easy to the Science Museum, moderate to Fort Point Channel; protected water

Round-Trip Mileage: 7.0 miles to the Science Museum or 10.0 miles to Fort Point Channel

Attractions: Boston skyline, Esplanade, Charles River Locks, picnicking, USS *Constitution*, Charlestown Navy Yard, Boston Inner Harbor, Fort Point Channel, restaurants

Precautions: Heavy boat traffic in river and harbor, significant wakes from large boats, refracting waves in Inner Harbor. Wind-generated chop often present in Inner Harbor and on Charles River between Longfellow and B.U. Bridges. Bring a whistle or horn to signal lock operators at the Charles River Dam.

Charts: NOAA 13272 (1:10,000), NOAA 13270 (1:25,000), or NOAA 13274 (1:40,000)

Tidal Information: Mean tidal range, 9.3 feet. Use Boston high tide.

Launch Site: Magazine Beach, Memorial Drive, Cambridge, free parking.

KAYAKING THE CHARLES RIVER holds magic to lovers of the city. Boston has always looked best from the water, and on a clear day (or night) the city is radiant from a kayak. While capturing a certain urban beauty, this trip never escapes the buzz of boats, trains, and automobiles. The contrasts, nevertheless, are delightful.

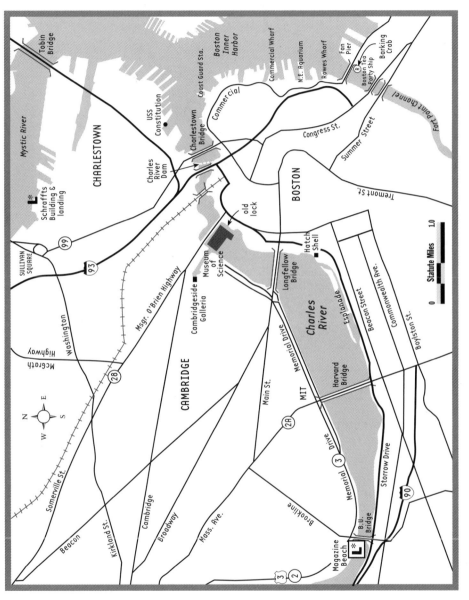

Trip 15: Charles River and Waterfront

One travels from the relative tranquillity of elite riverside universities to the bustling public playground of the Esplanade, under classic bridges to the construction site of the most ambitious and costly highway in the country. From the Jetson-like maze of freeways in the air, one moves through the byzantine lock system of the Charles River Dam. From the berth of "Old Ironsides" to the dark facade of the new federal courthouse, this trip spans many ages and moods.

Begin the trip at Magazine Beach. Launch amid a gaggle of geese whose feathers and droppings make the put-in a bit putrid. Watch carefully for barely submerged rocks near the beach which are difficult to see in the sepia-toned water. Paddle left (east) and proceed under the graffiti-ridden Boston University Bridge, the first of many bridges large and small across the Charles River. East of the B.U. Bridge is considered the Charles River Basin. From the B.U. Bridge to the Charles River Dam three miles east the river widens considerably, resembling a long lake.

Continuing east, pass under the Harvard Bridge at Massachusetts Avenue after another mile. Beyond the bridge, look to the right for a footbridge. Pass under this small bridge to the tributary of the Charles that flows along the Esplanade. Weeping willows gracefully frame a series of arching footbridges. The willows keep their leaves well into the fall, making this trip an attractive late-season paddle. The quiet ponds are fun to paddle through, especially by moonlight. A fountain in one of the ponds is romantically lit and the preciousness of the scene resembles a "Lover's Lane" carnival ride. Picnic spots abound.

If you forgot a picnic, refreshments are available (in season) at stands near the Hatch Shell, found just after the fourth footbridge. On many summer weekends, open-air concerts are staged under the beautiful wood-lined half-dome. Always interesting are the gatherings of roller-bladers, cyclists, joggers, dog-walkers, and strollers on the expansive lawn and footpaths. The Esplanade is the most visited riverfront park in the nation. In the water, oblivious to the commotion, mallard families glide by. (A must-read before the trip is Robert McCloskey's *Make Way for Ducklings*.)

After the Hatch Shell pass under one more small bridge, then merge into the main flow of the Charles just west of the Longfellow Bridge. Before the bridge, pass the home of Community Boating, with its large regatta of small sailboats and earnest sailors. Paddle under the

Longfellow Bridge, an underrated work of art, with four turrets shaped like salt-and-pepper shakers, sadly in need of a thorough cleaning. Beyond the bridge, paddlers approach the backside of the Boston Museum of Science and the old Charles River Dam. Before passing the museum on its south side, paddle up to the museum, then turn northwest down a narrow channel to explore the well-landscaped urban park behind the Cambridgeside Galleria shopping center. Pass under another bridge, then paddle around a large fountain. It is great fun to circle the fountain and surprise the strolling shoppers!

To continue down the Charles, paddle to the south side of the river to find a long stone corridor, the lock of the original Charles River Dam, built in 1910. The waterway is only forty feet wide, so watch for refracting waves created by motorboat traffic (duck boats pass frequently, and not always slowly). Before the completion of this

The B.U. Bridge from Magazine Beach, Charles River.

dam and the massive filling that created Boston's Back Bay, a magnificent tidal basin extended up the Charles from Boston to Watertown. Each low tide, however, exposed extensive mud flats that were offensive to Boston's expanding population. The city thus built the first Charles River Dam, which kept the river at a more constant level and allowed the filling of the flats and the creation of the Esplanade. This dam did not alleviate frequent flooding, however, because it could not release water at high tide. Severe flooding during storms and spring runoff required the building of a new dam with pumping capabilities. Thus a new dam was constructed about a half-mile east. Those out for the seven-mile round-trip paddle should turn around at the end of the old lock. All others should proceed to the second dam.

To reach the new dam, kayakers have to pass through an unattractive and noisy wasteland of new and crumbling bridges and highways. Pass first under the very low (four-foot vertical clearance!) railroad drawbridge that carries the commuter train into North Station. Then paddle beneath an emerging sky-high system of overpasses. The old and ugly mixes with the new and outrageous, creating a chaotic mess of rust and concrete, traffic and jackhammers. When highway construction is completed, this area may undergo a renaissance, but now it is a huge construction site which simply must be endured.

Next comes the exciting part. To reach the Inner Harbor, you must pass through the locks of the "new" Charles River Dam. Paddle under the I-93 Bridge and up to the dam, keeping to the right until the dam's traffic light is visible. From windowed control rooms above the dam, operators can observe incoming traffic. Watch the traffic signals. Official protocol requires boaters to sound a horn for the operators, two long blasts and two short. Without a horn or whistle, you simply have to wait to be noticed. Operators can be contacted also by radio (VHF 16) or cell phone (617-727-0488).

There are three locks, two for recreational boats (those farthest to the right) and a third larger lock for commercial traffic. When the water level in the lock meets the basin level, the doors slowly open and a green light signals boaters to enter. Upon entering the lock, secure a place along the side of the 200-foot-long compartment and hold on to a floating beam. Two curved doors shut behind, and the water level adjusts slowly, rising or falling, to the level of the harbor. The Charles River Basin is kept at a near constant 107" (about 7 feet above low tide). After five to ten minutes, the forward doors open and you must exit. Paddle carefully but powerfully when leaving the lock. A tricky current may pull boats to one side or another.

Going through the locks is quite fun. They feel medieval—the closing of the steel doors, the motelike quality of the brown water that fills the lock, and the weathered beam and rope to which one clings. In actuality the dam was completed in 1979, not at all ancient by Boston standards. A visitor center at the dam has interesting historical displays, and personnel can answer all your questions. (For more information, call the Charles River Director of Navigation; 617-727-0488.)

The procedure for passing through the locks is, of course, the same when traveling in the opposite direction. A set of traffic lights signals boats to wait or advance. Traveling west, the recreational locks will be the two farthest to the left. The only time passing through these locks might not be enjoyable is on the Fourth of July, when the dam handles more than 3,000 boats in a single night!

After exiting the locks, pass under the Charlestown Bridge and watch for heavy traffic. To the left is the Charlestown Navy Yard, where kayakers can paddle by the USS *Constitution*, the oldest commissioned battleship in the world. The ship, made famous as "Old Ironsides" in the War of 1812, looks marvelous from the water, and one gets a sense of its ferociousness by looking up at its rows of gun ports. In the next berth is the relatively modern USS *Cassin Young*, a navy destroyer built in 1943 that served in WWII and Korea. The destroyer was actually hit twice by kamikaze pilots during WWII. It was named for a war hero who earned the Medal of Honor for his heroism following the bombing of Pearl Harbor.

To tour Boston's Inner Harbor, carefully cross south to the Boston side of the harbor. Continue south past the U.S. Coast Guard base on the right. East Boston is on your left. Looking southeast there are good views of the Boston Harbor Islands. Continue to paddle south, passing Boston's many diverse wharfs. Some have been converted to expensive condominiums, others are working piers, and a few stand in a surprising state of dilapidation. About a mile from the *Constitution*, paddlers approach the New England Aquarium. Just north of the aquarium is a tour-boat terminal, so watch for large boats entering and exiting.

Continue south past India Wharf and Rowes Wharf, the latter distinguished by the impressive rose rotunda of the Boston Harbor Hotel. In stark contrast to the prettiness of this building is the Darth

Waiting in the locks of the Charles River Dam.

Vader–like facade of the new federal courthouse, looming across the water at the entrance to Fort Point Channel.

Turn right into Fort Point Channel, passing under the bridge at Northern Avenue. Immediately to the left is the striped awning of the Barking Crab, a channel-side restaurant welcoming kayakers. Paddlers can pull up to its low dock, stow their kayaks atop the dock, and duck into the Crab for some hot chowder or libation. Of interest in Fort Point Channel are the replica of the *Beaver* (the Boston Tea Party ship), the Children's Museum, and a fascinating amalgam of old and new Boston. Small rusting and peeling structures, interesting to look at and human in scale, compete with new, gleaming "improvements" like the tinselly International Place and the streamlined Fort Point Channel Bridge.

Fort Point Channel makes a good turnaround point (round trip about ten miles). Those who wish to continue farther to explore Boston's Inner Harbor can proceed southeast to view more commercial piers. Mammoth container ships use this channel, so paddle with extreme caution. Heading southeast, arrive first at Commonwealth Pier and the World Trade Center. Next is the Boston Fish Pier,

love that muddy water

The Charles River Watershed Association

The Charles River Watershed Association (CRWA) was formed in 1965 in response to public concern about the shockingly dismal condition of the Charles River. In the 1960s the river regularly ran in "toxic color," degraded by raw sewage discharged from outmoded wastewater treatment plants. Since its earliest days of advocacy, CRWA figured prominently in major cleanup and watershed protection projects, working with other citizen groups and with local, state, and federal officials.

Thanks in large part to the CRWA, water quality of the Charles has improved dramatically. In 1998, the river met the boating standard 84 percent of the time and the swimming standard 55 percent of the time. This represents significant improvement. In contrast, the 1995 boating and swimming standards were met just 39 percent and 19 percent of the time, respectively. This improvement is reflected in the EPA's annual "report card" for the Charles. The river's D rating in 1995 was upgraded to a C- in 1996, a C in 1997, and a B- in 1998.

Storm-water runoff, nevertheless, continues to have a severe impact on the river. When it rains, pollutants such as oil, grease, gasoline, cleaning agents, pesticides, fertilizers, pet waste, and trash on streets, parking lots, and other hard surfaces wash into storm drains. These pollutants can then discharge into the Charles. They seriously degrade water quality for fish and wildlife habitat and for recreation.

Thus there is still much to be done. CRWA has an active agenda of programs involving environmental management, advocacy, research, education, and recreation. Members of CRWA help support these activities and receive an informative newsletter which alerts them to volunteer and recreational opportunities. Support the important works of CRWA with your membership. Contact CRWA, 2391 Commonwealth Avenue, Auburndale, MA 02466; 617-965-5975 or www.crwa.org.

which can be smelled as well as seen. Those kayakers continuing southeast will see the U.S. Naval Reservation, the Containerport, and the Reserved Channel (stay out!). About two miles from Fort Point Channel, finally reach Fort Independence at Castle Island, the site of the oldest continuously used military fortification in the United States. (For a more scenic approach to Castle Island, see Trip 18.)

Those kayakers heading back to Magazine Beach from Fort Point Channel should retrace their strokes to the locks. Returning up the Charles on its north bank offers good views of M.I.T. and frequently a monster sunset. Be prepared, nevertheless, for a long slog home, because an opposing wind often picks up in the afternoon. In addition, the return paddle is a little less interesting without the Esplanade ponds to paddle through.

Lastly, for a magical tour, try the seven-mile round-trip paddle from Magazine Beach to the Museum of Science on a moonlit night. When paddling the river at night, be sure to paddle in a group, stay close to the bank, wear reflective clothing, and carry a light and whistle or horn. To park after dusk at Magazine Beach, secure prior permission from the Cambridge Police Department (617-349-3300).

Those kayakers launching from the boat ramp of the Schraffts Building in Charlestown will paddle the described route in reverse. From the put-in on the Mystic River, opposite the power plant, turn right (east) and paddle under the Tobin Bridge. On the other side of the bridge, round the corner heading south to the Charlestown Navy Yard. To the east, the skyline of Boston shines like Oz in contrast to the dour scenery of the industrial Mystic River. Paddle south past the USS *Constitution*, then explore the Charles River by traveling west through the locks, or paddle southeast to tour Boston's Inner Harbor.

Directions to Launch Site: Magazine Beach is located off Memorial Drive, just east of the B.U. Bridge. Approaching from the east, drive west on Memorial Drive past the B.U. Bridge, then change direction by turning around in a parking lot (e.g., Micro Center) and turning left onto Memorial Drive. Driving east on Memorial Drive, stay right (do not go on the overpass) and turn right into the parking lot *just before the bridge*. Drive to the end of the lot. The small beach is adjacent to the ballfield.

Alternate Launch Sites: Boat ramp behind Schraffts Building, 529 Main Street (at Sullivan Square), Charlestown. The boat ramp is open weekdays, 6:00 to 8:00 A.M. and 5:00 to 8:00 P.M. and weekends and holidays 6:00 A.M. to 8:00 P.M. From the north, take the Tobin Bridge (Route 1) to the I-93, Somerville/Charlestown exit. At the end of the ramp, turn left onto Rutherford Avenue. Drive Rutherford Avenue to the Sullivan Square exit which takes you to a rotary. From the rotary, *immediately* take the first right onto Main Street. The Schrafts Center is immediately on the left. Enter the parking lot. The parking attendant will direct you to the boat ramp at the back of the lot.

From Boston and points south: Take I-93 into Boston and exit on the Causeway Street exit. Turn right onto Causeway Street then immediately left onto North Washington Street which becomes the Charlestown Bridge. Cross the Charlestown Bridge and follow Rutherford Avenue to the Sullivan Square exit as described above.

From Route 128: Take I-93 to Exit 28 (Sullivan Square/Charlestown). Merge onto Mystic Avenue, then bear right onto Mt. Vernon Street. Turn left immediately onto Broadway. At the next rotary, take the first exit onto Main Street. Although the boat ramp is a bit tricky to find, the landmark Schraffts Building is tall and well-marked.

trip 16   BOSTON HARBOR— OUTER ISLANDS

Level of Difficulty: Strenuous; open water

Round-Trip Mileage: 11.5 miles to the Graves; 6.7 miles to Little Brewster via Georges Island and Great Brewster

Attractions: Boston Harbor Islands (Georges, the Brewsters, Green, Calf, and the Graves), historic lighthouses, views, picnicking, camping, fishing. Bring $10 per group for tour of Boston Light on Little Brewster.

Precautions: In Hull Gut, there is strong current (maximum ebb current 2.6 knots) and possible standing waves and/or confused waves created by boat wakes. Watch for boat traffic, especially when crossing busy shipping lanes. Do not paddle alone, and make yourself as visible as possible.

Charts: NOAA 13270 (1:25,000), and NOAA 13267 (1:80,000)

Tidal Information: Mean tidal range, 9.5 feet.

Launch Site: Pemberton Point (Windmill Point), Hull, free parking.

THERE'S NEVER A DULL MOMENT kayaking Boston Harbor. Its fifty square miles include more than thirty islands hosting historic forts, lighthouses, and view-filled trails. Its waters offer up a variety of currents, refracting waves, and challenging wakes from the multitude of boats that daily churn its surface. Kayaking the scenic outer islands can test the skills of even the most-experienced paddlers. Yet there are great rewards. Paddlers enjoy intimate views of two very different lighthouses, one at the eerily desolate Graves, the second at cheery Little Brewster Island. There are superb camping opportunities and panoramic views of the entire harbor and Boston skyline, as well as the full reach of Massachusetts Bay. For lovers of the city and its history, for boaters who enjoy watching (and dodging) other boats, and for those who enjoy a challenge, this dynamic paddle is custom made.

At Hull's Pemberton Point, the first challenge occurs at the put-in. The most convenient place to launch is directly across from the high school parking lot near the boat ramp. There is also parking at the very end of Pemberton Point, providing easy access to the beach on the east side of Hull Gut. The disadvantage of these put-ins is the necessity to pass through the gut to enter Boston Harbor. To avoid paddling through the gut, kayakers must carry their boats along the beach to the north side of Pemberton Point. This carry is awkward when the shore is lined with fishermen (as it often is on weekends), but it may be the safest option when the gut is crowded with boats or when standing waves jeopardize safe passage.

Since most kayakers choose to paddle through Hull Gut, consider the following safety tips. (1) Remember the "rule of twelfths" (page 33), which states that the greatest tidal flow occurs in the hours on either side of midtide. Consequently, paddle the gut at high or low tides to avoid maximum flow. (2) Observe conditions before entering. Watch the water and other boats to appraise the current, wave height, location of eddies, etc. Then plan your route before proceeding. (3) Remember that wind blowing against the tide steepens the waves. If there's a strong opposing wind, consider an alternate course. (4) Hug the shoreline, where the current is weaker. Don't paddle into the middle of the gut unless absolutely necessary; use the eddies on either side. (5) Lastly, know your skill level. Avoid the gut if you can't handle it. It's not a good place to capsize (especially in traffic). Kayakers can always avoid a dangerous crossing by carrying or paddling around the gut.

Most of the difficulties in the gut arise not on the passage to the islands early in the day, but on the paddle home. In late afternoon on the weekends, there is likely to be heavy motor and sailboat traffic. Kayakers must be alert to their wakes and unpredictable courses. To complicate matters, fishermen may crowd the shore, preventing kayakers from eddy-hopping or sneaking through the shallows to avoid traffic. If wave, current, and traffic conditions are truly dangerous, paddlers should land before the gut and carry in.

Once through Hull Gut, Georges Island is clearly visible to the

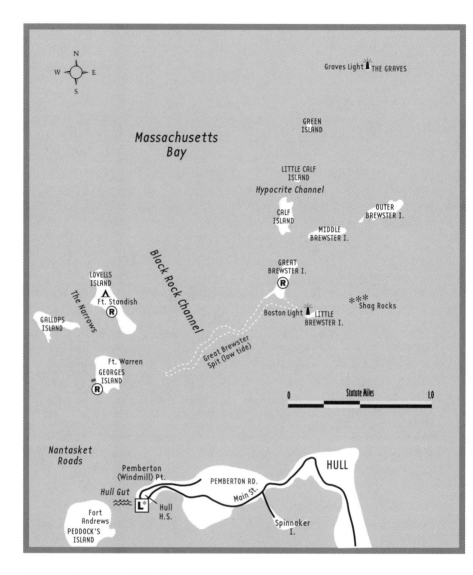

Trip 16: Boston Harbor Outer Islands

north, distinguished by the large dock and red brick building on its west side and the granite walls of Fort Warren. Between Pemberton Point and Georges Island is a shipping channel, so exercise caution paddling north. Take note of the location of the red and green buoys, and paddle in a direct line across the channel, minimizing time in the lane. Before making the crossing, determine the direction and strength of the current and plot your course accordingly, anticipating some drift in the direction of the current. After crossing the lane, paddle toward the beach just south of the pier. Georges Island is the transportation hub for the Boston Harbor Islands. Keep alert to ferry traffic around the pier.

Georges Island is a wonderful island to visit, and a walk through Fort Warren is highly recommended. Built of Quincy granite in 1833, the immense fort was used as a prison for more than 1,000 Confederate soldiers during the Civil War. Step through cool, interior spaces created by its ten-foot-thick walls, then enjoy the sunny expanse of its sweeping parade grounds and the awesome views from its ramparts, accessible by a spiral staircase within the fort. Fort Warren is positioned at the historic entry to Boston Harbor. It stands at the end of the Narrows, a narrow but naturally deep channel used by ships for centuries before the dredging of the harbor's North and South Channels. Guns, mounted every ten feet along the north and west walls of the fort, greeted all ships entering the harbor. Its walls rise almost seventy feet above the harbor water, prompting one early historian to compare the fort favorably with England's Rock of Gilbraltar. In 1957, the historic fort fell on hard times when it was sold to a group interested in using its subterranean prison for storage of radioactive waste. Fortunately, the Society for the Preservation of Fort Warren successfully lobbied for the fort, and the MDC acquired the island in 1961. Georges Island and Fort Warren are now the shining centerpieces of one of our nation's newest national parks.

Paddle around the north end of Georges for good views of Gallops Island to the northwest and Lovells Island directly north. (For more information on visiting the latter two islands, see Trip 17.) One can also pass around Georges Island to the south, but watch for rocks off the island's east and southeast side. To reach the outer islands, kayakers must carefully cross the Narrows to the northeast, staying north of the Great Brewster Spit. At low tide, there's a mile-long stretch of sand reaching west-southwest from Great Brewster. At high tide, the spit disappears and may be noticeable only as a line of ripples or breaking waves. The trip to Great Brewster is especially nice at low tide, since the gracefully arching spit creates the feeling of a small bay, though one is nearly two miles from Pemberton Point.

Paddle west-northwest to Great Brewster, readily identified by its 104-foot, shrub-covered bluff. In the middle of Great Brewster's

Pemberton Point, Hull.

eastern shore is a good landing area. A rocky beach provides a nice picnic spot with an excellent view of the Boston skyline. A rock cairn just upland from the beach marks a trail that climbs to the top of the bluff. Don't miss this short hike for the magnificent 360-degree view at its peak. As you ascend, note the concrete remains of the bunkers built in WWII. Bring along a chart to study the layout of the islands. This will assist navigation later, when your low vantage point makes it considerably harder to recognize the islands. Notable from the lookout is Boston Light to the southeast, Middle and Outer Brewster to the west, Little Calf and Green Islands directly north, and the Graves (with lighthouse) 1.5 miles to the northeast.

Kayakers choosing the shorter tour (6.7 miles round-trip) should head directly to Little Brewster and Boston Light. If the tide is in and covers the Great Brewster Spit, simply paddle south, then east around Great Brewster to the wharf at the west end of Little Brewster. The rocks by the wharf make landing difficult but not impossible if surf is not heavy. If the Great Brewster Spit blocks passage, paddle around the north end of Great Brewster Island, then head south to Little Brewster (See below for more on Boston Light and Little Brewster.)

From Great Brewster, kayakers headed for the Graves (2.6 miles north of Great Brewster) should paddle the 0.25 mile north to Calf Island. A brick chimney marks the island's south end (remains of the 1902 Cheney estate) and provides a useful landmark for navigation. Two easily accessible coves on Calf's east side provide good picnic spots. In the summer of 1998, a colony of more than fifty harbor seals took up residence on Calf Island, solid evidence of Boston Harbor's successful cleanup. Although the seals may have moved on, watch for their return to Calf or other harbor islands. Massachusetts's harbor-seal population is steadily increasing, at a rate of about 9 percent a year. Just 100 yards north of Calf Island is Little Calf, an inhospitable outcrop of bedrock that provides a nesting area for double-crested cormorants.

Graves Light, Boston Harbor, Outer Islands.

Just 0.5 mile north of Little Calf is Green Island, another rocky outcrop. Passing through the Hypocrite Channel between Little Calf and Green Island, one can see the lighthouse atop the Graves, 1.5 miles to the northeast. Look south-southeast for the Middle and Outer Brewsters just 0.6 mile away. If conditions allow, paddle out to the Graves. Ninety-three-foot Graves Light was built in 1905 on Graves Ledge, a jumble of dark, weed-covered rocks at the entrance to Boston Harbor. A popular misconception is that the ledge was named for the resemblance of its jagged rocks to a jumbled mass of gravestones or for the sailors' lives these rocks have claimed. It is true that on even on the sunniest of days, the ledge and its mottled stone tower have a macabre feel, yet the ledge was named not for its malevolent ambience or the many ships that have wrecked here, but for Thomas Graves, an early Winthrop Puritan.

This lonely outpost was manned until the mid-1980s. Kayakers are likely to feel isolated at the Graves, though early- or late-season paddlers may find a harbor seal or two. If conditions allow, slip through the circle of ledge on its open south side to a relatively sheltered spot at the base of the lighthouse. Then paddle around the ledge to drink in the full effect of its remoteness. Eastward there is only horizon; inhabited land is 3.5 miles away. The tiny barred windows of the lighthouse, as well as its dark exterior, resemble an eerie prison. The effect is haunting and a little creepy, and soon the green profiles of the Brewsters lure kayakers south to civilization.

On the way back to Hull, visit Boston Light on Little Brewster Island. From the Graves, either retrace your strokes southeast to Great Brewster or head for Outer Brewster, almost directly south of the Graves. Edward Rowe Snow, who wrote extensively about the Boston Harbor Islands and who was instrumental in their preservation, believed Outer Brewster to be the prettiest of all the harbor islands. He wrote, "A day spent at this site of chasms and caves will never be forgotten by the visitor." Outer Brewster is the largest outcrop of solid bedrock in the harbor. Paddle over to a cove on its northwestern side to find Pulpit Rock, a flat-topped rock that makes strange sounds as the wind passes over it. Grass and brush cover the wind-swept island, blighted a bit by the concrete remains of Battery Jewel, a military installation constructed during WWII. In any event, the ruggedness and remoteness of the island is worth a paddle. Kayak around the island, looking carefully for Snow's chasms and caves, and perhaps be surprised by its beauty.

From Outer Brewster continue south toward the lighthouse on Little Brewster. Northeast of Little Brewster beware of Shag Rocks, an area of sharp ledges barely covered at high tide. At low tide, a spit extends east from the southern tip of Great Brewster almost to Little Brewster Island. Exercise caution in the rock-studded area between the two islands.

Little Brewster Island is light-years from the gloom of the Graves. The green manicured lawn and immaculately painted tower more closely resemble a miniature-golf-course ornament than a working lighthouse. Land near the dock on the island's south side to tour the second-oldest and last-manned lighthouse in North America. The first lighthouse in the New World was built on this site in 1716, but it was destroyed by the British in 1776. The lighthouse standing today was built in 1783. The climb up the spiral stairs of the ninety-eight-foot-high tower will set your group back $10, but the reward is a million-dollar view. The island is steeped in history, and your national-park guide will gladly impart a few words of wisdom.

Those ready to end their tour should head southeast from Little Brewster to Hull. Those wishing to continue to explore the harbor can head east-southeast toward Georges Island and then north to Lovells and Gallops islands or west to Rainsford and Long islands (see Trip 17). Paddlers heading to Hull must carefully recross the boat channel between the harbor islands and the mainland and then carefully enter Hull Gut. If traffic is heavy and the current strong, land on the northwest side of Pemberton Point and carry in.

Directions to Launch Site: From Route 3 south, take Exit 14 (Route 228 north). Drive north on Route 228 6.5 miles to its intersection with Route 3A. Turn left (south) on Route 3A and drive 1.3 miles to the rotary. Drive one quarter around the rotary, then turn right on Summer Street, following signs for Nantasket. Bear left on George Washington Blvd., and then left again on Nantasket Avenue. Follow Nantasket Avenue past the beach to a fork where signs indicate School to the left. Take the left fork and follow it to its termination at Pemberton Point. Park in the Hull High School parking lot or along the beach at the end of the road.

Alternate Launch Site: Hingham Harbor; see Trip 19.

Camping: See Boston Harbor Island Camping Information, page 176.

trip 17 BOSTON HARBOR— INNER ISLANDS

Level of Difficulty: Strenuous; protected and open water

Round-Trip Mileage: 4.1 miles from Hull to Georges, Gallops, and Lovells islands; 9.4 miles to these islands plus Long, Rainsford, and Thompson islands

Attractions: Boston Harbor Islands (Georges, Gallops, Lovells, Long, Rainsford, Thompson), historic fort, views, picnicking, camping, fishing

Precautions: In Hull Gut, beware of strong current (maximum ebb current, 2.6 knots) and possible standing waves and/or confused waves created by boat wakes. Watch for boat traffic and carefully cross busy shipping lanes. Do not paddle alone, and make yourself as visible as possible.

Charts: NOAA 13270 (1:25,000), and NOAA 13267 (1:80,000)

Tidal Information: Mean tidal range, 9.5 feet.

Launch Site: Pemberton Point (Windmill Point), Hull.

KAYAKING BOSTON'S BUSY INNER HARBOR ISLANDS is a terrific urban adventure. Brimming with history, traffic, noise, and urbane beauty, this trip is challenging and stimulating. Learn a bit of the rich history of the islands, and this demanding tour will stir both head and heart.

Those launching from Hull's Pemberton Point should consult Trip 16 for passage to Georges Island. Tour, then depart Georges Island, as described in Trip 16. (Kayakers leaving from City Point in

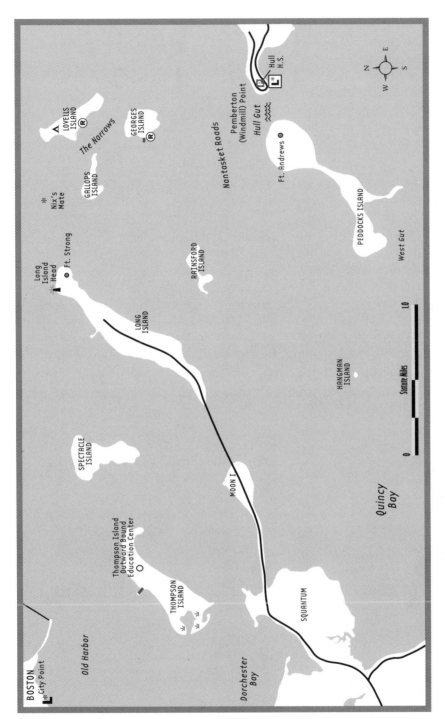

Trip 17: Boston Harbor—Inner Islands

South Boston should read Trip 18 for passage from City Point to Thompson Island, then follow this trip description in reverse.)

After departing Georges Island, paddle northwest through the Narrows, a naturally deep channel between Lovells and Gallops Islands. In the Narrows, beware of strong currents and heavy boat traffic. Southwest of the channel lies mutton-shaped Gallops Island. Gallops Island's diverse history includes use as a quarantine and immigration station, a WWI prison for German soldiers, a WWII training station, and as a Civil War training camp. The Massachusetts Fifty-Fourth Colored Regiment drilled there (immortalized in the movie *Glory*). Legend also has it that seventeenth-century pirate Ben Avery buried a yet-to-be-discovered stash of priceless diamonds on the island. For those without spades, Gallops also offers trails, picnic areas, a sandy beach, a heron rookery, and fabulous views from its grassy bluff.

Lovells Island borders the Narrows to the east. The island is long and narrow, with an attractive sandy beach stretching nearly the length of its southwest-facing shore. Like Gallops and many of the other Boston Harbor Islands, Lovells was the site of military installations, including Fort Standish, built in 1900 to defend the city of Boston. Remains of the fort can still be found. The island is also home to "Lovers Rock," a large rock in the center of the island where, in December 1786, thirteen people took refuge after a shipwreck. The group huddled together through a blizzard and was discovered the following day, all frozen to death at the rock. "Lovers Rock" is so-named for the young couple found frozen there in icy embrace. Lovells Island is famous also for its vigorous populations of wildflowers and rabbits, as well as its marshes, woods, and eleven-site campground.

Continuing northwest past Gallops and Lovells, reach the striking black and white cone atop Nix's Mate. The cone marks the southern terminus of the main channel into Boston Harbor, but its appearance has an incongruous resemblance to a monstrously proportioned toddler's toy. This bizarre structure towers over fellow kayakers, and its presence at the harbor's chaotic entrance is surreal. The history of the rocks it sits upon constitutes one of the most colorful tales of the harbor islands. (While contemplating this tale, watch for traffic, wakes, and refracting waves off the cone.)

According to legend, Captain Nix was murdered by one of his mates. When the accused was taken out to this island to be hanged, he claimed before dying that as proof of his innocence the island would one day disappear. Today little remains of Nix's Mate, although historians question the veracity of the account. It is unrefuted, nevertheless, that this tiny bit of island has seen the corpses of quite a few notorious pirates. In the eighteenth century, after several famous pirates were hanged at the Boston Harbor gallows, their bodies were transported to the island. Some were displayed as a warning to passing ships; others were buried in the sand. Boston Harbor historian Edward Rowe Snow wrote, "Many an honest sailor has been startled by the skeleton of a buccaneer hanging in chains" upon Nix's Mate.

From Nix's Mate continue west with care, crossing another shipping lane between Nix's Mate and the north end of the Long Island. Long Island, just 0.5 mile east, stretches south for 1.75 miles, where a bridge connects Long with Moon Island and Squantum in Quincy. A lighthouse at its north end easily identifies the island. Also visible on Long Island are the old hospital buildings currently used as a homeless shelter and alcohol treatment center. Significant in military history, Long Island was the site of Fort Strong during the Revolutionary War and was used for the training of conscripts during the Civil War. The camp was located on Long Island because of the obstacles it posed to would-be deserters. Today, access to the island is prohibited. Long-range plans for the island include the construction of a public pier near the lighthouse.

The ruins of Fort Strong at the north end of Long Island conjure up another strange tale. In March of 1776, thousands of Tories fled Boston to return to England. (Bostonians still celebrate "Evacuation Day" annually on March 17.) The refugees boarded ships until the harbor was filled with almost 200 England-bound vessels. One of the last ships to leave was anchored near Long Island and was fired upon before departing. The cannon volley mortally wounded a woman who pleaded with her husband not to be buried at sea. To respect her wishes, the ship raised a flag of truce and wrapped her body in a red blanket and transported her to Long Island. There the patriots agreed to a burial. Her husband then sailed off, never to return. Subsequently, at her grave, where a stone cairn marked the spot, several claim to have seen the "woman in scarlet." Strikingly similar accounts describe the ghostly appearance of a moaning woman wrapped in a red cloak with blood streaming from her head.

About one mile west of Long Island is Spectacle Island. Originally the island consisted of two drumlins connected by a sandbar.

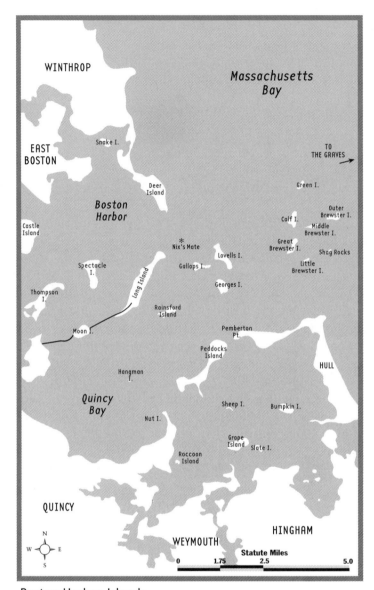

Boston Harbor Islands

Thus, from above, it resembled a pair of spectacles. In the early 1800s, Spectacle Island hosted gay summer resorts and gambling establishments, but by midcentury its use turned grim. In 1857, a horse-rendering plant occupied the island, and a hundred years later it became Boston's municipal dump. This tradition continued, and the island recently received massive amounts of fill dredged from Boston's "Big Dig." Today engineers are attempting to stabilize its

save the harbor/save the bay: an impossible dream realized

In 1986, Save the Harbor/Save the Bay (SH/SB), a small nonprofit environmental advocacy group, sponsored tours in Boston Harbor, then the filthiest harbor in America. SH/SB dubbed these trips "Sewer Tours." Thirteen years later the same tours, now showcasing a considerably cleaner Boston Harbor, won a "Best of Boston" award from *Boston* magazine. This new and improved harbor today encompasses one of the nation's newest national parks.

How did this miracle occur? The catalyst was a lawsuit, the solution was a $5 billion sewage treatment plant, and the players were a dedicated group of activists, including Judge Paul Garrity (the "sludge judge"), Quincy City Solicitor Bill Golden (whose lawsuit resulted in the Boston Harbor cleanup), and reporter Ian Menzies, all founders of SH/SB. Today SH/SB's membership has blossomed to more than 1,000 active members, and the group continues to advocate for restoration and protection of Boston Harbor and Massachusetts Bay.

bloated terraces, which will someday provide a visitors center, marina, and park. Kayakers should steer clear until work is completed on its 250-foot-high slopes.

Paddle on to handsome Thompson Island, 0.5 mile southwest of Spectacle Island. Thompson's history as a Native American settlement is documented in the significant collection of Indian artifacts found on the island. To visit privately owned Thompson Island, kayakers must call ahead to request permission (617-328-3900). The island provides a home for the Thompson Island Outward Bound Education Center. TIOBEC is housed in the brick buildings of the former Boston Farm and Trade School sitting atop the island's grassy slopes. The towers and rope course are visible at the south

SH/SB's considerable success is quantified not only by the completion of the Deer Island Treatment Plant, but by the reinvigorated marine environment to which harbor porpoises, harbor seals, striped bass, and sea and shore birds have returned in droves. With the return of good water quality, millions of visitors have also returned to swim, stroll, and tour the Boston Harbor Islands National Park.

SH/SB believes that the best way to *save* the harbor is to *share* the harbor. Having largely achieved their goal of meeting federal clean-water standards for fishing and swimming, SH/SB is building a broad-based constituency to restore, protect, and celebrate Boston Harbor and Massachusetts Bay. Specifically, SH/SB is working to increase public access to the water and has begun a comprehensive effort to establish a series of public open spaces from Winthrop to Hull for boaters, pedestrians, and cyclists.

Users of this book know the excitement and beauty of kayaking Boston Harbor. A membership in SH/SB supports the efforts of this dedicated and effective grassroots organization. For more information, call 617-451-2860; write SH/SB, 25 West Street, Boston, MA 02111; or e-mail shsb@bostonharbor.com.

end of the island.

Paddle around this large 157-acre island to view saltwater marshes and wooded drumlins. At high tide, kayakers can paddle into the saltwater marsh at the island's southwest end through a narrow channel. The area is quite lovely and variety of waterfowl may be seen. The island's boat landing is located on the west side of the island. Circumnavigation of Thompson is best done at half-tide or higher because of shallow areas on the island's south and east sides. Low tide uncovers sand, rocks, and a sharp mussel bed at the island's south end where Thompson Island nearly touches Squantum. Low tide necessitates a short carry, but the footing is precarious due to the sharp-edged mussels occupying the bed.

From Thompson Island one can continue east to tour the "Old Harbor" area south and east of Pleasure Bay or paddle north to Castle Island. From Castle Island, kayakers can paddle to Fort Point Channel along the Boston waterfront. This tour is described in Trip 15. Those paddling west from Thompson Island should cross the boat channel with extreme care. High-speed ferries and other large boats pass the island frequently.

More likely, paddlers will be ready to head back toward Georges Island and Hull. To return to the Pemberton Point put-in, paddle east from Thompson Island, passing under the Long Island Bridge after 1.1 miles. The bridge spans the gap between Long and Moon Islands. Moon Island is used for training the Boston and Quincy Police and Fire Departments, and visitation is discouraged. Pass under the bridge, then paddle about 0.9 mile east to tiny Rainsford Island. One can pass either north or south of the island. On Rainsford are buried hundreds of victims of smallpox from the quarantine station operating there from 1737 to 1852. One gravestone on the island reads: *Nearby these grey rocks/Enclosed in a box/Lies Hatter Cox/Who died of smallpox*. When the quarantine station was no longer needed in 1866, it was converted to a municipal poorhouse. Today the remnants of these structures still stand on the island, as well as two gravel beaches.

From Rainsford Island, paddle southeast 0.75 mile to the northeast shore of Peddocks Island. Paddle northeast around the head of Peddocks and arrive at the west side of Hull Gut. Carefully cross the gut to return to the put-in at Pemberton Point. If crossing appears hazardous, kayakers can paddle counterclockwise 1.2 miles around Peddocks and enter Hull Bay from the south end of Peddock's Island (through the wider and generally calmer West Gut). Paddlers taking this route must exercise caution crossing the boat channel east of Peddocks. The high-speed ferry from Hingham uses this channel, as well as boats frequenting the Quincy/Weymouth boatyards.

For more information on Peddocks Island and the islands of Hingham Bay, just south of Hull, see Trip 19.

Directions to Launch Site: See Trip 16.

Alternate Launch Site: City Point, South Boston; see Trip 18.

Camping: Camping by permit on Lovells Island; call 617-727-7676. See page 176.

camping on the boston harbor islands

Three of the Boston Harbor Islands, Lovells, Grape, and Bumpkin, provide camping opportunities. All three are accessible by ferry as well as by kayak.

Camping Permits
To camp on the islands, a free camping permit is required. From late June through Labor Day, daily camping is available on Lovells, Grape, and Bumpkin Islands. Early and late in the season (from May to mid-June and Labor Day to Columbus Day), Saturday night camping is available on Lovells and Grape Islands. For permits on Lovells Island, call 617-727-7676. For reservations on Bumpkin and Grape Islands, call 877-422-6762. Each island has ten to twelve individual campsites and one group campsite.

Transportation
For those not kayaking, ferries leave daily from Long Wharf in Boston and Hewitt's Cove in Hingham. Weekend ferry service is available from Lynn Heritage State Park. For schedules, call 617-227-4321. Overnight garage parking is available near Boston's Long Wharf. Hewitt's Cove provides free overnight parking.

Facilities
All of the islands have composting toilets. Campers must bring their own drinking water. Carry-in/carry-out policy is enforced on all islands.

Restrictions
Fires are permitted in camp stoves, hibachis, or grills at the campsites. Beach fires (but not bonfires) below the high-tide line are also permitted. Pets, alcohol use, and amplified sound are not allowed.

Any Questions?
For general information on camping on the Boston Harbor Islands, call 617-223-8666.

trip 18 BOSTON HARBOR CITY FROM POINT

Level of Difficulty: Easy; protected water

Round–Trip Mileage: 4.0 miles to tour Old Harbor, 4.0 miles to circumnavigate Thompson Island, 6.0 miles to Fort Point Channel (all distances from City Point)

Attractions: Castle Island, Thompson Island, Boston Inner Harbor, Old Harbor, Carson Beach, Harbor Point Park, Fort Point Channel, restaurants

Precautions: Heavy boat traffic in harbor. Watch especially for ferry and commercial traffic west of Thompson Island and around commercial piers in Inner Harbor. Kayakers may encounter significant wakes from large boats, and refracting waves off the seawalls of Castle Island, Pleasure Bay, and Harbor Point Park.

Charts: NOAA 13272 (1:10,000), NOAA 13270 (1:25,000), or NOAA 13274 (1:40,000).

Launch Site: City Point (M Street Beach), Day Boulevard, South Boston. Free parking.

Tidal Information: Mean tidal range, 9.3 feet. Use Boston high tide. Plan to circumnavigate Thompson Island between mid and high tide.

FROM CITY POINT, one can paddle to the Boston Harbor Islands for a strenuous full-day outing or take a spin around Old Harbor and Thompson Island for a short and easy paddle. Many kayakers also paddle from City Point to Fort Point Channel to a popular dockside restaurant (see Trip 15). Dorchester Bay and Old Harbor are filled with activity. High-speed ferries, cargo ships and a multitude of pleasure boats rock the water around City Point. An extension rather than a respite from the traffic and noise of Boston, this area is nonetheless filled with interesting sites and fascinating history. It's a fun and convenient paddle for Boston area kayakers.

Touring Old Harbor

Launch into Old Harbor from the stony M Street Beach at City Point (just right of the "Sugar Bowl"). The City Point peninsula, and even this very beach, have a fascinating history. This point of land, originally named Mattapannock, was once a large Native American settlement, where Indians grew maize, beans, squash and gathered seeds, nuts, berries, and shellfish. Before the arrival of the Puritans, 25,000 Indians lived in the vicinity. Attracted by a fresh-water spring and the shade of weeping willows, the region's Indians met regularly at today's City Point, once called Pow Wow Point.

In 1630, just a stone's throw from this beach, settlers from Dorchester, England first came ashore. Three years later, a small pox epidemic killed the majority of local Native Americans, leaving so many dead that bodies were left on the ground unburied as survivors fled. For many decades, Indians returned to the peninsula to hold a commemorative ceremony and feast.

After the departure of the Indians, the peninsula turned to a common pasture used for decades by settlers' livestock. Because this area was used as a common, its development was delayed in comparison with the residential and industrial settlement of neighboring areas. As a result, South Boston looks remarkably different from the rest of Boston, readily apparent by looking at a street map. The rest of the city grew rapidly and haphazardly, with little planning, and its crooked streets are telltale signs. In contrast, real estate investors carefully planned South Boston. They laid out streets in an orderly grid, numbering and lettering them sequentially.

From the put-in, take a quick 2-mile tour of Old Harbor. Turn right and paddle past four yacht clubs, one after another. The first, the South Boston Yacht Club (SBYC), is the oldest chartered yacht club in the country. It occupies a handsome wood shingle building with arches and an impressive porch. In 1882, M.F. Sweetser wrote in the King's Handbook to Boston Harbor, "The low promontory of City Point is the paradise of yachtsmen. Here scores (and sometimes

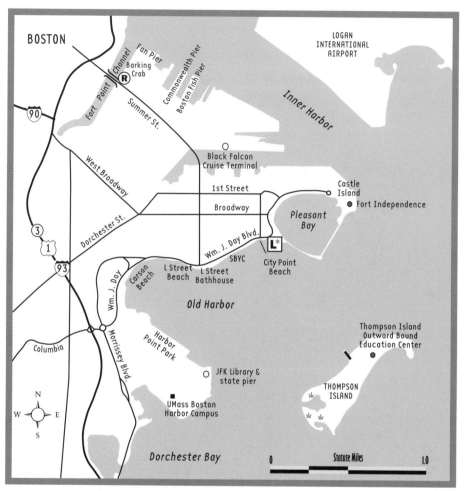

BOSTON

LOGAN
INTERNATIONAL
AIRPORT

Fan Pier

Fort Point Channel

Barking
Crab

Commonwealth Pier

Boston Fish Pier

Summer St.

Inner Harbor

West Broadway

Black Falcon
Cruise Terminal

1st Street

Broadway

Wm. J. Day Blvd.

Dorchester St.

Castle
Island

Fort Independence

Pleasant
Bay

SBYC

City Point
Beach

L Street
Beach

L Street
Bathhouse

Carson
Beach

L Street
Beach

Wm. J. Day

Old Harbor

Morrissey Blvd.

Harbor
Point Park

Columbia

Thompson Island
Outward Bound
Education Center

JFK Library &
state pier

THOMPSON
ISLAND

UMass Boston
Harbor Campus

N

W ←→ E

S

Dorchester Bay

0   Statute Miles   1.0

Trip 18: Boston Harbor from City Point

hundreds) of pleasure boats of all classes are to be seen...straining at
their cables in the blue waters offshore, graceful, dainty and apparently full of bounding life and pride."

Continue west, dodging the prideful pleasure boats. Weave
through their many moorings to arrive at the tall wooden fences
demarcating the beaches of the L Street Bathhouse, a famous South
Boston landmark. Lined with cormorants, these walls lend an air of
privacy to the beaches they screen. Shortly after the Civil War, the

City of Boston built the L Street Bathhouse to improve the health and welfare of its Irish immigrant population. A large number of Irish immigrants lived in tenements lacking both hot water and bathtubs.

The public bathhouse was terrifically successful. By 1900, it was no longer needed for hygiene but required for recreation. The new building, seen plainly from the water, was constructed in three sections, one for women and girls, one for men, and another for boys. Its fences promoted the tradition of swimming and sunbathing in a minimum of clothing (or none at all). L Street Bathhouse patrons came, in fact, to be known as "Brownies" because of their suntans. Today, the group is most famous for their annual plunge into the harbor on New Years Day (albeit with bathing suits). Fall paddlers are likely to see a few diehard Brownies working on their tans or even swimming in the cool waters.

Toward the west end of Old Harbor is Carson Beach, distinguished by a handsome red brick beach house. In 1975, Carson Beach was the site of an ugly race riot between South Boston natives and their black neighbors in Dorchester. The incident occurred at the height of the school busing crisis.

Past Carson Beach on Columbia Point are the new amenities of Harbor Point Park. At the tip of the point sits a housing development, the campus of U-Mass Boston and the stunning I. M. Pei-designed Kennedy Library. Watch for refracting waves off the rip-rapped shores of the point.

Touring Thompson Island

Kayakers should now turn eastward to explore the Boston Harbor Islands. Due east just 0.5 mile from Columbia Point is Thompson Island. (For those paddling directly from City Point, Thompson Island is 0.9 mile to the southeast.) The distance is short, but kayakers need to watch boat traffic carefully. High speed commuter catamarans, tugs and large cargo ships travel in a well-marked channel west of Thompson Island. Wait until the coast is clear, then paddle with efficiency across the shipping lane.

Thompson Island is owned by a nonprofit trust and is open on a limited basis for guided tours, picnics, and hiking. Kayakers interested in stopping on the island must call first to request permission to picnic or explore (617-328-3900). Find a dock and easy-landing beach on the island's northwest side. Just uphill from the dock is the site of the nation's first vocational school, founded in the 1830s. Its brick campus still stands and is today used as a private middle school serving Boston youngsters, most by scholarship. In the summer, Thompson Island is the home of the Outward Bound Education Center. Their rope course is visible above the marsh reeds at the south end of the island.

For more information on circumnavigating Thompson Island, exploring its scenic pond at high tide, and visiting other Boston Harbor Islands, consult Trip 17. A circumnavigation of Thompson Island from City Point is approximately 4 miles. Add 2 miles for touring Old Harbor.

Touring Castle Island and Fort Point Channel

From the northern tip of Thompson Island, cross the shipping lane to the west to reach the dam at Pleasant Bay after 0.6 mile. Paddle in a northerly direction around the dam (watch for refracting waves) to reach Castle Island in 0.4 mile. For those leaving from City Point, turn left and paddle east along the seawall then north along the Pleasant Bay dam to reach Castle Island in 0.9 mile.

In 1634, the Puritans built a small mud-walled fortification on Castle Island. Ship captains named the island, not for its small fort, but for its impressively jagged silhouette. From a mud fort, English military engineers built Castle William in the early 1700s which became Fort Independence in 1799. The site of the oldest continuously occupied military installation in North America, Fort Independence has many tales to tell. A must-read is Edgar Allan Poe's grisly "Cask of Amontillado." A Castle Island incident involving a young army officer buried alive in the fort's subterranean dungeon served as inspiration for Poe's famous story. Edgar Allen Perry (later changed to Poe) was stationed on Castle Island in 1827. Other incidents involving ghosts, murders, and suicides color the fort's long history. Adding to its macabre reputation, Castle Island was also home of the commonwealth's first prison. The island has been attached to the mainland since 1927.

To enter Boston's Inner Harbor, continue north to the end of Castle Island, then turn northwest. On the way to Fort Point Channel, kayakers must pass a series of large commercial piers, frequented by very large ships. Those not comfortable in the company of

protecting boston harbor

As you paddle the Boston Harbor Islands, help protect the harbor by contacting the appropriate authorities if you see a potential problem. Report unusual odors or discharges, discoloration of the water, floating debris, or other problems to one of the following organizations as soon as possible (most of the numbers operate 24 hours):

❖ Problems concerning Marine Life: New England Aquarium, Marine Animal Rescue Hotline, 617-973-5200 x5247.

❖ Oil or Hazardous Waste Spill: National Response Center 1-800-424-8802, US Coast Guard, Boston Marine Safety Office, 617-223-3000, or Mass Dept. of Environmental Protection, 24 Hour Notification Line, 1-800-304-1133.

❖ Illegal Environmental Activity: Mass Environmental Strike Force, 617-556-1000 or 1-888-VIOLATE.

❖ Problems concerning Public Access: Mass Dept of Environmental Protection 617-292-5686.

❖ Sewage Pollution Problems: Boston Water and Sewer Commission, 617-330-9400 or Mass Water Resources Authority, 617-539-3666.

❖ Boston Harbor—General: The Boston Harbor Association, 617-482-1722 or Save the Harbor/Save the Bay, Baywatch Program, 617-242-1542.

huge cargo ships, military vessels, and ferries should retreat to Old Harbor. Watch out for wakes and refracting waves.

From Castle Island, the one-way distance to Fort Point Channel is 1.9 miles. Pass first the Reserved Channel that terminates at the US Naval Reservation (do not enter!). Next cruise by the Boston Fish Pier, a working pier with a historic stone headhouse and fish processing businesses. Early morning (weekday) paddlers may catch fishermen arriving with the daily catch. The next pier is Massport-owned Commonwealth Pier, distinguished by the stately 1912 Beaux Arts headhouse and World Trade Center. Cruise ships and the Boston to Provincetown ferry dock here. Paddle another 0.4 mile from Commonwealth Pier to Fort Point Channel. Recognize the channel by the new federal courthouse at its entrance. Paddle under the Northern Street bridge to find a low dock and the Barking Crab Restaurant on the left. For more on paddling Boston's Inner Harbor, see Trip 15.

To return to City Point, simply retrace your route around Castle Island.

Directions to Launch Site: From Boston, take I-93 south to the Columbia Road exit. Turn left at the end of the ramp and go straight through the rotary. You are now on Day Boulevard (pass the State Police station on your right). Drive Day Boulevard past the L Street Boathouse and South Boston Yacht Club to the sandy beach on your right, just before the seawall. Free parking.

trip HINGHAM HARBOR
19 AND BUMPKIN AND GRAPE ISLANDS

Level of Difficulty: Moderate; semiprotected and protected water

Round-Trip Mileage: 7.2 miles (add about 2.3 miles to visit Grape Island)

Attractions: Harbor Islands for picnicking, camping, and exploring; World's End Conservation Area, fishing

Precautions: Busy boat traffic, especially on weekends, including high-speed ferry from Hingham.

Charts: NOAA 13270 (1:25,000), and NOAA 13267 (1:80,000), Maptech Chart 21.1 (1:33,333)

Tidal Information: Mean tidal range, 9.5 feet. High tide same as Boston high tide. At low tide, Hingham Harbor has large areas of exposed mud, and paddling is restricted to a dredged channel.

Launch Site: Hingham Harbor Park, Hingham.

HINGHAM HARBOR is an excellent starting point for kayakers who want to visit the Boston Harbor Islands but wish to stay within relatively protected waters. This trip offers two interesting harbor islands, a smattering of Hingham's own tiny islands in Hingham Harbor and World's End, a beautiful park owned by The Trustees of Reservations. Additional attractions include Nantasket Beach, with its historic carousel and boardwalk, and some quiet, very scenic paddling on the Weir River on the east side of World's

End. Though very much an urban paddle, filled with views of the Boston skyline and the lingering noise of highways, the trip is lovely in places and historically interesting. It also is a good introduction to island camping. Nearby Bumpkin Island offers waterfront sites at an excellent price (free), just 2.3 miles from the put-in.

Starting from the boat ramp at Hingham Harbor Park, kayakers paddle north to pass tiny Button Island, the first and smallest of the four Hingham Harbor islands. At low tide, paddlers must make a jog to the east (right) to follow the boat channel out of the harbor. At high tide the shallow harbor is full and paddlers can roam its attractive shores. Hingham's islands are little more than bedrock outcroppings covered with underbrush and trees, but Sarah and Langlee Islands are large enough to provide a nice picnic or rest stop.

Passing to the east of Langlee Island, heading north, find to the east (right) the handsome profile of World's End. Four glacially formed drumlins make up a 250-acre park of carriage roads, fields, forest, marsh, and scenic viewpoints. It is an exceedingly lovely place to stroll and well-worth a visit. The landscaping was designed by the famous landscape architect Frederick Law Olmsted. In the late 1880s, Olmsted laid out his trademark curving carriage paths and hardwood plantings for a planned development of 163 house lots. Fortunately, the development was never built, and the property eventually came to be owned by The Trustees of Reservations. Kayakers can stop to picnic and enjoy the four miles of carriage paths and three miles of footpaths that weave through the marsh and rocky ledges. It is an especially delightful place in fall when foliage is bright and hawks and falcons survey the fields for prey. An easy place to land is the beach between the two drumlins.

From the northern tip of World's End, paddle northwest to pass the end of Hull's Sunset Point after 0.3 mile. Shortly thereafter arrive at Bumpkin Island, just off Sunset Point. Hundreds of years ago a sand spit connected the island to the point. (At low tide one can walk between the two.) The rocky beach on the south side of Bumpkin provides easy landing. To pick up island information (or check in, if camping), paddle west to the new boat dock. There kayakers can pick up a brochure for a self-guided island tour, browse the outdoor exhibits, or talk with the island staff.

Of interest on Bumpkin Island are pleasant trails with excellent views to Boston, Hull, and the outer islands; picnic areas; apple trees; the ruins of an exceedingly well-built stone farmhouse; the

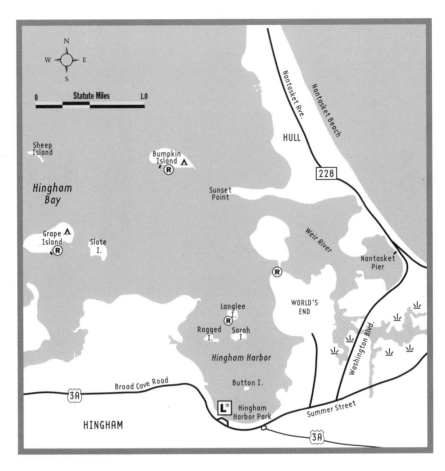

Trip 19: Hingham Harbor and Bumpkin and Grape Islands

more homely ruins of the large mess hall of a WWI naval installation; and the old foundation of a hospital that in 1900 provided respite for handicapped children. Amid the ruins grow an abundance of salt-spray rose, bayberry, and staghorn sumac, all providing edible delights for resourceful paddlers (rose hips for tea, bay leaves for seasoning, and fuzzy red berries for "sumac-aid," a drink resembling lemonade).

For more edibles, kayakers can stop to fish for stripers off green bell buoy number 3 on the west side of the island (infamous) or visit nearby Grape Island. Just 0.9 mile to the southwest, Grape Island

Hingham Harbor.

consists of two large drumlins covering fifty acres, just 500 yards from the mainland at Weymouth. A dock and beach on its south side provide easy access. Grape Island was named for the grapes grown there by the colonists. Today there is an abundance of wild berries in late summer, including red raspberries, huckleberries, and blackberries. It is a great place to find berry-loving birds (including quail and pheasant) and small mammals (most notably, a *very* large population of skunks). Revolutionary War buffs may recall the Battle of Grape Island in 1775, in which South Shore minutemen ran off a group of British soldiers who attempted to gather hay on the island for their horses. A superb picnic area high atop the island's drumlin offers exquisite views north, east, and west and is reached by following the well-defined trail north up the hill from the dock. Campsites on the island are located inland.

Just east of Grape Island is twelve-acre Slate Island. This small but attractive island provided colonists with slate for gravestones and foundations as early as 1650. A small beach on its southwest corner provides access, but visitors must avoid the abundant poison ivy.

From Slate Island, paddlers can head east once more to the north end of World's End to explore its eastern side. Paddling southeast, enter the Weir River, its channel marked by buoys. The Weir River provides entry to a pretty, quiet area where again kayakers have access to the shady trails of World's End. For a more urban stop, kayakers can paddle southeast to Hull and visit Nantasket Beach. Look for the round building with the conical green roof next to a larger red-roofed building. The smaller structure houses an antique carousel and sits just off Nantasket's boardwalk, where an assortment of frozen treats, hot dogs, etc., can be found. To reach Nantasket Beach, kayakers must land, then cross the road.

the way they were

Kayakers offended by the dull roar of Route 3A or the brown haze smothering the Boston skyline can reflect back to a quieter time and imagine the harbor before the onslaught of highways, condominiums, jet skis, and even white-skinned intruders. The scene was quite different and quite beautiful. The sea level was lower. A marsh grew where Hingham Harbor waters are now. Today's islands were dry uplands of the marsh. On these highlands, Native Americans pursued deer, fox, and raccoon and raised corn, beans, and squash. Indian artifacts found on Grape Island date back to 4000 B.C., providing clues to their simple existence.

Centuries later, as the sea level rose, Button, Sarah, Langley, Grape, Slate, and Bumpkin became islands. But the climate was colder and the harbor frequently froze over, permitting hunting to continue on the islands. Birch-bark canoes crossed the water. Fire from Indian camps on World's End sent thin lines of smoke to the clouds above the harbor.

Aim your birch-bark canoe toward this place in time. Look down into the depths of Hingham's brown water. Find a place to set your gaze where little has changed.

To return to the put-in, paddle back up the Weir River, around World's End, and back to Hingham Harbor to the launch ramp.

Kayakers who want to paddle farther from the put-in can venture northwest from Bumpkin Island 1.6 miles to view Peddocks Island. This island is not yet open to the public because of the many private homes still in use. In the 1800s, the large island was a fashionable resort destination, sporting inns, gambling establishments, and boxing matches. Still standing on the northeast end of the island is a white church and a red brick gymnasium. Paddlers to Peddocks must be very careful crossing the shipping channel east of the island and cautious when paddling near Hull Gut (the narrow channel between Peddocks and Hull's Windmill Point) because of strong currents and rips. Kayakers can also paddle directly north from Bumpkin to explore Hull Bay and Hull's Allerton Harbor, sheltered by the condo-covered Spinnaker Island.

Directions to Launch Site: From Boston, take I-93 south to Route 3 south. Take Route 3 south to Exit 14 (Route 228). Drive Route 228 east 6.7 miles to Route 3A. Turn left on Route 3A and drive 1.5 miles to the Hingham Rotary. Follow 3A north around rotary and find Hingham Harbor Park on the right, just before Hingham's bathing beach. Free parking is available at the landing.

Camping: Overnight camping is permitted on Bumpkin and Grape Islands. Permits are required, but reservations are free. Campsites are first-come, first-served. Bumpkin has several attractive waterfront sites, so arrive early. For more information call 617-223-8666 or check the Boston Harbor website at www.nps.gov/boha/. See page 176.

THE SOUTH SHORE

NORTH RIVER— HANOVER TO SCITUATE

Level of Difficulty: Moderate; protected water

Mileage: 11.1 miles one-way (car shuttle recommended)

Attractions: Protected salt marsh, beautiful vistas, bird-watching, fishing, sandy beach for picnicking

Precautions: Avoid low tide, and paddle *with* the tide. Do not attempt to paddle against the tide under the Washington Street bridge. Below the Route 3A bridge, boat traffic is heavy in the summer and tidal currents can be strong. Avoid New Inlet at the mouth of the North River because of hazardous waves.

Charts: NOAA 13267 (1:80,000 and 1:20,000), NOAA 13269 (1:10,000). In addition, an excellent map of the North River is published by the North and South River Watershed Association (see box on page 195).

Tidal Information: The upper reaches of the North River are navigable three hours on either side of high tide. To determine high tide, see below. Mean tidal range in Scituate is 9.0 feet.

Launch Site: Hanover Canoe Launch, Hanover (to paddle north to Marshfield); ample free parking. To paddle south to Hanover, begin at Mary's Boat Livery in Marshfield.

COURSING THROUGH expansive marshlands beneath wooded drumlins, the North River is a superb place for a quiet paddle. In early summer or fall, when boat traffic is light and the marsh is alive with birds, this trip is truly magical. The finest time is autumn, when golden grass surrounds your boat, oak- and maple-covered hills light up the horizon, and red-tailed hawks hang in the sky above. Drift up- or downriver with the tide, and the North River's eleven scenic miles seem almost effortless.

This beautiful paddle is best done one-way, using a two-car shuttle. Depending on the tide, start either at the Hanover Canoe Launch or downriver at Mary's Boat Livery in Marshfield. The distance between the two is 11.1 miles one-way. For a slightly shorter one-way paddle, kayak between the Hanover Canoe Launch and the Marshfield Canoe Ramp (8.6 miles one way). Novice paddlers should avoid the lower reaches of the North River (below the bridge over Route 3A) where tidal current is strong and boat traffic heavy. If two cars are not available, an excellent round-trip paddle of 11.2 miles begins at the Hanover Canoe Launch, with a turnaround point at Couch Beach.

All paddlers must plan their trips carefully to coincide with the tides. Low tide should be avoided because portions of the river fall too low to paddle. The upper reaches of the North River are navigable for three hours on either side of high tide. When planning, use the following tide differentials calculated from the Boston tide chart (don't rely on Boston tide times!):

- Mary's Boat Livery (Route 3A bridge): add twenty-five minutes
- Marshfield Canoe Landing (Union Street bridge): add 1 hour
- Route 3 bridge: add 2 hours
- Hanover Canoe Launch: add 3–3.5 hours

For example, a good time to put in from the Hanover Canoe Launch would be 3–3.5 hours after Boston's high tide. For an easy upriver float, launch from Mary's Boat Livery about 2.5–3 hours after Boston's low tide. Since most paddlers opt for a one-way paddle, the following describes a trip beginning at the Hanover Canoe Launch and ending at Mary's Boat Livery. To plan an alternate route, consult the accompanying map.

From the Hanover Canoe Launch, kayakers enter the Indian Head River. The banks of this narrow creek are crowded with nar-

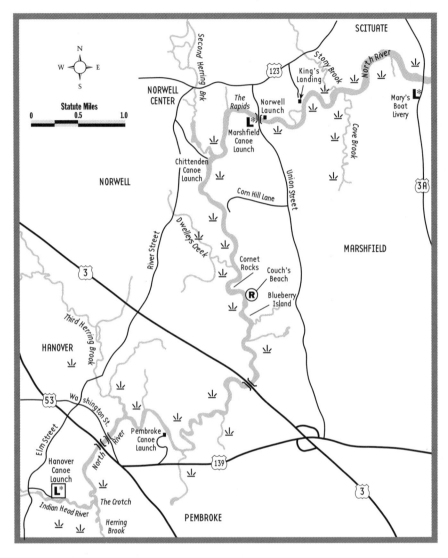

Trip 20: North River—Hanover to Scituate
Trip 21: North River to Cove Brook, Marshfield

row-leaf cattail, swamp maple, and speckled alder. Floating on nearly still, tea-colored water, one feels far from the ocean. In this quiet spot, where conservation land flanks the river, listen for birds that thrive in the freshwater tidal marsh such as the Baltimore oriole, goldfinch, kingfisher, and ubiquitous red-winged blackbird. Follow the river east about a half-mile to its junction with Herring Brook. This confluence marks the head of the North River and is known as the Crotch. The surrounding marsh is one of only three freshwater tidal marshes in the state. Turn north (left) and begin your paddle down the North River.

From the Crotch, paddle nearly 0.75 mile to pass under the Route 53 bridge and, shortly thereafter, the Washington Street bridge. Due to the constriction of the river under the Washington Street bridge, kayakers may encounter fastwater. Exercise care under the bridge, and do not attempt to paddle upstream against the tide at peak tidal current. At this site in 1656, settlers built the first bridge across the North River. Although no trace of the original bridge remains, stone abutments from a horse-and-cart bridge built in 1682 can still be seen just upstream from the existing stone bridge at Washington Street.

While today the view from the bridge is dominated by a lovely emptiness, this area was once a thriving shipbuilding center. For more than a century, beginning in the mid-1700s, eleven active shipyards could be seen from the bridge. During their years of peak production, from 1800 to 1808, the shipyards employed 400 carpenters and completed ten ships per year. Just around the bend, shipbuilders at the Brick Kiln Yard built the infamous *Beaver* of Boston Tea Party fame. (To kayak past a replica of the *Beaver*, see Trip 15.) Watch for plaques along the river marking the sites of the various shipyards.

Continue paddling north, passing Third Herring Brook on the left. After a bend to the southeast, the North River flows through the thirty-three-acre Pembroke Town Forest; a canoe launch is visible on the south bank. North of the launch, paddlers can enjoy the scenic North River Salt Marsh, nearly seventy acres of marsh conserved by the town of Norwell.

After passing under the noisy Route 3 bridge (once the site of a prehistoric Native American campground), kayak through an expansive swath of conservation land; including marsh owned by The Trustees of Reservations (Two Mile Reservation) and land owned by the towns of Norwell (Stetson Meadows) and Marshfield (Mounce's Meadow). Because of the many acres of conserved marsh and uplands, this stretch is particularly beautiful.

Approximately 5.4 miles from the Hanover Canoe Launch, pass Blueberry Island on your right, an easily recognized clearing of upland above the river. Just past this popular picnic area, find sandy

Couch Beach on the river's right bank. Couch Beach is an excellent place to stop, picnic, swim, and take in the beauty and serenity of the marsh and river. The beach is also a good turnaround point for one-way paddlers.

After a break, continue north, passing the sites of more ship-yards. At 1.7 miles from Couch Beach, pass a canoe launch on the river's west bank at Chittenden Yard in Norwell. Just after the launch, Second Herring Brook enters on the left. Continue north about 0.6 mile to a bend in the river. As the North River turns sharply east, encounter the Rapids, a short stretch of usually mild whitewater. When traveling with the tidal current, this stretch should not cause undue concern. Just after the Rapids, arrive at the Union Street bridge. Before the bridge, on the right (south) side of the river, is the Marshfield Canoe Launch. The Norwell Town Land-ing is on the opposite bank after the bridge.

From the Union Street bridge, it's a 2.5-mile paddle through slightly more developed marshland to the Route 3A bridge. One and a quarter miles from the Union Street bridge, find Cove Brook enter-ing from the right. At high tide, kayakers can take a lovely detour and follow tiny Cove Brook deep into the reaches of the salt marsh (see Trip 21).

Reach Mary's Boat Livery just before the Route 3A bridge on the south side of the river. Mary's Boat Livery is a good place to end this paddle, especially on a summer weekend. Summer motorboat traffic beyond the bridge gets quite intense, and the tidal current strength-ens significantly. Off-season, kayakers can continue 0.5 mile on the North River to the takeout at Damon's Point (a town pier located adjacent to an abandoned railroad trestle). Travel east of Damon's Point is not recommended for novices, because tidal influence builds and hazardous waves and currents plague the mouth of the North and South Rivers at New Inlet. New Inlet is a very dangerous area for small boats and is the site of serious accidents each year. The most hazardous conditions occur during an ebb tide and strong onshore winds. Under any water and weather conditions, this area deserves the utmost respect.

Directions to Launch Site: From Boston, take Route 3 south to Exit 12 (Route 139) in Marshfield and drive west 1.9 miles to Route 53 north. Turn right onto Route 53 and drive 0.8 mile to the first traffic light. Turn left and proceed about 0.2 mile to a fork and bear

the north and south rivers watershed association (nsrwa)

The North and South Rivers Watershed Association (NSRWA) is a nonprofit organization whose mission is to work for the preservation, restoration, maintenance, and conservation of the waters and natural resources within the watershed of the North and South Rivers. Founded in 1970 by a handful of river-lovers bound by a fierce devotion to the rivers' natural beauty and environmental health, today the NSRWA is a thriving organization of more than 1,300 members. Through the efforts of the NSRWA, the North River gained recognition in 1975 with its designation as a National Natural Landmark. Four years later, the Massachusetts Department of Environmental Management declared the river the state's first Scenic River under the Massachusetts Scenic Rivers Act.

The NSRWA enthusiastically welcomes new members. Its projects and activities include monitoring water quality, restoring natural resources, promoting recreation access, and providing environmental education. The group also sponsors a broad range of social, recreational, and educational opportunities. Such activities include river cleanups, canoeing, bird-watching, kayak skill training, picnics, book clubs, and an annual North River boat race. Lastly, NSRWA publishes two absolutely indispensable maps of the North and South Rivers which are loaded with information critical for paddlers' enjoyment and appreciation of the rivers. For information on membership, publications, and activities, contact the NSRWA at 781-659-8168, or check out their terrific website at www.nsrwa.org.

left onto Elm Street. After 0.5 mile, again bear left as the road forks (staying on Elm Street). After 0.1 mile, reach Luddams Ford Park and turn left onto Indian Head Road. (If you cross small stone bridge, you have gone too far.) Then proceed 0.2 mile to the parking lot and launch on the right.

Alternate Launch Sites: (1) Mary's Boat Livery, Marshfield (to paddle south); fee for launching. To find Mary's Boat Livery, take Route 3 south to Exit 12 (Route 139). Drive 1.2 miles east on Route 139 to Furnace Street and turn left. In 0.7 mile reach Route 3A. Turn left on Route 3A and continue 3.9 miles north to Mary's Boat Livery on the left. (2) Marshfield Canoe Launch. Take Route 3 south to Exit 12 (Route 139). Turn right (east) on Route 139. Take the first left (Union Street), and drive north 3.5 miles to the Union Street bridge over the North River. Before crossing the river, find the Brooks-Tilden Picnic and Canoe launch on the left. Parking is free.

trip 21 NORTH RIVER TO COVE BROOK, MARSHFIELD

Level of Difficulty: Easy; protected water

Round-Trip Mileage: 4.5 miles

Attractions: Narrow tidal river through salt marsh; bird-watching

Precautions: Tidal creek passable only within three hours of high tide. Greenhead flies and no-see-ums present early July through mid-August. Boat traffic at marina put-in can be heavy.

Charts: NOAA 13267 (1:80,000 and 1:20,000), NOAA 13269 (1:10,000). In addition, an excellent map of the North River is available from the North and South Rivers Watershed Association (see Trip 20).

Tidal Information: See Trip 20 for tide differentials from Boston high tide. Note that high tide at the Union Street bridge (launch site) is one hour *after* Boston high tide. Mean tidal range, 9.5 feet.

Launch Site: Mary's Boat Livery, Marshfield.

THIS VERY SHORT PADDLE is a pleasant and relaxing excursion at high tide. It takes paddlers to a small tidal creek bordering the Nelson Memorial Forest. On narrow, meandering Cove Brook, in the noisy company of birds and insects, disappear briefly into the isolation and beauty of the salt marsh. The trip is of particular interest to naturalists, for over the course of a mile the brook travels from saltwater estuary to freshwater marsh. This brief trip can stand alone or be paddled in conjunction with Trip 20. For greatest ease of paddling, launch very close to high tide to take advantage of slack tide and to enjoy the greatest amount of water in the tidal creek.

Cove Brook can be accessed easily from the east using the ramp at Mary's Boat Livery. From Mary's Boat Livery, kayakers paddle about 1.25 miles west on the North River to find the entrance to Cove Brook on the left. Paddlers will spot the Riverside Circle Club near the mouth of the inlet. By departing Mary's Boat Livery near the end of the flooding tide, kayakers can paddle with the current to Cove Brook. Leave the brook as the tide is beginning to ebb to float back to the put-in.

To explore Cove Brook, turn left (south) and head up the narrow inlet. Pass several docks as the brook winds deeper into the marsh. In these quiet wetlands, look for ducks, geese, swans, great blue and green herons, and egrets. During migrations, a variety of shorebirds may also be seen. As one progresses, the grasses grow taller until reeds and cattails take over as the brook terminates at the Cove Creek Nature Area. Dragonflies as large as small birds bounce from reed to reed. Retrace your route to return to the North River.

Those launching from the Marshfield Canoe Launch are using the site of the Brooks-Tilden Shipyard, one of the North River's historic shipyards, active from 1784 to 1860. To reach Cove Brook, turn right (east) from the put-in, and paddle the curvaceous North River about 1.25 mile (about a half-hour). On the left (north) side, pass King's Landing Marina and King's Landing Conservation Land. Shortly after the marina, look on the right (south) side of the river for the entrance to Cove Brook. Paddlers launching from the Marshfield Canoe Launch must paddle against the tide in the North River to take advantage of high water in Cove Brook.

Directions to Launch Site: Mary's Boat Livery is located on the North River at Route 3A. From Boston, take I-93 south to Route 3; take Route 3 south to Exit 12 (Route 139) in Marshfield. Drive 1.2 miles east on Route 139 to Furnace Street and turn left. In 0.7 mile reach Route 3A. Turn left on 3A and continue 3.9 miles north to Mary's Boat Livery on the left. $10 parking/launching fee.

Alternate Launch Site: Marshfield Canoe Launch at Brooks-Tilden Shipyard Picnic Area, Union Street bridge, Marshfield. Take Route 3 south to Exit 12 (Route 139) in Marshfield. Turn right (east) on Route 139 and pass under the expressway. Take the first left (Union Street) and drive north 3.5 miles to the Union Street bridge over the North River. Before crossing the river, find the Brooks-Tilden Picnic Area and Canoe Launch on the left, parking is free.

trip 22 SOUTH RIVER, MARSHFIELD

Level of Difficulty: Easy to moderate; protected water

Round-Trip Mileage: 11 miles

Attractions: Salt marsh, bird-watching, fishing, lagoon for swimming and picnicking

Precautions: Avoid low tide, and paddle *with* the tide. Do not attempt to paddle against the tide at midtide under the Julian Street or Marshfield Avenue bridges. Avoid New Inlet at the mouth of the North River because of hazardous waves.

Charts: NOAA 13267 (1:80,000 and 1:20,000), and NOAA 13269 (1:10,000). In addition, two excellent maps of the South River: *South River Recreation Guide* and *North and South Rivers Guide* are published by the North and South Rivers Watershed Association; see Trip 21.

Tidal Information: Paddle at high tide. High tide at Julian Street bridge is 45 minutes after Boston high tide. Mean tidal range, 9.5 feet.

Launch Site: South Shore Stern Drive Marina, 1240 Ferry Street, Marshfield, MA; $5 launching/parking fee. Off-season, see alternate launch site.

THE SOUTH RIVER is a lovely place to paddle, nearly equal in beauty to the North River but more intimate in scale. At high tide, kayakers can paddle south about five miles one-way from the put-in before the river becomes too narrow to navigate easily. The wonder of the South River is the way it slowly reveals itself. At the put-in the river is busy, its banks crowded with homes and businesses. As one paddles south, buildings fall away to reveal a beautiful marsh surprising in its expansiveness. On a warm summer day, observant kayakers can find a lovely lagoon tucked away in the marsh, perfect for swimming and picnicking. Easy, scenic, and fun, this paddle is ideal for families.

Put-ins are hard to find on the South River, since parking is largely restricted to residents and those who have purchased ramp stickers. The easiest launch for nonresidents is from South Shore Stern Drive, a marina located at 1240 Ferry Street in Marshfield. A ramp fee of $5 covers parking at the marina. Do not launch from the adjacent Marshfield Town Landing without a ramp or beach sticker between Memorial Day and Labor Day—you will be ticketed. Off-season, stickers are not usually required and parking is free. Before you park and launch from the town landing, call the Marshfield Harbormaster (781-834-5541) to determine if a sticker is required. Ramp stickers cost $5 and are available at the harbormaster's office located at the Marshfield Town Pier at the end of Town Pier Road in Green Harbor. If you're planning to buy a sticker, call ahead to make sure the office is open.

Secondly, local knowledge of the tides is essential when paddling the South River. High tide at the Julian Street bridge occurs forty-five minutes after Boston high tide. For high tide at Willow Street (the turnaround point), add 1–2 hours. Passage under the Julian Street bridge is not recommended at mid-tide because of the strong tidal current. Kayakers who plan to spend time at the lagoon should plan accordingly. Optimally, if one leaves the put-in at approximately the time of Boston's high tide, it is possible to ride the tidal current up and back, assuming a rest stop at the lagoon.

From the ramp at South Shore Stern Drive (or Marshfield Town Landing), paddle to the right (south) and reach the bridge at Julian Street in about a half-mile. When passing under the bridge, beware of dangling fishing lines from bass fishermen on the bridge. As one paddles south from the bridge, the vista blooms. About 0.5 mile past the bridge (before Rexhame Dunes on the left), Clapp Creek enters on the right. At or near high tide, paddlers can explore this small waterway for a short distance to search for birds, fish, or simple solitude on the marsh. Prior to 1898, the stretch of barrier beach across from Clapp Creek was the location of the mouth of the North River. Since the Portland Gale of 1898, however, the mouth of the North River (New Inlet) moved about three miles north. Just after Clapp Creek, paddlers pass Rexhame Dunes, a large town park offering a variety of coastal habitats from saltwater estuary to ocean dune to barrier beach. Kayaks can

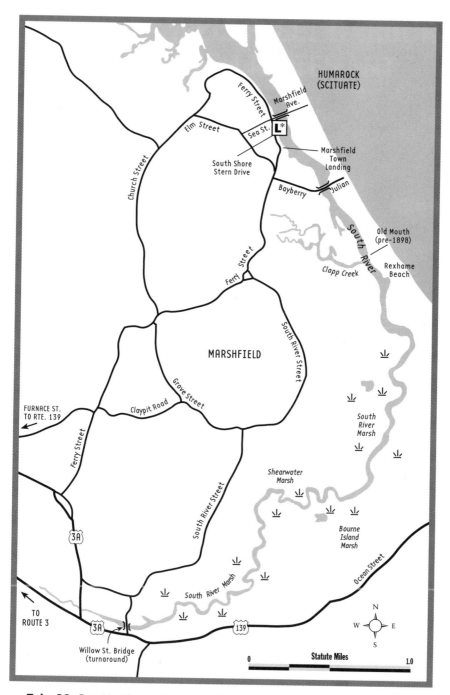

Trip 22: South River, Marshfield

be launched from Rexhame Dunes, but a long (200 yards) carry is required and a parking fee is charged in the summer.

About a half-mile after the dunes (before you pass a massive brown house overlooking the river), look to the right to view an osprey nest on a platform above the marsh. The nest stands in the South River Marsh, a collection of protected parcels encompassing more than 150 acres of salt marsh on both sides of the South River. From April to November, osprey inhabit New England's coastal estuaries. Their nests are a large mass of sticks, occasionally supplemented with odd objects found along the shore. Straw hats, milk bottles, rubber boots, and other beach debris are fair game. Paddlers often observe nesting ospreys, and at high tide the creek to the right can take kayakers closer to the platform.

Ospreys are a thrill to watch, especially while fishing. Their superlative eyesight allows them to scout for prey from as high as 200 feet before they dive for fish beneath the surface. With half-folded wings, an osprey enters the water, then carries off its prey in large

south river s.o.s.

In 1997, the North and South Rivers Watershed Association (NSRWA) created the "South River Initiative," a collaborative effort whose goal is to restore the South River. Through education, study, and broad community participation, the South River Initiative aims for measurable improvements in water quality, fisheries, and recreational opportunities. Day-tripping kayakers can do their part as stewards of the South River by scooping out debris found floating in the water or caught along its banks. By securing to the deck an errant plastic bag, six-pack ring, or aluminum can, paddlers remove potentially deadly hazards to sea creatures and unsightly blemishes on the river. Each year the NSRWA removes hundreds of pounds of debris from its watershed during well-attended cleanup events. For membership information or to help the NSRWA in its important mission to protect, preserve, and maintain the natural integrity of the North and South Rivers, call 781-659-8168 or visit its website at www.nsrwa.org.

talons. The raptors have brown backs, white crowns, and a distinctive black band running across their eyes. Their wingspans can be greater than 5 feet. Devastated by DDT forty years ago, ospreys fortunately are making an impressive comeback since the pesticide was banned. Platforms like the one on this marsh provide valuable space for the ospreys to build their large and unwieldy nests.

About 3 miles from the put-in, look for a channel on the left (east) bank. (This channel is narrow and easily missed. Look for the channel in the vicinity of an "island" of trees, east of the river.) A very short paddle down this channel (about thirty yards) brings paddlers to a tree-rimmed lagoon. An easy takeout on the right bank leads up to a comfortable picnic spot. The lagoon's isolation and warm water make it perfect for swimming and playing.

Returning to the main channel, the river becomes more winding and narrow as it progresses south-southwest. South of the lagoon, pass through more of the South River Marsh, as well as the small Shearwater and LeBlanc Marshes, the latter managed by the Wildlands Trust of Southeastern Massachusetts. Red-tailed hawks are commonly seen, and great blue herons may be observed feeding. At about 5.2 miles from the put-in, pass the remains of an old railroad bridge. Look for garter snakes and Northern water snakes sunning on the rocks of the bridge. Immediately following that, watch for submerged and partially submerged rocks in the river. A keen observer may spot large snapping turtles along the riverbank.

A progressively narrower river and higher grasses mark the end of this trip. A good turnaround is the old Willow Street bridge, built in 1646. Limited on-street parking is available here, but the put-in at the northwest corner of the bridge is steep, muddy, and often choked with poison ivy. The best option is to retrace your strokes and enjoy the return trip downriver to the put-in.

Directions to Launch Site: From Boston, take I-93 south to Route 3 south. Take Route 3 south to Exit 12 (Route 139) in Marshfield. Drive east on Route 139 to Furnace Street. Bear left on Furnace Street and drive to Ferry Street. Turn left on Ferry and follow it to the South Shore Stern Drive Marina.

Alternative Launch Site: Marshfield Town Landing. Adjacent to above launch site; ramp sticker required Memorial Day through Labor Day.

trip 23 COHASSET HARBOR

Level of Difficulty: Easy-moderate; protected and open water

Round-Trip Mileage: 4.0–6.0 miles (depending on route; 2.0 miles additional to Minots Light.

Attractions: Minots Lighthouse, quaint harbor, sandy beach for picnicking, shallow Little Harbor for swimming.

Precautions: Breaking surf near base of Minots Lighthouse. Heavy boat traffic on summer weekends at mouth of harbor.

Charts: NOAA 13269 (1:10,000), and NOAA 13267 (1:80,000). Also Maptech Chartkit 21.1.

Tidal Information: Use the tide tables for Boston. Mean tidal range, 9.5 feet. At low tide, the harbor drains to large areas of sand and mud flats.

Launch Site: Cohasset Launching Ramp, Parker Avenue, Cohasset. Free on-street parking.

COHASSET OFFERS PADDLERS hidden delights. Its obvious amenities—a quaint village center and ocean-front mansions—are easy to find, but its subtle beauty demands a closer look. Exploring Cohasset at high tide reveals its hidden wonders. Paddlers can discover the quiet, lush reaches of its shallow harbor and the warm waters and birdlife of lovely Little Harbor, a gem nearly invisible from the coast. At high tide one can swim, play, and explore for a few delightful hours. For an exciting expedition, able and adventurous kayakers can paddle to historic Minots Ledge Light, an impressive beacon just one mile off the Cohasset coast.

Trip 23: Cohasset Harbor

Cohasset Harbor's limited access requires kayakers to launch at the town launching ramp behind Bassing Beach. From the ramp, kayakers can turn right to explore a meandering creek through marsh or head left to reach Cohasset Cove. Those paddling to the left must turn north (right) after clearing the beach and paddle through an impressive array of sailboats moored at the south end of the harbor. After 0.3 mile, kayakers arrive at the end of the cove.

The view beyond the breakwater changes dramatically with the tide. At low tide kayakers must stay close to the narrow boat channel to reach the entrance to Cohasset Harbor. At high tide the mile-wide area in front and east of Bassing Beach floods to provide a wide area for exploration. Gunkholing is particularly nice at the east end of Bassing Beach (called Briggs Harbor), in the lush marsh behind the beach (paddle east along the length of the beach and then south), and along Scituate Neck to Strawberry Point. When paddling east in front of Bassing Beach, watch for submerged rocks, usually easily seen in the clear water.

Depending on the weather and your skill level, kayakers can leave Cohasset Harbor to view Minots Ledge Light, one mile offshore. (Do not undertake this excursion alone, and all group members must possess rescue skills and the ability to paddle in rough water and wind and, of course, be dressed for immersion.) Paddle first to Strawberry Point, the point of land at the northeast end of the harbor (the end of Scituate Neck). A large red building dominates the point. From Strawberry Point, kayakers can paddle north-northeast 1.0 mile to the 165-foot granite lighthouse, built upon a rocky reef. The story of this lighthouse's ill-fated predecessor, constructed in 1848, and its unfortunate lightkeeper is legendary. Each night, the lonely keeper of that original lighthouse sent his wife a message of blinking lights in the pattern 1-4-3 (I-LOVE-YOU). Their love was star-crossed because only two years after the lighthouse was built, a storm destroyed it and swept away its keeper. The present stone lighthouse has stood on this reef since 1860, surviving a 170-foot wave that crashed over it in the Christmas storm of 1909. To this day it still flashes 1-4-3.

The stone lighthouse is an impressive site—perhaps more so when you imagine the keepers who braved the storms alone in this towering beacon. The reef around the base of the lighthouse throws back some interesting waves—fun for advanced kayakers to play in but potentially treacherous for novices. Less competent paddlers should keep a safe distance away.

Back at Cohasset Harbor, paddlers can turn northwest (left) and paddle past the beach at Sandy Cove to the next large cove. If the water is high enough, kayakers can enter Little Harbor, a beautiful and relaxing detour about 2.0 miles from the put-in. To find Little Harbor, look for a concrete bridge barely visible as one looks west into the cove. Head for the bridge, but stop in an eddy to the left of the bridge to judge the depth and speed of the water flowing under the bridge. One hour on either side of high tide should allow most kayakers to paddle through with little difficulty. The current is swift, however, so it is necessary to be able to control a kayak in moving water. Don't attempt passage under the bridge at two hours on either side of dead low. Rocks prevent safe passage, and in any event, Little Harbor will be too shallow to paddle.

Once past the bridge, Little Harbor reveals itself as a graceful swath of shallow, warm water surrounded by beautiful homes. You are likely to see a small cotillion of locals paddling, enjoying the quiet beauty and looking for the egrets and herons that frequent the harbor. Kayakers can usually picnic atop a sandbar in the middle of the harbor (and perhaps watch their picnic spot shrink in the rapidly rising water!). Unfortunately, no public land fronts Little Harbor, so kayakers must be content with a shifting sandbar picnic (think moveable feast) and a delightful swim in the warm water.

If passage back under the bridge is not possible due to low water or an opposing current (do not attempt to paddle against the current), there is an alternative way out to open water. At the north end of Little Harbor, where the shore turns marshy, there is a path through the marsh grass where a kayak can be easily portaged. The path leads to Atlantic Avenue directly across from Sandy Beach. The kayak can be carried across the street and launched off the beach. Unfortunately, this option is available only during the off-season. Between Memorial Day and Labor Day, lifeguards prohibit boats within the swimming area.

From Sandy Beach, kayakers can continue northwest to tour the Cohasset coastline. One and a half miles northwest of the beach, paddlers reach Hull and shortly thereafter can see the stone breakwater protecting Hull's Crescent Beach on the left. To the right, a storm-beaten cottage sits precariously atop a tiny island just offshore at Black Rocks. Paddling farther northwest brings Nantasket Beach clearly into view. Kayakers can continue north to tour the beach (about 4.5 miles from Cohasset Harbor) or turn around and retrace their strokes to the put-in.

Directions to Launch Site: From Boston, take I-93 south to Route 3 south. Follow Route 3 south to Exit 14 (Route 228). Turn left at the end of the ramp to access Route 228 North to Hingham. Drive Route 228 North for 6.7 miles to its intersection with Route 3A. Turn right on Route 3A and proceed 1.1 mile to Sohier Street in Cohasset (watch for sign for Cohasset Village). Turn left on Sohier and drive 1.1 mile to Main Street. Turn right on Main Street and proceed 0.4 mile, then take a soft left on Elm Street. Follow Elm Street 0.3 mile to Border Street. Bear right on Border and drive 0.6 mile to Parker Avenue. Turn left on Parker Avenue and proceed 0.2 mile to the ramp at its end. Unless you have a parking sticker, do not park in the lot. Offload your boat, then park along the side of Parker Avenue.

Alternate Launch Site: Cohasset Town Landing, Border Street. With permission from the harbormaster, kayaks can be launched from the town dock located on Border Street adjacent to the Olde Salt House. Follow the directions above to the intersection of Elm and Border Streets and drive just 0.25 mile on Border to find the landing. On-street parking available along Border Street. The harbormaster prefers that kayaks use the launching ramp off Parker Avenue (see above).

trip
24

DUXBURY BAY
AND BACK RIVER

Level of Difficulty: Easy–moderate; protected and open water

Round-Trip Mileage: 4.0–11.0 miles

Attractions: Salt marsh, bird-watching, fishing, island, beautiful barrier beach for picnicking and swimming

Precautions: For the best paddling in Duxbury Bay, paddle within three hours of high tide. To explore the Back River and Marsh, paddle within two hours of high tide.

Charts: NOAA 13253 (1:20,000)

Tidal Information: Use high tide for Boston. Mean tidal range, 9.0 feet. Extensive mud flats at low tide.

Launch Site: Powder Point Bridge, Duxbury. Free parking.

DUXBURY BAY is an extraordinarily lovely place to paddle. The bay and tidal rivers of the Great Salt Marsh offer exceptional natural beauty and serenity. Duxbury's seven-mile-long barrier beach is a natural breakwater that protects the bay and marsh and creates a paddling haven for kayakers. Arrive early in the morning to explore the marshes and islands of the Back River for terrific birding. At midday paddle across the bay to Saquish Beach for a picnic and swim. In any season, Duxbury Bay has a jewel-like quality; its sapphire water and soft sand beaches make one feel gloriously far from home.

Begin your trip on the beach at the west end of Powder Point Bridge. Two hours on either side of high tide, there's ample water to explore the tidal rivers of the Great Marsh. To reach the marsh, paddle left (north) under the wooden bridge, watching for fishing lines from above. Originally erected in the late 1800s, the present bridge was reconstructed in 1984. It is said to be the longest wooden bridge in the United States. Just past the bridge, enter the 750-acre Great Salt Marsh. This marsh and adjacent barrier beach create one of the top twenty East Coast stopover sites for migratory birds in North America. Commonly seen species include great and snowy egrets and several species of heron. In addition, the barrier beaches of Duxbury and Plymouth supply annual nesting grounds for rare and threatened species, including the least tern and piping plover.

To explore the reaches of the Back River and narrow Duck Hill River, follow the shoreline in a west-northwest direction. Pass elegant shore-front homes and head toward a wooded point about 0.75 mile from the bridge. To the right are low islands of cordgrass. In summer, they are lovely patches of dark green sitting barely above the blue water. Along the edges of the grass look for the snow-white silhouettes of feeding egrets, often visible a great distance away. Once past the forested point, continue to hug the shore to reach the entrance to the Duck Hill River. Alternately, one can paddle north from the point around a small island (Great Harry Foot Island) and then paddle west to find the river's mouth. Duck Hill River meanders about a mile through protected marshlands, becoming progressively narrower as one paddles deeper into the marsh. The scene is serene, with homes hidden unobtrusively in the tall trees above the marsh. Among the Spartina marsh grass, look for warblers, herons, and egrets. Overhead look for red-tailed hawk, northern harrier, and osprey.

Chances are the water will run out before your interest in the marsh. In any event, after less than a mile, head out the way you came in. For more marsh exploration, try the Wood Island River and Pine Point River just to the north. By hopping in and out of these short tidal rivers, novice paddlers can spend a few pleasant hours playing in these protected waters. The round-trip distance for this brief marsh exploration (depending on the route) is 4.0–6.0 miles. Paddlers seeking more-open water and broader horizons should move to the bay side of the bridge.

To explore the bay, paddle back under the bridge and past the put-in. From the vicinity of the put-in, Clarks Island is visible to the south, Saquish Beach is just beyond the island, and Gurnet Light is to the southeast. One can immediately cross the bay and paddle southeast along the backside of Duxbury Beach, then paddle around

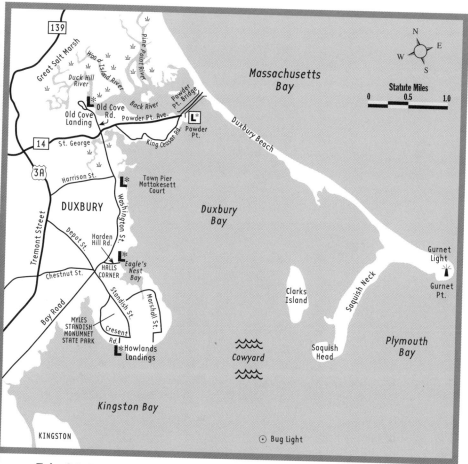

Trip 24: Duxbury Bay and Back River

the back (east) side of Clarks Island to reach the sandy point of Saquish Beach. This route is likely to avoid heavy boat traffic, but kayakers have to be careful of the current running between Duxbury Beach and Clarks Island. If choosing this route, time the trip to paddle *with* the current entering and exiting the bay.

Alternatively, one can choose a longer route that tours the scenic shore of Duxbury. Hugging the shoreline, kayakers first view the impressive bayside homes along King Caesar Road. Arriving at the mouth of the Bluefish River, paddlers are presented with an interesting detour. Possible only at high tide, this one-mile-round-trip distraction gives kayakers the true flavor of this genteel and historic town. Assuming readers have taken the bait, turn right into the Bluefish River and pass more magnificent homes. Follow the river through a small and elegant archway of an old stone bridge under Washington Street. Emerge in a picture-perfect New England scene, deep green in summer, bright foliage in fall, birds singing and a white church steeple poking above the trees. The setting is like a painting, a little surreal in its preciousness. This fairy-tale environment ends all too quickly as the Bluefish River rapidly becomes too narrow to paddle. Follow it back to the bay and continue the shoreline tour.

About a half-mile south of the river entrance, pass the Duxbury Yacht Club, often surrounded by a profusion of children in small sailboats. Next pass Duxbury's bustling town pier, where boat traffic can be intense. Continue south to leave the activity and pass several town landings. About 1.2 miles from the town pier, find usually quiet Eagles Nest Bay. The land just south of the bay hosts the Miles Standish Monument. Built on a hilltop, the monument is visible from most places within the bay. Directly across the bay about 1.5 miles from the monument is Clarks Island and Saquish Beach.

Head east toward Clarks Island. Exercise caution when crossing the buoyed boat lane and the Cowyard. The Cowyard, located just southwest of Clarks Island, was named for the confusing chop generated by boat wakes and waves refracting off the island. Unfortunately Clarks Island is private, and kayakers should not land without permission. The wooded island sports a few large homes, one of which housed Truman Capote when he wrote *In Cold Blood*.

Paddle south from Clarks Island about 0.5 mile to reach Saquish Beach at Saquish Head. Owned by the town of Plymouth, this lovely beach is a jewel of the south shore. On a sunny day its waters are a Caribbean blue, a color rarely seen in New England. Consequently, Duxbury Bay is a haven for water sports, including sailing, windsurfing, fishing, shellfishing, swimming, and water-skiing. Take a break on Saquish's soft and spacious sand. Once refreshed, return to Powder Point Bridge or enjoy further exploring. Try heading east from Saquish Head to view Gurnet Light (see Trip 25). Your only limitation will be the return of low water to Duxbury Bay.

Directions to Launch Site: From Boston, take I-93 south to Route 3 south. Follow Route 3 south to Exit 11 (Route 14) in Duxbury, and drive Route 14 east 0.6 mile to a fork in the road. Bear right to remain on Route 14 (do not bear left, even though the sign indicates Duxbury Beach). Proceed on Route 14 east (West Street) another 1.2 miles to its intersection with Route 3A. Continue straight (it becomes St. George Street) another 1.1 miles to its termination at a Y intersection with Washington Street and Powder Point Avenue (at the flagpole). Bear left onto Powder Point Avenue, and drive 1.1 miles to the parking lot at the west end of the Powder Point Bridge. Parking is free, but be forewarned that the lot fills quickly (by 10:00 A.M.) on warm summer weekends.

Alternate Launch Sites: If the parking lot at Powder Point Bridge is full, the following put-ins can be used (consult map for location). (1) Old Cove Landing, off Old Cove Road has limited parking (four cars). (2) Duxbury Town Pier at Mattakeesett Court off Washington Street has ample parking but is very busy in summer. (3) Harden Hill Landing is on Harden Hill Road off Washington Street. (4) Howlands Landing is located off Crescent Road near the Miles Standish Monument and has parking for twenty cars. Access from Howlands Landing is to Kingston Bay.

trip PLYMOUTH
25 HARBOR

Level of Difficulty: Easy, protected water to moderate-strenuous, open water

Round-Trip Mileage: 5.8 miles; add 4.0 miles to paddle to Saquish Head and 8.0 miles to Gurnet Point.

Attractions: Historic harbor including *Mayflower II* and Plymouth Rock, sandy barrier beach, public parks, bird-watching

Precautions: Summer boat traffic is extremely heavy in Plymouth Harbor. Exercise great caution when crossing boat channels. Avoid one hour either side of low tide, because much of the harbor empties or is extremely shallow. Watch for tidal current and small rip off the north end of Plymouth Beach. In an outgoing tide, the current around Bug Light can run three to four knots. Proceed with utmost caution through the Cowyard. Chop, wakes, and waves can make it a dangerous place for kayakers.

Charts: NOAA 13253 (1:20,000), and NOAA 13246 (1:80,000). Also available on Maptech Chartkit 20.1.

Tidal Information: Use the tide tables for Boston. Mean tidal range, 9.5 feet. At low tide, the harbor drains to leave large areas of sand and mud flats.

Launch Site: Stephens Field, Plymouth. Free parking.

PLYMOUTH IS AN ATTRACTIVE and interesting harbor to paddle, offering unique historical sights as well as scenic waters teeming with bird life in season. History buffs are treated to excellent seaside views of Plymouth Rock and the *Mayflower II*. Naturalists are

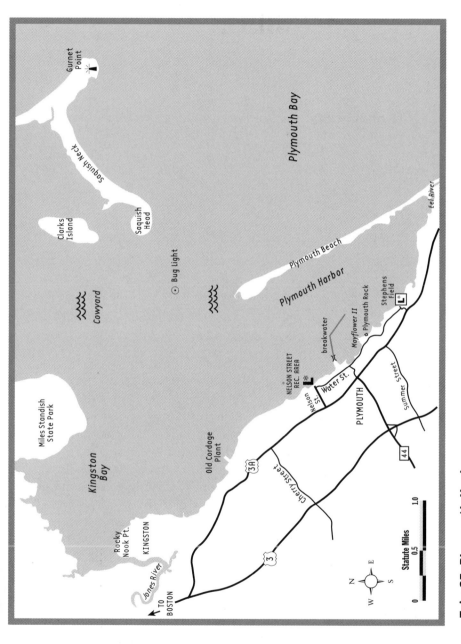

Trip 25: Plymouth Harbor

thrilled by Plymouth Beach, a three-mile-long barrier beach which supplies prime nesting areas for terns and piping plovers, as well as sandy picnic spots for paddlers. Side trips from the harbor include a visit to Gurnet Point Lighthouse (the oldest wooden lighthouse in the U.S.), Clarks Island (the first landfall for the Pilgrims in Plymouth Harbor, and beautiful Saquish Beach. To enjoy Plymouth Harbor, kayakers must paddle at mid- or high tide, because sand flats significantly limit paddling at low tide.

Begin the trip at Stephens Field, paddling left (north) from the launch. Immediately pass the Plymouth Yacht Club and Brewers Marina. Hug the shore to stay clear of the boat channel, which is marked by red and green buoys. Kayakers should avoid the channel except to make necessary crossings. Ferries to Provincetown, as well as large tour boats and a plethora of pleasure boats, frequent the channels, creating a dangerous environment for paddlers.

On the shore, just past the marina, find the columned portico built around Plymouth Rock. Paddle in for a closer look. The rock is surrounded by water at high tide. At low tide, the beach seaward of the rock is easy to land on, enabling kayakers to get a good look on foot. Although its legitimacy as the first steppingstone of the Pilgrims may be shaky, the rock nevertheless played a solid role in early American history. First identified in 1741 by a ninety-five-year-old Pilgrim descendant who claimed that he learned of the rock's identity from his forefathers, the rock was revered from that year onward. During the Revolutionary War, patriots sought to protect the rock, a symbol of the emerging nation, from destruction by the British. When thirty yoke of oxen attempted to move it to safety, however, the beloved rock split in two, leaving the crack visible today.

Just a few paddle strokes north of Plymouth Rock is the *Mayflower II*, a replica of the original ship that carried the Pilgrims to Plymouth in 1620. Docked at the state pier, the wooden, square-masted vessel is strikingly small. During the rough voyage across the Atlantic, its 102 passengers spent nearly the entire sixty-five-day passage under the decks! Although no plans of the original *Mayflower* survived, this replica was built in England in the tradition of a seventeenth-century merchant vessel and was painted in the fashion of the time. The replica actually sailed from England, arriving in Plymouth in 1957. Next to the *Mayflower II* is a replica of the shallop, a thirty-two-foot open boat which served as the Pilgrim's exploratory vessel as they sailed along the Cape Cod shoreline.

Leave the *Mayflower II* to continue north to the small bridge at the end of the breakwater. Passage under the bridge is possible at all times except dead low tide. (Just 0.3 mile north of the breakwater is Nelson Street Recreation Area, the alternate launch site.) Above, to the right, the immense National Monument of the Forefathers rises above the city and harbor. The 1889 gargantuan monument represents Faith. Her forefinger, pointing to the heavens, is more than two feet long! Outside the breakwater, turn northeast and paddle one mile toward the north end of Plymouth Beach. Near the end of the beach is a good place to cross the boat channel, because it is fairly narrow at that point. Use caution and be aware of increasing current in this area.

The dunes of Plymouth Beach provide an important nesting ground for terns. In 1995, the Massachusetts Division of Fisheries and Wildlife counted more than 4,700 pairs of common terns on Plymouth Beach. Lesser numbers of the endangered least, roseate, and arctic tern also nest here. Avoid disturbing terns during spring and early summer when they are nesting. Terns are highly protective breeders and will dive at invaders. When they fly up and scream at kayakers, they are leaving their nests unprotected. Eggs and chicks left unguarded are easy prey for gulls, foxes, skunks, raccoons, and other predators on the beach. Also nesting here from late March to August is the endangered piping plover. This small, sand-colored bird is hard to see from a distance when still, but kayakers may notice its characteristic feeding motions: run-pause-peck, run-pause-peck, run-pause-peck, up and down the wet sand.

Kayakers wishing to stay within the protective reach of the barrier beach and avoid areas of strong current can head southeast along Plymouth Beach (keeping out of the boat channel!). Alternatively, more-experienced kayakers can venture out into Plymouth Bay, past Bug Light and on to Saquish and Garnet Point Lighthouse (2.0 miles and 4.0 miles round-trip, respectively, from the end of Plymouth Beach). In this trip description, the longer trips are described first, so those heading south along the beach can skip the following three paragraphs.

To reach Saquish Head, kayakers once again must cross a busy boat channel. Cross the channel by paddling first east along the end of Plymouth Beach until clearing Bug Light, then paddle north, perpendicular to the channel. Use utmost caution because the boat channel is much wider in this area, about 0.2 mile across. In addi-

Plymouth Rock, Plymouth Harbor.

tion, currents running out of the harbor can reach three to four knots in the vicinity of the light. Once past Bug Light, head northeast to Saquish Head. Clean blue water and lovely sand beaches are found on its west-facing shore. Also, just 0.5 mile north lies Clarks Island, which was actually the first place the Pilgrims landed in 1620. The Pilgrims observed their first Sabbath on the island and, in commemoration, named that place of worship Prayer Beach. Today the island is privately owned and, although kayakers cannot land on its shores, it is fun to circumnavigate.

When leaving Clarks Island or Saquish Head, beware of the area denoted as "Cowyard" on the chart. This area of water was so named because the chop from boats, refracting waves, and converging currents creates a rough and irregular surface, resembling a muddy yard trampled by cattle. This area can be hazardous for kayakers, so proceed cautiously, stay close to fellow paddlers to increase visibility, and pass through quickly.

Those paddling to Gurnet Point can simply follow the shoreline of Saquish Neck northeast for about two miles. Paddling farther from shore in a direct line from Saquish Head shortens the trip, but paddlers might miss the delights of the clear and shallow waters close to shore. Small fish abound amid large, seaweed-covered rocks. Pat Long, a kayak aficionado from the excellent Billington Sea Craft in Plymouth, poetically likens the scene to one observed from a biplane over northern New England. The seaweed-covered boulders resemble Vermont's green hills, and their clusters of small, white shells mimic its whitewashed villages. Pat also observes that paddling this section is a bit like mountain-biking. The sea floor and rocks rise and fall below the boat like a rocky mountain trail. At Gurnet Point, kayakers can admire Gurnet Light, the oldest wooden lighthouse in the country. Watch out for submerged rocks and refracting waves at the point. After enjoying the view, retrace your path back to Plymouth Beach, once again watching for tide rips and boat traffic.

From the north end of Plymouth Beach, hug the shore and paddle south to its southern end, almost three miles from the tip. About halfway down the beach, a handful of stalwart houses line the shore, braving the hostile environment of the barrier beach. At the southern end of the beach, the Eel River flows into the harbor, and paddlers can explore its marshy mouth. After touring this quiet end of the harbor, kayakers can paddle north along the Plymouth shoreline. About one mile from the Eel River, paddlers will recognize their launch site, Stephens Field. If Nelson Park was the put-in, paddle north past Plymouth Rock and the *Mayflower II*, exiting through the breakwater to reach Nelson Park, just 0.3 mile north of the breakwater bridge.

If a longer trip is desired but you're reluctant to leave the safety of the harbor, paddle up the Plymouth shoreline north to Kingston Bay. About one mile from the breakwater pass the vacated Cordage plant (watch for rocks opposite the plant). After another mile, paddlers round Kingston's Rocky Nook Point. On the west side of the point, kayakers can explore the Jones River, a relatively wide tidal river traveling through moderately developed marshland. Leaving the river, paddlers can tour the residential shore of Kingston Bay or cross Kingston Bay to Duxbury. The entire paddle is overseen by the stern figure of adventurer Miles Standish, whose figure tops an exceedingly tall monument capping Miles Standish State Park in Duxbury. Consult Trip 24 for additional paddling routes from Duxbury.

Directions to Launch Site: From Boston, take I-93 south to Route 3 south. Follow Route 3 south to Exit 6A (Route 44 east) in Plymouth. Drive on Route 44 east 0.8 mile to its termination at Route 3A (Sandwich Street). Turn right following sign for Downtown/Harbor, and proceed 1.0 mile to Stephens Field on the left. Free parking; bathrooms; easy beach for launching. Long carry at low tide.

Alternate Launch Site: Nelson Street Recreation Area, Nelson Street, Plymouth. Follow above directions to the end of Route 44 east. Turn left onto 3A and proceed 0.5 mile to Nelson Street. Turn right. Nelson Park is at the end of the street. Free parking; sand/gravel beach provides easy launching; long carry at low tide. At dead low tide, try Plymouth Town Wharf or State Pier and Boat Ramp, both located on Water Street.

CAPE COD BAY

BARNSTABLE HARBOR AND GREAT MARSH OF WEST BARNSTABLE

Level of Difficulty: Moderate; protected water

Round-Trip Mileage: 9.0–10.0 miles

Attractions: Salt marsh, bird-watching, sandy beach for picnicking, swimming

Precautions: Beware of strong currents and tide rips off Beach Point; novices should avoid the area. Boat traffic in the harbor is very heavy in summer. Strong southwest winds can create rough water throughout the harbor and breaking waves on Sandy Neck, especially at high tide. Watch the weather.

Charts: NOAA 13251 (1:20,000), and NOAA 13246 (1:80,000)

Tidal Information: Use high tide for Boston. Mean tidal range, 10 feet. High tide in Great Marsh is delayed 1–1.5 hours after Boston high tide. Paddle at high tide to have sufficient water to explore salt marsh and to avoid extensive mud flats in the harbor.

Launch Site: State boat ramp, Blish Point, Barnstable.

PADDLE BARNSTABLE HARBOR and the Great Marsh in the fall or spring for superb bird-watching, terrific vistas, and a good dose of solitude on the magnificent beaches of Sandy Neck. The best paddle allows time for exploring Sandy Neck Beach on foot, but paddlers must remember, to return Cinderella-like, before low tide turns the harbor to mud. Although the trip is wholly within protected waters, note that an east or northeast wind creates significant chop in the harbor and a southwest wind at high tide creates waves that can make both the return trip a chore and your mid-trip landing difficult on Sandy Neck.

Start at the state boat ramp at Blish Point. Turn right to paddle into the harbor. Whale-watch boats leave from an adjacent marina, so watch for traffic. Paddling toward the harbor, note the long poles and/or trees marking the channel. Given the huge (ten-foot) tidal range, buoys would poorly serve the narrow lane because the current would pull them grossly off course. Consequently the town of Barnstable plants poles to mark the channel. The poles (as well as a flashing green buoy) help kayakers identify Blish Point on their return.

Barnstable Harbor is long and narrow, bordered to the north by Sandy Neck, a seven-mile stretch of barrier beach, and to the west by the Great Marsh. From Blish Point, located nearly in the center of the harbor's southern boundary, kayakers can easily explore the Great Marsh, 2.5 miles to the west, and Beach Point, 1.5 miles east. A fine harbor tour of 9.0-10.0 miles round-trip easily encompasses both. Plan your direction of travel to coincide as much as possible with the flow of the tide. Paddle to Great Marsh on a rising tide and explore the marsh at high tide.

Assuming an incoming tide, turn left (west) for the marsh. Enjoy the view north to the high dunes of Sandy Neck. Not much spoils the scene. Numerous grassy islands dot the harbor, but they disappear from view at high tide. Paddling west, watch for submerged rocks near the shore west of Blish Point. Avoid also the marked areas of aquaculture along the harbor's south shore, starting about a mile west of the point. Continue to the northwest corner of the harbor, where you'll find the major channel flowing into Great Marsh.

The main channel, Scorton Creek, meanders west into the marsh. If the water is high enough, paddlers can explore numerous other smaller channels flowing north and south off the creek. In all seasons, the marsh is a superb place to find birds. In late May, sharp-tailed and seaside sparrows nest in the western end of the marsh. In summer and early fall, migrating shorebirds feed throughout the marsh. Visit as the first high tide of the day is receding to see birds gather on the banks to feed. Summer also brings osprey and raptors, as well as marsh wrens and Virginia rails. In *Birding Cape Cod*, the

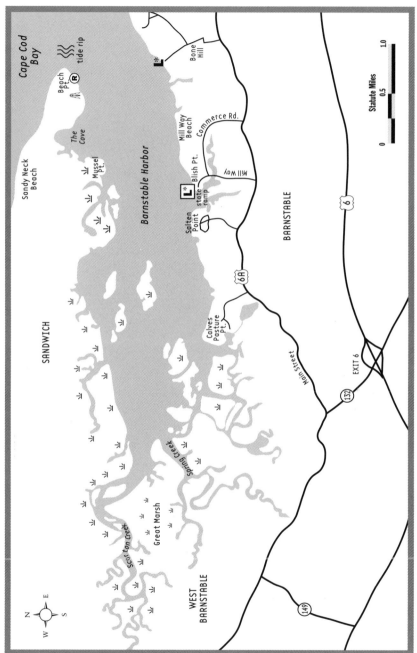

Trip 26: Barnstable Harbor and Great Marsh of West Barnstable

Massachusetts Audubon Society advises the following. When a Boston tide is eleven feet or more, arrive in Great Marsh just *before* high tide. As the spring tide crests, rails, heron, and shorebirds "get pushed up out of the ditches...[creating] a thrilling show if you time it just right." In the fall, expect also to see a variety of ducks, including eiders, old squaw, scoter, and pintails. Both early and late in the season, keep an eye out for harbor seals.

Paddle as far west as you can, enjoying the quiet, isolation, and calm. Each season brings its own mood to the marsh. In spring, the look is drab and severe. The marsh has the appearance of a badly mowed field, shorn and sad. In early summer, grasses bloom to an intense green, which changes slowly to gold, russet, and scarlet in fall. During a flood tide, kayakers can paddle about two winding miles into the marsh. For additional exploring, paddle Spring Creek, just south of Scorton Creek.

Leaving the marsh, head back into the harbor and paddle east, aiming for Beach Point about three miles away. The views north are lovely, filled with marsh, dunes, and a few uplands supporting wind-sculpted pine and oak. Only a handful of weather-beaten homes, their facades baked and faded to the color of sand and rock, interrupt the natural scene.

Pass numerous grassy islands and creeks heading north. Keep your sights on the houses of sandy Beach Point (they seem to recede with your approach). Clam flats on the left near the point are good places to view more shorebirds. From late September to mid-October, look for peregrine falcons. Finally a small pebbly bay (the Cove) opens to the north, and paddlers arrive at Beach Point. A cluster of about eighteen summer homes occupies the point. Paddle just beyond the houses to land on sandy public beach. Do not venture east-northeast around the point due to strong tide rips at the outer edge.

The estuaries of rivers appeal strongly to an adventurous imagination. From the offing the open estuary promises every possible fruition to adventurous hopes.

Joseph Conrad, *The Mirror of the Sea*

The beach is a wonderful place to stop for lunch, especially in the off-season. By September, the point's summer community is a ghost town and only shorebirds, gulls, and ducks remain. Walk up the inland road to see the magnificent dunes of Sandy Neck, or stroll around the edge of the point for marvelous views of Cape Cod Bay. Sandy Neck Beach extends seven miles west.

On the return, cross over to the south side of the harbor. Paddle by Barnstable's spacious public beaches and the green bluffs that define its southeastern shore. At the flashing green buoy just north of Blish Point, turn south to follow the narrow channel back to the put-in.

Directions to Launch Site: From Boston take I-93 south to Route 3 south. Follow Route 3 across the Sagamore Bridge to Route 6. Take Route 6 to Exit 6 (Route 132) in Barnstable. Take a left off the ramp, and drive Route 132 north 0.8 mile to Route 6A. Turn right on Route 6A and proceed 2.6 miles to Mill Way. Turn left and drive 0.6 mile to the state boat ramp on the left.

Alternate Launch Sites: There are several other landings along Barnstable Harbor, but most are restricted to resident-only parking. Also, many of the town landings require long carries at low tide. One landing that is advisable at high tide only is located at the end of Bone Hill Road. Using the above directions, proceed on 6A east about 1.5 miles from Mill Way to Bone Hill Road. Turn left on Bone Hill and find a landing and very small parking lot at the end of the road.

trip 27   PAMET HARBOR AND WEST PAMET RIVER, TRURO

Level of Difficulty: Easy–moderate; protected and open water

Round–Trip Mileage: 3.5 miles (including Pamet River and inner harbor); add 1.5 miles round-trip for Corn Hill and 4.0 miles round-trip additional for Cape Cod National Seashore

Attractions: Tidal river, salt marsh, bird-watching

Precautions: Paddle at two to three hours before or after high tide only. Strong current at harbor entrance. Bring bug repellent.

Charts: NOAA 13249 (1:20,000). See also *Trails Illustrated* Topographic Map 250.

Tidal Information: Mean tidal range, about 9.5 feet. sHigh tide is fifteen minutes after Boston high tide. Paddle within two to three hours of high tide.While it is easier to paddle with the tide, one can also paddle against the current.

Launch Site: Town wharf, Depot Road, Truro. Parking fee, late May to September.

THIS SHORT PADDLE allows kayakers to explore both sandy Pamet Harbor and the marshy reaches of the Pamet River. The two destinations stand in high contrast. Travel first up the quiet, winding Pamet River, whose turbid waters, brown mud banks, and green grass close in on paddlers bent on reaching its navigable end (at Route 6). Down at the Pamet Harbor breezes are fresher and horizons substantially broader. There kayakers greet other boaters, enjoy sandy beaches, and gain views north to Provincetown Harbor

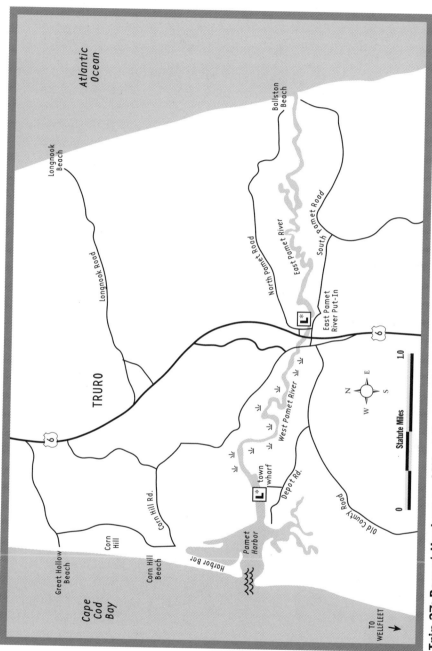

Trip 27: Pamet Harbor and West Pamet River, Truro
Trip 28: East Pamet River, Truro

or south down Cape Cod Bay. Paddle at high tide for the best paddle in this shallow waters.

The original name of the town of Truro was Pamet, or Payomet, from the name of the Native American tribe that inhabited this part of the cape. In 1620, this tribe played a critical part in the history of the Pilgrims. It was in Truro, on what is today Corn Hill, just north of Pamet Harbor, that the Pilgrims found ten bushels of seed corn. The Pilgrims stole the corn, believing that the bounty was left for them by God, and the seed provided them with a lifesaving crop the following year. In Truro, the Pilgrims also found their first source of fresh drinking water in the New World, not far from the course of this paddle.

To explore the Pamet River, turn right (east) from the launch. Travel up the main river channel, easily found by following the docks of the houses along the river. The route is peaceful and relaxing, although the scenery is not memorable. The twisting course of the river, nevertheless, keeps the trip interesting by presenting different views at each bend. The river is a good choice for a windy or inclement day. On warm days, however, the still air below the banks of the slow-moving river can be quite stifling.

Paddle a meandering course of about 1.25 miles to the spot where a road crosses the river (just short of Route 6). If paddlers were able to land and climb up the steep embankment to the road, they would find an excellent gourmet shop, Jams, with an exceptionally attractive array of lunch offerings. At the time of this writing, however, such a move is not easily accomplished. Instead, paddlers must retrace their strokes to the harbor.

Back in the harbor, paddle by the put-in, but this time head west. Looking at the unusually quiet harbor, it is hard to believe that it once rivaled Provincetown as a whaling and codfishing port. In the 1700s, Pamet Harbor was a prominent shipbuilding center, producing vessels bound for the Grand Banks. In the 1850s, the harbor hosted a fleet of more than sixty mackerel-catchers, and its docks hummed with commerce from Boston. By 1860, however, the harbor was quiet. Several violent storms had swept into the harbor, taking many lives and filling the inlet with sand. Due to declining harbor conditions, companies went bankrupt and the fishing industry went elsewhere.

Today the shallow harbor is left to small boats, kayakers, and those fishermen who wade the shallows. Paddlers can explore what is left of the harbor and enjoy its sandy banks. Just north of the mouth, behind Gull Island (Harbor Bar), kayakers can play in warm, protected water.

Those who want to explore Cape Cod Bay should follow the buoys leading out of the harbor's narrow mouth. Watch for strong currents at the outlet. From the harbor entrance, Provincetown Harbor is about eight miles north, on a course that closely parallels the shoreline. Along the way, kayakers pass numerous public beaches below fifty-foot bluffs rising steeply from the bay. Paddling north just 0.75 mile places one directly under the infamous moors of Corn Hill. (The moors [coastal heathlands], an environment increasingly rare on the Cape, are glorious in fall. Their low, woody shrubs turn scarlet with a burning intensity.) Just north of Corn Hill, kayakers can visit Great Hollow Beach.

Traveling south from Pamet Harbor, the coastline is less dramatic. A popular and beautiful destination, nevertheless, is Wellfleet's Great Island, about 4.5 miles south (see Trip 30). Kayakers can also enjoy the lovely bay-side beaches of the Cape Cod National Seashore, which begin in South Truro, just 2.0 miles south of Pamet Harbor.

To explore the freshwater portion of the Pamet River, see Trip 28.

Directions to Launch Site: From Boston, take I-93 south to Route 3 south. Cross the Sagamore Bridge, and take Route 6 to Pamet Roads exit in Truro. Turn west on South Pamet Road, take the first left on Castle Road, then the first right immediately onto Old County Road. Drive about 0.5 mile on Old County Road to Depot Road, and turn right. Follow Deport Road to the town wharf at its end. Fee charged for launching.

trip 28 EAST PAMET RIVER, TRURO

Level of Difficulty: Easy; protected water

Round-Trip Mileage: 2.5 (approximate) miles

Attractions: Narrow river through a freshwater marsh, bird-watching

Precautions: The very narrow, twisting nature of this stream makes maneuvering difficult for long sea kayaks. Best for short plastic boats that can withstand a few bangs from launching and submerged logs. Bring bug repellent.

Charts: See *Trails Illustrated* Topographic Map 250.

Tidal Information: The dike at Route 6 keeps the tide out, consequently making the East Pamet River a freshwater stream.

Launch Site: Highway overpass between North and South Pamet Roads, Truro. Free parking.

WHY KAYAK DOWN A TWISTING, tree-choked stream? You can barely travel a mile before branches grab your paddles. Yet paddlers come because it's quiet, earthy; alive with bugs, birds, and flowers; and totally different from other trips on the Cape. The east branch of the Pamet River doesn't offer much paddling (hardly any!), but it does provide an hour of escape into a lush, wild garden of freshwater marsh. Best for Walden wannabe's, miniaturists, naturalists, and loners, this brief excursion clears the head and renews the spirit for one's next adventure into the noisy, open spaces of Cape Cod Bay or the Atlantic Ocean. Take a short plastic kayak and breakdown paddle for greatest flexibility in this narrow stream.

After hoisting your kayak over the guardrail, launch from the bank just feet from the highway. From this inauspicious beginning, head east (right) into the narrow, tree-lined river. In midsummer, paddlers are greeted by hundreds of iridescent blue dragonflies. Huge and hovering, they flit like tinkerbell from leaf to leaf. A large variety of other insects, most not as enticing, are also likely to welcome kayakers. Damselflies, midges, mosquitoes, and deerflies thrive in the freshwater wetland.

A midsummer paddle feels like a float through Monet's *Waterlily*. The Pamet's dark, still water reflects clouds and overhanging trees in awesome complexity. Waterlilies choke the stream. Layers upon layers of green make up the riverbank, from lush grasses to shiny-leafed shrubs to pale deciduous trees to dark pines. Even the green water is layered with pine pollen, fallen leaves, and water weeds. In places, a paddle raises weeds like forkfulls of green spaghetti.

Listen through the buzz of the insects for the bird life of the Pamet. Watch for red-winged blackbirds, yellow warblers, kingfishers, wood ducks, and members of the heron family. Overhead, look for birds of prey attracted to the rodents living in the half-mile-wide Pamet River valley, through which this narrow stream meanders. Mammals enjoy this stream as well. Muskrats make their homes in lodges of canes on the banks of the river. Also on the banks, look for painted turtles and frogs.

Before you travel a truly satisfying distance, the Pamet narrows to a ridiculous width. Barely wider than a paddle length, the river challenges tenacious kayakers to shorten up and paddle canoe-style. But this only forestalls the inevitable. Paddle backward to a spot wide enough to turn around. Perhaps lingering will be rewarded by one more sighting of a bright yellow warbler, downy or hairy woodpecker, or the sight of a butterfly making love to a white pond lily.

To learn more about the flora and fauna of the Pamet River, take a guided trip with Massachusetts Audubon. For information call the Massachusetts Audubon Wellfleet Bay Wildlife Sanctuary at 508-349-2615. To explore Pamet Harbor and the west half of the Pamet River, see Trip 27.

Directions to Launch Site: From Boston, take I-93 south to Route 3 south. Take Route 3 south, across the Sagamore Bridge, to Route 6. Drive Route 6 to Pamet Roads exit in Truro. Between South Pamet and North Pamet Roads, a short connecting road travels over the Pamet River. Park on the west side of this road, taking care to park completely off the road, close to its intersection with South Pamet Road. (Approaching from the south on Route 6, turn right after exiting at Pamet Roads to reach the overpass.) To launch in the river, kayakers must carry their boats over the guardrail on the east side of the road and launch near the cement off the riverbank.

trip
29

WELLFLEET HARBOR AND LIEUTENANT ISLAND

Level of Difficulty: Easy to moderate; protected water

Round-Trip Mileage : 3.8 to 8.0 miles

Attractions: Massachusetts Audubon Wildlife Sanctuary; salt marsh; bird-watching; sandy beach for picnicking, swimming

Precautions: South and southwest winds can produce difficult waves. Boat traffic in harbor can be heavy in summer. Extensive mud flats can ground kayakers a few hours on either side of low tide.

Charts: NOAA 13250 (1:40,000), and NOAA 13246 (1:80,000)

Tidal Information: High tide is fourteen minutes after Boston high tide; low tide is thirty minutes later. Mean tidal range, 10.0 feet. Paddle two hours on either side of high tide to have sufficient water for exploring and to avoid extensive mud flats.

Launch Site: Town Landing at Old Wharf Point, Old Wharf Road, Wellfleet. Free parking.

THIS IS A BEAUTIFUL TRIP, particularly in late summer or early fall. At that time, shorebird viewing is at its prime, boat traffic diminishes, and the changing colors of the marsh add to Wellfleet's already considerable beauty. For the Cape, the area is unusually quiet; the natural environment is aided substantially by the presence of the 1,000-acre Massachusetts Audubon Wildlife Sanctuary on the south side of Lieutenant Island.

Launch into the harbor off Old Wharf Point. The best route around Lieutenant Island depends upon the phase of the tide. In order to have maximum kayaking time, start the trip one to two hours before high tide. Paddle counterclockwise around the island so that you are paddling *with* the current under the Lieutenant Island bridge.

From the put-in, paddle west across Loagy Bay to the sandy northern tip of Lieutenant Island. Continue west around the end of the island, then head south. In the eighteenth century, whalers scouted pilot whales from the hills of Lieutenant Island. Much later these hills were again lookouts, but for an entirely different reason: local lore has it that the island was a trafficking spot for illegal alcohol during Prohibition.

Three-quarters of the way around the island (paddling southwest), kayakers arrive at the Massachusetts Audubon Wildlife Sanctuary. A variety of terns feed in the offshore water. The island's south side is characterized by marsh and is an excellent place to watch birds. Heron, egret, and migrating shorebirds frequent the marsh. From August to October, watch particularly for the whimbrel, a large sandpiper with a very long, distinctively down-turned bill and dark stripes through its eyes. Toward evening large numbers of whimbrels gather, and groups of 200 birds have been counted! In September, kayakers may also see large concentrations of greater yellowlegs and snowy egrets. Many of the birds feed on the abundant fiddler crabs that inhabit the marsh. (See Trip 30 for more on fiddler crabs).

Paddle east along the marshy south edge of the island. The sanctuary extends east to the marsh surrounding Fresh Brook on the mainland, an area also worth exploring. When ready to return, head north to pass under the narrow bridge leading from the mainland to Lieutenant Island. Passage under the bridge is easier when the basin is filling, but it can be accomplished against the current as long as there is sufficient water. If paddlers leave Old Wharf Point before high tide, there should be sufficient time to make it under the bridge (a distance of approximately 3.8 miles, including sanctuary exploration) before the water runs out.

After paddling north under the bridge, head up through Loagy Bay back to Old Wharf Point. Kayakers can then continue north to explore the Blackfish Creek drainage and more salt marsh. To continue, paddle north around the point, then head east to Blackfish Creek. The creek is often the site of pilot whale strandings. Pilot

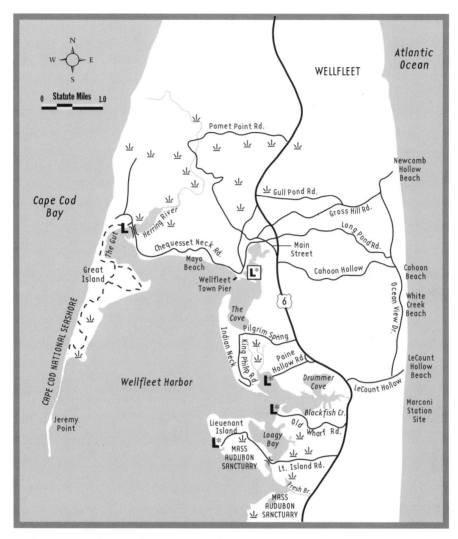

Trip 29: Wellfleet Harbor and Lieutenant Island
Trip 30: Wellfleet Harbor and Great Island

whales average about thirteen feet and 1,800 pounds and are found in significant numbers in the western North Atlantic. The whales are almost completely black, explaining the origin of the creek's name. Wellfleet's outer harbor offers plentiful food sources for the whales, including squid and small fish. It is hypothesized that the whales chase the fish into the harbor at high tide, then find themselves without sufficient water when the tide recedes. Wellfleet Harbor also sees frequent strandings of harbor porpoises and white-sided and common dolphins.

Explore the channels and marshes of Blackfish Creek, then paddle north to Drummer Cove, where large homes surround the quiet water. Another protected area worth exploring is the marsh behind Indian Neck. The long, sandy barrier beach of Indian Neck protects a small marsh just west of Drummer Cove. Peak into its meandering channels to observe more birds and wetlands. If all this marsh exploration is a bit too precious, head north to paddle along the sandy west shore of Indian Neck and north to explore Wellfleet's busy harbor (see Trip 30).

Directions to Launch Site: From Boston, take I-93 south to Route 3 south. Take Route 3 south, across the Sagamore Bridge, to Route 6. Take Route 6 to Wellfleet, then turn west onto Old Wharf Road and follow it 1.3 miles to its termination at a small landing on Old Wharf Point. The last 0.6 mile is on sandy road. Parking is limited; if no parking is available, check alternate launch sites, below.

Alternate Launch Sites: (1) Town landing at Paine Hollow Road. Turn west from Route 6 (near the 100-mile mark) onto Paine Hollow Road and proceed to the town landing at its end. Parking is limited. (2) Lieutenant Island put-in. At high tide, kayakers can launch from the island by taking Route 6 to Lieutenant Island Road, and proceed over the bridge to the island. Turn left on Meadow Avenue East (a sand road) and drive to the parking lot at its end (a 2.4-mile drive from Route 6). Park near the end of the road. Because of soft sand, do not attempt to drive closer to the beach. There is about a 100-foot carry to the water. (3) Kayakers can also launch from the Wellfleet Town Pier (see Trip 30) and paddle around Indian Neck, adding about 4.3 miles round-trip to the paddle.

Camping: Massachusetts Audubon members can enjoy woodsy harborside camping at Massachusetts Audubon's Wellfleet Bay Wildlife Sanctuary off Route 6. Call 508-349-2615 for reservations.

trip 30

WELLFLEET HARBOR AND GREAT ISLAND

Level of Difficulty: Easy to moderate; protected water

Round–Trip Mileage: 4.0–10.0 miles

Attractions: Cape Cod National Seashore, salt marsh, bird-watching, sandy beach for picnicking, swimming

Precautions: South and southwest winds can produce difficult waves. Boat traffic in harbor can be heavy in summer.

Charts: NOAA 13250 (1:40,000), and NOAA 13246 (1:80,000)

Tidal Information: High tide is 14 minutes after Boston high tide, low tide is 30 minutes later. Mean tidal range, 10 feet. Paddle two hours on either side of high tide to have sufficient water for exploring harbor.

Launch Site: Wellfleet town pier, Wellfleet. Free parking.

WELLFLEET HAS an aesthetically pleasing harbor that begs for exploration by kayak. Opening to the south and protected by the long arm of Great Island to the west, it feels big but not overwhelming. Paddlers can look out at the attractive landforms bordering the harbor and think, I'd like to go *there*, and do it, returning in time for a terrific sunset. One such trip is the moderately ambitious trek to Great Island and Jeremy Point, part of the Cape Cod National Seashore. For the best trip, visit in September when shorebirds and seals replace the tourists and crisp, dry air supplants summer's mugginess.

Although Wellfleet Harbor is often a gentle place, be mindful of the wind and tides. A south or southwest wind can kick up waves, and low tide makes paddling a chore, especially around Great Island. Also beware of fog, which often shrouds the harbor on summer mornings. It obscures obstacles and, more importantly, hides your presence from other boaters.

Launch from the beach next to the town pier and paddle west along Wellfleet's Mayo Beach. The harbor's ten-foot tidal range is apparent here. At low water, one could walk a half-mile into the harbor on the sand flats. At high water, on the other hand, the beach is exceedingly narrow. At high tide, beware of refracting waves from a sea wall about 0.5 mile west of the put-in.

At 1.2 miles west of the Wellfleet pier, arrive at the mouth of the Herring River. If the water is high turn north to paddle up to the Herring River dike. (Near the north end of the bridge is the alternate put-in.) At low water, this area drains to mud and kayakers must immediately turn south toward Great Island. Inconvenient for navigation but gastronomically important, the area's mud flats produce the famous Wellfleet oyster. In fact, the town's first European name, coined by the French explorer Samuel de Champlain in 1606, was Port aux Huitres, French for "port of oysters." At low water, this is an excellent place to observe shorebirds, herons, and gulls feeding. In the fall, look for ospreys and a variety of ducks.

Great Island is a knob, or large mound of glacial debris, originally forested in white pine and American chestnut but today covered by pitch pine and bearberry. In the 1700s, European settlers cleared the island to supply their ships, homes, and industries. Bears and wolves originally roamed the land, but the animals went the way of the hardwood forests. By 1800 Great Island was pasture for pigs, horses, and sheep. The island's denuded slopes rapidly eroded until pitch pines were planted in the 1830s. Great Island *was* an island until 1831, when sand blocked the mouth of the Herring River and created a natural land bridge at Herring Gut.

Rising sixty feet above the harbor, the bluffs of Great Island were used in whaling days as a lookout for pilot whales. In the 1800s, Wellfleet was a good-sized whaling port. Whale boats launched off the shores of Great Island to catch whales feeding in the fertile shoals southwest of the island. An eight-mile National Park Service trail starts at the north end of Great Island, climbs the knob, then travels three miles south to Jeremy Point. Along the way, hikers can visit the site of an eighteenth-century tavern which once served whalers on the island.

Paddle south around the edge of Great Island. The marshes east of Great Island are home to a remarkably large population of fiddler crabs. It is quite a sight to watch the crabs during their noisy march home to their burrows in the marsh. On a flooding tide, watch (and hear!) the little crabs *tap-tap-tapping* their way home, appearing in a royal panic. Called fiddler crabs for the male's one magnificently out-sized violin-shaped claw, the crabs live by the thousands in the marsh. Males display their huge claws to attract females, to protect their tiny territories, and to fight other males. All male crabs are born with an outsized *right* claw. If they lose this claw in battle, a new one grows on the left. When observing a population of crabs, one sees a fair distribution of right and left fiddlers, evidence of a healthy pugnacious nature. Check the mud flat for lost limbs. What looks like D-Day on the marsh is simply natural adaptation. The crabs practice self-amputation of their ten legs if caught by a predator. Legs grow back during the next molt.

The activity of fiddler crabs is timed with the tides. On an ebb tide, the crabs come out to the mud flats to feed. When the tide floods, they retreat en masse to their surprisingly deep (two to three feet!) tunnels in the mud. If disturbed by your approach, their noisy retreat is an act of self-preservation. When walking in the marsh, avoid stepping on the crabs or their holes.

From the eastern tip of Great Island, it's a straight shot 2.8-mile south to the far end of Jeremy Point. If the tide is in, kayakers will be able to slip west through a break between the mainland and Jeremy Point to take a look at Cape Cod Bay. Paddle out for long bay views. Provincetown is visible to the north. Alternatively, beach the kayak on the Wellfleet side and hike west to the bay side of the island to gain views and enjoy superb picnic spots along the magnificent national-seashore beach.

The area from Great Island to Jeremy Point is incredibly rich in bird and wildlife activity. The beach along the bay side is one of the most productive nesting areas on Cape Cod for the threatened piping plover. Spring and summer paddlers will note the cordoned-off areas and wire cages that protect the plover nests. When walking on the beach, kayakers must stay clear of the restricted areas and watch where they step. The tiny, fledgling plovers are sand colored and often get stuck in the weak depressions made by footprints and vehicles.

the mystery of the wellfleet oyster

The rich salt marsh of Wellfleet Bay supports an abundance of oysters, soft-shell clams, and quahogs. Wellfleet oysters, in particular, are world renowned. For hundreds, perhaps thousands of years Native Americans (in this area, the Punonakanits) ate oysters. The Pilgrims followed suit. But European settlers discovered that the oyster's commercial value was not limited to its sweet flesh. Oyster shells were burned to make lime for mortar.

Thus came the rub. The Wellfleet oyster gained international fame by the early 1800s. As demand swelled, Wellfleet's riches and population expanded. But by the mid-1800s the Wellfleet oyster had vanished.

Today we can guess what happened. Although it was not well understood at the time, oysters need old shell surfaces to propagate their spat. The removal of their shells for lime likely caused their dramatic disappearance. Oysters from southern coastal areas were reintroduced, and they re-established themselves firmly in Wellfleet Harbor. Whether this replacement stock matches the flavor of the original Wellfleet oyster is a question no one can answer.

Paddlers from August to October can enjoy shorebirds along the beach and in the marshes of Great Island and Jeremy Point. The Wellfleet area is a significant stopover area for migrating birds. (For more opportunities to see birds in Wellfleet, see Trip 29.) In fall, Jeremy Point is also a significant haul-out for both gray and harbor seals. When viewing seals, maintain a respectful distance (at least 200 feet). If seals enter the water to avoid your approach, back away—you are too close.

Late-fall paddlers may even witness one of the Cape's most amazing wildlife phenomena, the stranding of sea turtles. Each year between 50 and 100 sea turtles wash up between Great Island and Jeremy Point. The strandings occur in late fall after a profound cold snap, when the turtles are inadvertently caught in colder water than they can handle. The cold-stunned green, Kemps Ridley, leatherback, or loggerhead turtles are rescued, when possible, by transport to the New England Aquarium. Observation of the stranding can be breathtaking; leatherbacks can weigh 1,000 pounds and grow to the size of a Volkswagen!

Paddling farther south takes kayakers to Billingsgate Shoal. Until the early 1900s this shoal was an island, lying just south of Jeremy Point. The island supported a lighthouse and small community of fishermen. It is now covered except at the very lowest of low tides, when kayakers can see the original foundation of the lighthouse.

Great Island's natural beauty and wealth of habitat for birds, mammals, and sea creatures draw kayakers back for many return visits. For additional Wellfleet kayaking, see Trip 29.

Directions to Launch Site: From Boston, take I-93 south to Route 3 south. Take Route 3 south to the Sagamore Bridge to Route 6. Drive Route 6 to Wellfleet, and turn left on Commercial Street (signed for Wellfleet Center). When road forks after 0.3 mile, bear left and continue on Commercial Street, following signs for harbor. One mile from Route 6, arrive at the town pier at the end of Commercial Street. There is free parking at the pier. Launch off the public beach to the right of the pier.

Alternate Launch Site: Chequessett Neck Road at Herring River, Wellfleet. Follow above directions to town pier. From the pier, turn right and continue west along the waterfront on Kendrick Avenue. At Kendrick Avenue's intersection with Chequessett Neck Road, turn left. Proceed on Chequessett Neck Road to cross the Herring River on a small bridge. Take the first left after the bridge to a dirt parking area and put-in (3.2 miles from Route 6). Park on the highest ground possible! At high water, the lower half of the parking lot floods! Avoid at low tide due to mud flats.

Camping: Massachusetts Audubon members can enjoy woodsy harborside camping at the Massachusetts Audubon's Wellfleet Bay Wildlife Sanctuary off Route 6. Call 508-349-2615 for reservations.

trip 31   PROVINCETOWN HARBOR

Level of Difficulty: Easy to strenuous (depending on distance); protected water

Round–Trip Mileage: 3.7 miles to Long Point, 8.0 miles to Woods End Light, 12.0 miles to Herring Cove, 15.0 miles to Hatches Harbor; add 0.7 mile to paddle around breakwater

Attractions: Historic harbor, wreck, picnicking and swimming at Cape Cod National Seashore and Race Point

Precautions: Watch for traffic in harbor, especially ferry and whale-watching boats. Both move at high speed and create large wakes. Watch also for riptides off Race Point and heavy and dumping surf on the Atlantic side of Cape Cod National Seashore.

Charts: NOAA 13249 (1:20,000), NOAA 13246 (1:80,000), NOAA 13267 (1:80,000)

Tidal Information: High tide is 15 minutes after Boston high tide. Mean tidal range, 9.1 feet.

Launch Site: Fisherman's Wharf (Cabral's Wharf), Commercial Street, Provincetown. Parking fee.

PADDLING OUT OF PROVINCETOWN HARBOR provides great views of the town as well as terrific opportunities to explore the magnificent Cape Cod National Seashore. Seldom can urban and natural adventures be combined so seamlessly. The trip's only drawbacks are summer crowds, boat traffic, and parking hassles. For a touch of serenity and sanity, visit before July 4 or after Labor Day. The trip described below stays within Cape Cod Bay, so kayakers avoid the heavy surf and currents encountered off Race Point.

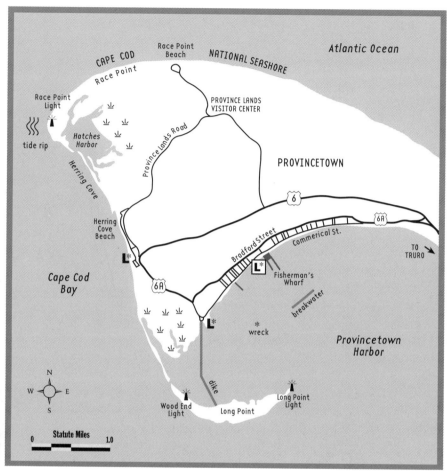

Trip 31: Provincetown Harbor

It's a cliché, perhaps, but there is indeed something special about Cape light. Particularly on the outer cape, light brings magic to ordinary space. For a kayaker, it means floating in a world where boundaries are enchantingly blurred. Sky reaches into water, water to the garden beneath, and sand to sky. The light is soft yet intense. One paddles *through* it—hot, shimmering, cool, foggy, a million shades of blue, lavender, and yellow. One can hate Cape Cod for its traffic, sprawl, noise, and crowds; but it begs forgiveness with its light. Paddle Herring Cove at sunset and watch the sun set into the bay. All will be forgiven.

Launch from the beach next to the pier. Provincetown is the deepest natural harbor on Cape Cod. Consequently watch out for the rapid comings and goings of large commercial boats. Once a major fishing port, Provincetown supported hundreds of fishermen harvesting great catches from nearby Stellwagen Bank and Georges Bank. As early as 1700, schooners filled the harbor, and windmills and saltworks lined the beaches. Today fishing, although diminished, is still excellent here, so paddlers are likely to encounter numerous fishing boats. When tuna are running, watch for a small but active fleet of tuna fishermen.

Paddle southwest on a route paralleling the shore. To the southeast lies a stone breakwater. Aim your bow at Woods End Light, a lighthouse with a flashing red light (and a frequently blasting horn) at the west end of Long Point. With this heading, kayakers will arrive at an interesting boat wreck in approximately 0.6 mile.

Historians believe that Woods End was so named because it marked the end of the forest that originally covered this eroding beach. According to European explorers of the seventeenth and eighteenth centuries, sizable hardwood forests blanketed Cape Cod. Centuries of European settlement, however, consumed the vast woods. Clearcut for agriculture and harvested for shipbuilding, home construction, and fuel, the trees rapidly disappeared. Gone also is the soil once held in place by their roots. The most dramatic change occurred here in the Provincelands, where the soil and forests were probably historically thinner than in other areas of the Cape. Consequently severe erosion plagues Provincetown today. Each year unstable dunes crawl closer to Route 6 and neighboring homes.

Looking out at the barren sand spit comprising Long Point, imagine the view 200 years ago. Until the mid-1800s, thirty-six families lived at the point, working the easily accessible fishing grounds. Isolation and winter storms finally convinced the community to leave, and around 1850 eighteen homes were floated across the bay to Provincetown. These old homes can still be seen in town, identified by a blue tile picturing a house upon a barge.

After about 0.6 mile, arrive at the wreck. Paddle its perimeter to study its skeletal remains. In this shallow water one can see crabs, fish, and the crisscrossing trails of moon snails in the sand. To the southwest, note the granite dike that runs more than a mile from the end of Route 6 to Long Point.

The sandy shores of Long Point provide lovely picnic areas. Paddle around Long Point Light, at the tip of Long Point. Be aware that whale-watch boats increase their speed dramatically once they reach the point. When presented with the large wakes thrown by these boats, turn into them bow first, and for greatest control, paddle forward through the wake.

North of Long Point, the beach as far as your eye can see is contained within the Cape Cod National Seashore. The 43,000-acre national seashore was created in 1962 to protect what was left of the man-ravaged landscape of the outer cape. Look for many varieties of terns, including common, roseate, and the endangered least. About two miles from Long Point, pass the Woods End Lighthouse. Quiet and beautiful picnic spots abound.

About four miles northwest from Long Point Light, paddlers arrive at Herring Cove Beach, an extremely popular summer destination. The water is cool, but the surf is usually gentle and the people-watching superb. For a more natural scene, continue to the north end of Herring Cove Beach to Hatches Harbor. This is a beautiful detour, but manageable only at high tide.

Hatches Harbor was once thriving, but sand has long taken over, making the harbor nearly too shallow even for kayaks. At high tide, nevertheless, kayakers can sneak through the shallow channel and paddle in a lovely salt marsh frequented by shorebirds, gulls, and terns. The pleasure is fleeting, however, and kayakers must exit quickly, before their water disappears.

Beyond Hatches Harbor is Race Point Light. The outer edge of the "elbow" to the northwest marks territory suitable only for kayakers secure in advanced ocean-going skills. Race Point is known for its tide rips and significant surf. For most kayakers, the south side of Race Point is a good place to turn around.

Head south back to the Provincetown Harbor. After passing Long Point Light, appreciate the view of the Provincetown skyline. The Pilgrim Monument is the town's centerpiece. Rising 352 feet, it is the tallest granite structure in the United States. Provincetown's spirit is not dampened a bit by this formidable reminder of its conservative forefathers or the fact that the federal government owns 90 percent of the town. Provincetown's remaining 10 percent bursts with vitality and (sometimes outrageous) creativity. Artists and writers have long flocked to its colorful streets. Notables include John Dos Passos, Norman Mailer, and Eugene O'Neill. Today art galleries, theaters, and cabarets line the main drag.

Paddle back toward the harbor, but this time pass on the outside of the breakwater. From late spring through fall, a line of double-crested cormorants sits atop the stones. A few stand with their

center for coastal studies and the stellwagen bank national marine sanctuary

The Center for Coastal Studies of Provincetown is a private, nonprofit organization dedicated to research, conservation, and education in coastal and marine environments. From roseate terns to right whales, the center is on the cutting edge of scientific investigation for the purposes of promoting conservation and environmentally supportive public policy.

The center's home in Provincetown is no accident. The fertile waters off Cape Cod are home to several different species of whales, many of which reside here seasonally. The whales use the area as a feeding ground and a safe place in which to raise their young. Provincetown is the closest port to Stellwagen Bank, an underwater deposit of sand and gravel located just a few miles north of Provincetown. The shallower waters of Stellwagen result in high levels of productivity, supporting huge quantities of plankton; and large numbers of fish upon which humpbacks, fin whales, and other large marine animals feed. Stellwagen Bank was dedicated in 1993 as New England's first National Marine Sanctuary. This designation was the result of ten years of hard work by the Center for Coastal Studies.

Kayakers can learn more about whales and Stellwagen Bank by joining CCS for a whale watch on the Dolphin Fleet or by attending one of CCS's natural history seminars. Membership is another excellent way to support the center's programs. For information contact the Center for Coastal Studies, 59 Commercial Street, Provincetown, MA 02657; 508-487-3622, www.coastalstudies.org.

wings outspread, drying their feathers in the sun. Unlike most other water birds, cormorants do not coat their feathers in water-repelling oil. Consequently cormorants are excellent divers. The downside is their need to dry their waterlogged feathers like laundry on the line.

Looking southeast from the breakwater, paddlers see Truro and its houses along the shore. The larger view, however, takes in a long line of beach, cliffs, dunes, and blue water. Paddle north and east to tour the shoreline or paddle northwest around the breakwater back to the put-in. As you return to the wharf, take note of boats entering and exiting.

TRIP TIP: Kayakers can make an easy trip from Herring Cove Beach to Hatches Harbor (at high tide) or south to Woods End Lighthouse. From Herring Cove Beach, the round-trip distance is about 3.0 miles to Hatches Harbor. To Woods End, it's about 3.5 miles round-trip. Both are spectacular around sunset. See *Alternate Launch Sites* listed below for directions to Herring Cove Beach.

Arrive in P-town without a boat? Off the Coast Kayak rents kayaks and runs excellent guided tours out of Provincetown Harbor. Contact them at 877-PT-KAYAK, 508-487-2692, or www.offthe-coastkayak.com.

Directions to Launch Site: From Boston, drive I-93 south to Route 3. Take Route 3 south across the Sagamore Bridge to Route 6. Drive Route 6 to Route 6A in Provincetown. Continue into Provincetown on Route 6A to Ryder Street. Turn left on Ryder Street, then cross Commercial Street to a large parking lot at the wharf. If the parking lot is full, drop your boat off and use one of the satellite parking lots a few blocks away. Parking is very limited July and August.

Alternate Launch Sites: (1) Boat Launch, Commercial Street, Provincetown. Follow above directions to Route 6A. Continue on Route 6A (Bradford Street) to West Vine Street at the end of town. Turn left and follow it to its end at Commercial Street (it turns into Soper Street). Turn right on Commercial Street and find the boat launch and parking immediately on the left. (2) Herring Cove Beach. Follow above directions to Route 6 and continue on Route 6 nearly to its termination. Signs will indicate the turnoff to Herring Cove Beach and parking. Fee for parking. From the parking lot, it's a short carry at high tide across the beach to the water.

NANTUCKET SOUND AND ENVIRONS

trip NAUSET MARSH,
32 EASTHAM

Level of Difficulty: Easy to strenuous; protected water

Round–Trip Mileage: 6.5 to 15.9 miles, depending on route

Attractions: Bird-watching, unspoiled vistas, Cape Cod National Seashore's Salt Pond Visitor Center and trails

Precautions: Shifting channels, sand spits, and shallow water create navigation challenges in hard-to-negotiate marsh. Bring a compass and memorize landmarks. Tide rips and breaking waves at inlet from the Atlantic at the break in Nauset Beach. Greenhead flies persistent July to early August.

Charts: NOAA 13246 (1:80,000). For larger-scale maps, try *Trails Illustrated* Topographic Map 250.

Tidal Information: Mean tidal range, 6.0 feet at Nauset Harbor; high tide delayed 3 hours in Nauset Marsh

Launch Site: Town Landing at Salt Pond, Eastham. Free parking.

N AUSET MARSH is one of the most beautiful places in Massachusetts for paddling serene, unspoiled, and protected water. Amid abundant bird and marine life, kayakers find sweeping vistas of low islands, narrow blue channels, and high green bluffs. The area's beauty more than makes up for its frustrating hydrography. The fall of the tides exposes sandbars and raises wide islands of

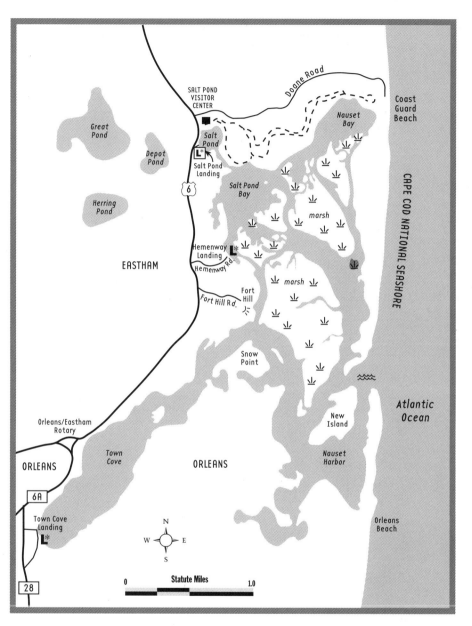

Trip 32: Nauset Marsh, Eastham

waving cordgrass, making navigation a challenge in this largely unmarked area. It is very easy to get lost in the maze, and a walk is likely at low tide. Regardless, the rewards of paddling this quiet, special spot far outweigh the difficulties.

To orient yourself in this difficult-to-negotiate marsh, make a pre-paddling stop at Fort Hill, part of the Cape Cod National Seashore. Park in the parking lot closest to the water and walk the trail to the top of the hill. Fort Hill overlooks Nauset Marsh. From its windy ridge top one gets an excellent overview of the channels, islands, and shoreline. Visible from the lookout are Town Cove to the south; the channel to Nauset Marsh from the cove directly below; the break in Nauset Beach that provides an outlet to the Atlantic to the east; Hemenway Landing to the north; and the old Coast Guard station and Coast Guard Beach two miles to the northeast. Knowing the location of these landmarks helps navigation considerably. In any event, Fort Hill offers brilliant views and great bird-watching. To reach Fort Hill, turn east off Route 6 on Fort Hill Road about 1.6 miles north of the Orleans/Eastham rotary or 1.4 miles south of the Salt Pond Visitor Center.

Part of the pleasure of paddling Nauset Marsh is aimless exploration. Consequently, this description highlights different areas of the marsh but does not dictate a certain route. Kayakers should consider the time and direction of the tides when plotting their course. Consider, always, the three-hour delay from high tide at Nauset Beach to high tide in the marsh. And although the current in the marsh is never so strong that one can't paddle against it, kayaking with the current makes the trip more pleasant.

From Salt Pond

Launch from the landing at the southwest shore of the round pond. Next to the landing is an aquaculture operation seeding quahogs and oysters. Above to the left is the Salt Pond Visitor Center and the trailhead for trails that run along the shore of Nauset Marsh. (One can walk to Coast Guard Beach, 1.5 miles northeast.) Paddle southeast toward the pond's outlet. Salt Pond was once a freshwater kettle pond, glacially created, that breached at its southeast end. When paddling through the breach out to the marsh, note the distinctive boathouses on the shore. These will help identify the inlet upon your return.

Enter Salt Pond Bay and enjoy an inspiring view of the marsh. Before the blizzard of '78, Henry Beston's "Outermost House" stood on the barrier beach to the southeast. His groundbreaking book, published in 1928, describes and exalts the seasons of the marsh and pleads eloquently for balance in man's relationship with nature. Still standing adjacent to the Salt Pond inlet is the handsome cape of author Wyman Richardson, who wrote the eloquent *House on Nauset Marsh.*

Following the shoreline north from Salt Pond about 1.7 miles takes paddlers to the back side of Coast Guard Beach at Nauset Bay. Above the beach sits the old white clapboard Coast Guard station high atop the bluff. Returning south, one can paddle closer to the backside of Nauset Beach, between the islands of the marsh. This northern portion of Nauset Marsh is navigable only an hour or so on either side of high tide. Even at high tide prepare for some meandering and dead ends. It is lovely paddling, nonetheless, away from all boat traffic and with only insects, marine life, and birds as traveling companions. Look for herons, oyster catchers, black skimmers, osprey, marsh hawks, gulls, and, of course, terns.

The authors of *Birding Cape Cod* christened the tern the "unofficial bird of Cape Cod." Just a century ago, tens of thousands of terns inhabited the Cape each summer. Three species of cape terns are still numerous today but far less abundant than 100 years ago, largely due to the destruction of their habitat. Frequently seen in Nauset Marsh is the common tern, a dove-sized white bird with a black cap and a red-orange, black-tipped bill. Also nesting in Nauset is the least tern, a smaller, swallow-sized bird with a yellow bill. Terns fly gracefully on long, slender wings, hovering before they dive bill first, wings folded, to pluck a small fish from the water. Their trilling call is pleasant to hear, a musical note compared to the catlike screeching of gulls.

While watching the skies, look also for easily identified laughing gulls. Their jet-black heads and red bill set them apart from any other Cape gull in the summer. Listen for their high-pitched voices calling *haaaah.*

From the outlet at Salt Pond, kayakers can also turn right (south). If you're paddling south from Salt Pond in low water, hug the western shoreline to find the deepest channels. Perhaps contrary to intuition, deeper water is found along shore, not in the middle of Salt Bay. A sea gull standing in inch-deep water in the center of the bay is a clear warning sign. Paddlers stuck at low tide must think positively. One advantage of the still, shallow water is an excellent view of the abundant fish (tiny striped killifish and mummichogs), crabs (fiddlers, marsh, and horseshoe), snails (moon), and blue mussels that inhabit this productive marsh. To keep afloat, look for flowing water and floating buoys. If south-traveling paddlers stay close

Nauset Marsh from Fort Hill.

to the Eastham shore, they will pass Hemenway Landing, readily identifiable by a large greenhouse-like building behind the landing. The rough distance from Salt Pond to Nauset Bay to Hemenway Landing and back to Salt Pond is 6.2 miles.

From Hemenway Landing

Hemenway Landing is a convenient put-in, but the landing can be difficult to find at the end of the day. A zigzagging channel between marsh islands takes paddlers to comfortably deep water and the outer marsh. Pay attention going out. Lobster buoys mark the deeper channels, and returning local fishermen (when present) lead the way back.

(Please note that this region is subject to great change, and this description may become obsolete as a result of those changes. For guided tours of the area, contact the Mass Audubon Sanctuary in Wellfleet, 508-349-2615, Fun Seekers of Wellfleet 508-349-1429, and Goose Hummock, 508-255-0455, of Orleans [located at the town landing at the south end of Town Cove].)

From the landing, one can paddle directly to the left (north) to reach Salt Pond Bay. Large areas of low water lie in this direction, so watch the tides. To one's immediate right is an obvious dead-end channel into the marsh. The third option, favored by most boaters, is the center channel heading east which turns between cordgrass islands to reach deeper water after about 0.7 mile. Once paddlers reach the wider channel, kayakers can travel north to Salt Pond Bay and Nauset Bay (see description above) or south toward Town Cove.

Paddling south, paddlers pass Fort Hill (distinguished by the undeveloped shoreline and high bluff) on the right. About one mile from Hemenway Landing, reach the entrance to Town Cove. If civilization is sought, paddlers can head down the busy cove to reach the Orleans town landing and wharf at its south end in 3.2 miles. Alternatively, kayakers can head southeast toward Nauset Harbor (watch for boat traffic). This direction leads to the marsh's outlet to the Atlantic. Kayakers should avoid passage through the outlet due to strong currents and breaking waves.

Within Nauset Harbor, south of the outlet, kayakers can view New Island. This sizable island hosts one of the largest tern colonies in New England. More than 1,100 pairs of terns were counted there in 1995. New Island is also a significant nesting site for laughing gulls. Do *not* attempt to land on the island when terns and gulls are nesting. Both are extremely protective of their nests and will attack if provoked! To explore the eastern side of Nauset Marsh, keep New

Nauset Marsh, Eastham.

Island on your right, and paddle north behind the barrier beach. Kayakers may find channels to take them north to Nauset Bay and Salt Pond Bay, or lack of water may force them back to the main channel to retrace their route to Hemenway Landing.

From Town Cove

All of the places mentioned above can be explored from the put-in at Town Cove. The large parking lot and easy-to-find landing (both from land and water) may be attractive to some paddlers. Kayakers will always have company launching from this busy landing. The 3.2-mile paddle out of Town Cove is developed, but pleasant.

Once kayakers reach Snow Point, at the end of Town Cove, they can either paddle north beneath Fort Hill to reach Salt Bay and Nauset Bay or paddle southeast to reach New Island and the outer marsh. Both routes are described above. From the landing at Town Cove, it is approximately ten miles round-trip to the top of Nauset Bay. Exploration of the eastern side of the marsh adds a few miles to the trip.

Check out the Salt Pond Visitor Center in Eastham to learn more about Nauset Marsh and its environs. The National Park Service runs an excellent series of lectures, walks, and even paddles from the Salt Pond facility. In addition, the bookstore at the visitor center has an extensive selection of natural history books as well as a good selection of maps.

Directions to Launch Site: From Boston, take I-93 south to Route 3 south. Take Route 3 south, across the Sagamore Bridge, to Route 6. Drive Route 6 to the Orleans/Eastham rotary. Continue north on Route 6 about 2.7 miles, then right down a short access road for Salt Pond Landing. The well-marked National Park Service's Salt Pond Visitor Center is 0.2 mile farther on Route 6, so if you see the visitor center, you know you've gone a little too far.

Alternate Launch Sites: (1) Hemenway Landing, Eastham. Follow the directions above to the Orleans/Eastham rotary and proceed north on Route 6 about 1.8 miles to Hemenway Road on the right. Turn right and drive 0.3 mile to the landing at its end. (2) Town Cove Town Landing, Orleans. Follow the directions above to the Orleans/Eastham rotary. Turn right on Route 6A and drive south to its intersection with Route 28. Turn left on Route 28 and find the town landing about 0.25 mile on the left, next to Goose Hummock.

trip PLEASANT BAY AND
33 LITTLE PLEASANT BAY

Level of Difficulty: Easy to moderate; protected water

Round–Trip Mileage: 5.5 miles to explore Little Pleasant Bay and 10.3 miles to explore Little Pleasant Bay and circumnavigate Strong Island in Pleasant Bay

Attractions: Cape Cod National Seashore, fishing, bird-watching, islands for picnicking

Precautions: Very heavy boat traffic in summer. Wind can generate rough water in Pleasant Bay. Avoid Chatham Harbor because of strong currents and boat traffic.

Charts: NOAA 13248 (1:20,000), and NOAA 13246 (1:80,000). Note that recent changes to the entrance to Chatham Harbor have rendered older charts of this area inaccurate. For a fairly accurate depiction (the sand shifts year to year), refer to NOAA 13248 (Edition 31, 10/31/95) or consult *Trails Illustrated 250*.

Tidal Information: Mean tidal range about 4 feet. High tide at Little Pleasant Bay is about 2.75 hours after Boston high tide. Paddle within 3 hours of high tide for ease of paddling.

Launch Site: Town Landing off Portanimicut Road, South Orleans. Free parking.

PLEASANT BAY offers hours of terrific kayaking, and a full day can be spent exploring its nooks and crannies. Especially beautiful are the quiet islands of Little Pleasant Bay and the passage along the bay side of Nauset Beach, all contained within the Cape Cod National Seashore. Much of the bay's shoreline is crowded with large homes, but the islands of the bay are mostly undeveloped. At high tide, Pleasant Bay encompasses 7,285 acres of salt water and is one of the most biologically diverse and productive marine habitats on the East Coast of the United States. Although the bay is protected from the Atlantic's big surf, don't underestimate the winds that can blow steadily across the bay and raise whitecaps. Summer winds often pick up in the afternoon, then diminish again at dusk. The best paddling is therefore in the early morning, when neither the wind nor the recreational boaters have yet risen. Tourist-free, bird-filled fall is the optimum season.

The long version of this trip circumnavigates Strong Island in southern Pleasant Bay and explores Pochet Island in the northern reaches of Little Pleasant Bay for a round-trip distance of about 9.0 miles. For a shorter, easier trip of about 4.8 miles round-trip, stick to Little Pleasant Bay and paddle to Sampson, Hog, and Pochet Islands. The best direction of travel depends upon the tide. While it is possible to paddle against the current in Pleasant Bay, the longer trip will seem much longer if one disregards the tides. Also, kayak Pleasant Bay around high tide; at low tide large areas of the bay are extremely shallow.

Launch into Little Pleasant Bay from tiny Paw Wah Pond. Many of the place names around the bay point originate from the Native Americans who first lived here. The Monomoyiks and Nausets lived and fished on Monomoyik, or "Great Bay." The road to the put-in, Portanimicut, was the Nauset name for "place of big rocks." Indeed, watch for large rocks just outside the entrance to Paw Wah Pond.

Paddle into Little Pleasant Bay and head east across the bay to Sampson and Hog Islands. At high tide, paddle between the islands on Hog Island Creek to reach Broad Creek, which runs along the backside of Nauset Beach at high water. It's a treat to paddle this quiet passage north to the top of Sampson Island. During most tides, kayakers must paddle around the west side of the islands.

From the north side of Sampson Island, continue north, paddling through the narrow passage between Pochet Island and Barley Neck to the cove below Pochet Neck. At low tide, there is little room to paddle, but at high tide kayakers can swing around the residential cove. Exiting the cove once again past Barley Neck, paddlers should avoid the aquaculture plots—marked by buoys, stakes, or ropes—where fishermen are seeding clams.

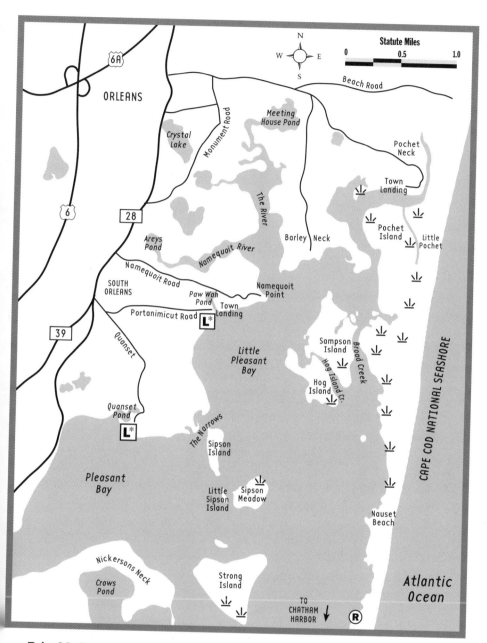

Trip 33: Pleasant Bay and Little Pleasant Bay

Traveling south, Pochet Island is on the left. Although the island is part of Cape Cod National Seashore, summer residents occupy the island from late May to October. Most do not mind the occasional visitor, but please ask for permission to explore this beautiful island. A 50-foot bluff at the south end of the island affords superb views of the surrounding bay and barrier beach. The best time to visit Pochet Island is in the fall when human residents have gone and kayakers are left with a prime viewing ground for a variety of raptors, including red-tailed hawks, harriers, and occasionally rough-legged hawks.

From Pochet Island, paddle back across Little Pleasant Bay to return to the put-in. For more exploring, head south, either down Broad Channel or around Sampson Island to the west. A few privately owned islands sit in Pleasant Bay southwest of Sampson and Hog Islands. The distance from Hog Island to the top of Strong Island (the southernmost island) is about 1.5 miles.

If paddling at high tide, the best option is to stay close to the backside of Nauset Beach, where Pleasant Bay is most quiet and beautiful. Fortunately, larger boats can't venture into these shallows. Directly south of Sampson and Hog, kayakers can hug the backside of Nauset Beach and look for a place to land. According to seasoned kayakers at Cape Cod Coastal Canoe and Kayaks, paddlers can find a good landing by heading south along the sand dunes a couple of miles. Just past a house with a cupola that stands alone is a beach where kayakers can land. From the beach, walk east to find a dirt road and turn left (north). Walk about 0.15 mile to a breach in the dunes. Once on the ocean side, enjoy the view up and down the long barrier beach. Reputed to be one of the prettiest and wildest beaches on the East Coast, Nauset Beach is well-worth the detour.

To take a look at the islands of Pleasant Bay, paddle southwest out of Little Pleasant Bay to Pleasant Bay. At the top of Pleasant Bay is a cluster of three islands, Sipson, Little Sipson, and Sipson Meadow. At high tide, you'll find only Sipson and Little Sipson Islands. Between the mainland and the Sipson Islands is a passage of water called the Narrows, where constricted tidal flow can cause rips. South of the Narrows, enter Pleasant Bay. Novices should consider winds and current before venturing to the south end of larger and less protected Pleasant Bay. From Sipson Island, it's a 0.7 mile paddle to Strong Island. If circumnavigating Strong Island, watch for rocks at its north and east ends.

From Nauset Beach or Strong Island, paddle northeast to return to the put-in. Paddling south of Strong Island into Chatham Harbor is not recommended due to strong currents and heavy boat traffic.

Both Massachusetts Audubon Society (508-349-2615) and Cape Cod Coastal Canoe and Kayak (508-564-4051) run excellent and highly recommended natural history paddling tours to Pleasant Bay.

Directions to Launch Site: From Boston, take I-93 south to Route 3 south. Follow Route 3 south, across the Sagamore Bridge to Route 6. Drive Route 6 to the Orleans rotary (Exit 12). From the rotary, turn right onto Route 6A for about 0.5 mile, then turn left onto Route 28. Drive south on Route 28 to Quanset Road on the left (at Route 28's intersection with Route 39). Turn left on Quanset Road, then take the first left on Portanimicut Road and follow to the town landing at its end. Limited parking.

Alternate Launch Site: Quanset Pond Town Landing, South Orleans. Follow above directions to Quanset Road. Follow Quanset Road to its end at Quanset Pond Town Landing. For information on additional town landings on Pleasant Bay, consult local town maps.

MONOMOY ISLANDS

Level of Difficulty: Strenuous; open water

Round–Trip Mileage: 11.0 miles from town landing at Mill Pond. Subtract 3.0 miles round-trip if launching from Harding Beach. Add up to 11.0 additional miles to explore South Monomoy Island.

Attractions: Monomoy National Wildlife Refuge, harbor and gray seals, shorebirds, unspoiled barrier islands, sandy beaches, lighthouse, swimming areas

Precautions: Strong tide rip off southeast end of South Monomoy. Breaking and dumping waves on east side of South Monomoy. Thick fog can roll in rapidly and unexpectedly, especially during the summer. Do not paddle without a compass and solid navigation skills. Note that most marine charts are not accurate as to location of sandbars and breaks that have occurred in the island in the last decade. Poison ivy is abundant on the islands, especially on South Monomoy. Ticks and mosquitoes are also prevalent in summer on the south island. On North Monomoy, greenhead flies abundant in July and August. Large portions of islands closed from May through September to protect piping plover and tern nesting.

Charts: NOAA 13248 (1:20,000), NOAA 13246 (1:80,000), NOAA 13229 (1:40,000), NOAA 13237 (1:80,000), Maptech Chart 5.1 (1:40,000). *Trails Illustrated* 250 (1:38,000), roughly reflects changes in shoreline but is *not* a nautical chart. NOAA 13248 (1:20,000), revised in 1995, provides the most up-to-date representation of the area but can not be relied upon to reflect the constantly changing conditions.

Tidal Information: Mean tidal range 3.7 feet at Monomoy Point, 4.0 feet at Stage Harbor, and 6.7 feet outside Stage Harbor. High tide at Stage Harbor is 55 minutes after Boston high tide and low tide is

48 minutes later. Outside the harbor, high tide is 30 minutes later, and at Monomoy Point it's 35 minutes after Boston high tide. Because extensive sandbars can impede progress around the islands at low tide, attention must be paid to the tides. Passage around the islands is also considerably easier when paddling *with* the current.

Launch Site: Mill Pond, Stage Harbor, Chatham. Free parking.

THE MONOMOY NATIONAL WILDLIFE REFUGE is the only federally designated Wilderness Area in southern New England. Paddling Monomoy brings kayakers in touch with a uniquely beautiful and ecologically invaluable place. The trip is one of the best in the state for unspoiled vistas, wildlife, birds, and challenging waters. The expansive beauty of Monomoy's sandy islands, bathed in Chatham's diffuse light, is inspiring in a region characterized more by runaway development than by natural phenomena. The islands are home to hundreds (sometimes thousands) of seals which provide unforgettable viewing by kayak. Bird-watchers can delight in the 285 species of birds that frequent the islands. The clear waters of Nantucket Sound reveal treasures and its fresh breezes breathe life into the body and psyche of all road-weary paddlers. The richness of this trip's challenges and the unfathomable depth of its beauty always make it worth the drive, again and again.

· *Note:* The circumnavigation of the Monomoy Islands (approximately twenty miles round-trip from Stage Harbor around Monomoy Point) requires solid ocean skills, great stamina, and knowledge of local waters. Even proficient kayakers benefit from paddling with an experienced guide in this confusing and sometimes dangerous area. Less demanding trips can be fashioned by limiting your circumnavigation to North Monomoy Island or by exploring only the quieter western shore of South Monomoy Island. These shorter routes are described in detail below.

The Monomoy Islands and adjacent beaches comprise a dynamic landscape. The current configuration is so new, in fact, that most NOAA charts are out of date. With each wave and, especially, with each nor'easter, sand is stolen from the Cape's Atlantic-facing beaches and is carried south to be redeposited on South Monomoy.

In the last fifty years, Monomoy has been a peninsula, an island (since 1958), and now two islands (since 1978).

North and South Monomoy are today classic barrier islands that extend southward off the coast of Chatham. Their total acreage, protected as a federal National Wildlife Refuge, is an impressive 2,450 acres. North Monomoy is 2.5 miles long and South Monomoy extends south about 6.0 miles. The islands' eastern shorelines are surf-battered dunes, and their western shores flatten gradually to broad areas of salt marsh and mud flats. To the east, lying parallel to North Monomoy, is South Beach, owned by the town of Chatham. South Beach was created in 1987 when a severe winter storm broke through North Beach directly east of Chatham Light, creating a 3-mile-long spit which has since connected to the mainland just below Chatham Light.

Launching from one of the boat landings in Stage Harbor ensures an easy, surf-free put-in and takeout. From the put-in at Mill Pond, paddle south through the narrow pond and under the old Mitchell River Draw Bridge. Continue southwest about two miles to the mouth of Stage Harbor, passing Stage Harbor Light (now a private residence) on the right. Northwest of the harbor mouth is Harding Beach, a beautiful 1.25-mile barrier beach on Nantucket Sound. Before Memorial Day and after Labor Day, kayakers can launch from the beach. Behind Harding Beach is a narrow salt marsh where kayakers can spy shorebirds, herons, terns, and seaside sparrows. On the flats at the entrance to the Oyster River, watch for American oystercatchers.

Once out of the harbor into Nantucket Sound, plot your course, taking into consideration the tide and direction of current. Toward low tide there are extensive sand flats west of Monomoy Island. Attempting to paddle through these flats likely will ground your kayak and necessitate a walk. If launching at low tide, avoid the west-side sandbars and mud flats by plotting a clockwise course around the island(s). To do so, follow the boat channel (marked by buoys) east past the northern tip of North Monomoy Island. As you pass the island, note the shallow water and mud flats at its tip. Thousands of migratory birds feed on the flats and nest on its sandy dunes. From mid-May to late September, kayakers can see hundreds of common and least terns, as well as endangered roseate terns in late summer. Continue to follow the buoyed channel to avoid flats on the island's east side. The channel continues south, running between South Beach and North Monomoy Island.

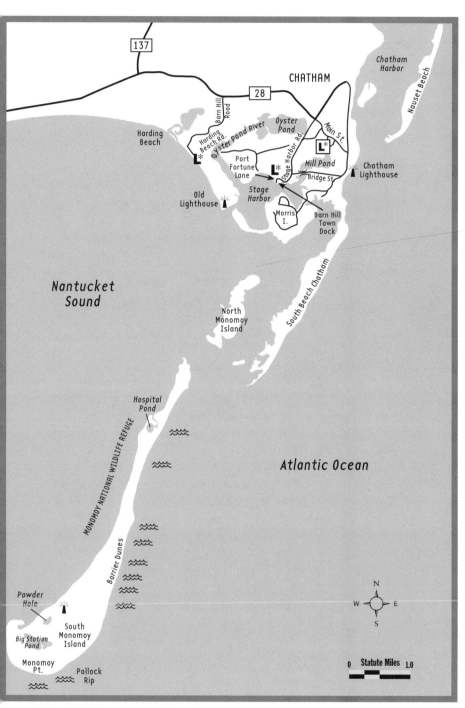

Trip 34: Monomoy Islands

In spring and fall, look for harbor seals. Harbor seals leave Monomoy in late spring to spend their summer in Maine. They return in droves in late fall and can number several thousand on North Monomoy! At the south end of North Monomoy, look east toward South Beach for the year-round population of gray seals. A large colony of about 450 gray seals lives between South Beach and the Monomoy Islands. Gray seals are readily distinguished from harbor seals by their size, the males approaching 1,000 pounds as compared to only 200 for a harbor seal. At low tide gray seals haul out and rest on South Beach, forming a crowded mass of groaning, blubbery bodies. The low drone of their guttural vocalizations reverberates across the water like an ancient chant. Paddle nearby for a view, but do not harass the seals. If seals take evasive measures because of your presence (i.e., dive into the water), back away. At high tide, kayakers are likely to find the seals in the water feeding. Dozens of huge-eyed heads may pop in and out of the water around your boat, looking like a life-size game of whack-a-mole. The seals are curious and may approach fairly close to your boat. Never chase them. Seals are much more sensitive to canoes and kayaks than they are to large pleasure or fishing boats.

Continue paddling south to reach the break between North and South Monomoy. At the break, kayakers have two alternatives. Those looking for challenging conditions can remain on the east side of the islands and continue paddling south, paralleling the east shore of South Monomoy. Swells off the Atlantic hit shoals offshore and generate lines of breaking waves. At the south end of South Monomoy, 7.1 miles from the channel, kayakers reach Pollock Rip. All paddlers must exercise great caution in this area. Strong tidal current can generate large and breaking waves, and fierce current can pull kayakers eastward through the Pollock Rip Channel. The trip to the south end of South Monomoy is rewarding, but the trip demands excellent ocean skills.

Those wishing to avoid these conditions should proceed through the channel to the west side of the islands. Although the channel is shallow in places, kayakers can usually make it through without walking. Once on the west side of the islands, kayakers can turn north to return to Stage Harbor (making a round trip of about 11.0 miles) or turn south to explore the west side of South Monomoy Island. The west side is generally more placid than the east side, because the islands shield paddlers from the Atlantic swells.

Paddling south from the channel, paddlers are likely to encounter broad areas of mud flats. At low tide, it may be necessary to paddle a mile to the west in order to find enough water to paddle south. At high tide, kayakers can find Hospital Pond, about 0.75 mile south of the north tip of South Monomoy near what used to be known as Wreck Cove (shifting sands have almost filled the cove). In the early 1700s, ships sat out storms at this west-side cove. A tavern for the stranded sailors did a booming business near Hospital Pond. The pond was named, not for injured sailors, but for wounded waterfowl. A century ago hunting was immensely popular here, and in the 1800s up to 8,000 golden plover and Eskimo curlew could be shot in a *day*. Wounded birds would retreat to the relative safety of Hospital Pond to nurse their wounds or die quietly. While plovers have recovered somewhat, the unfortunate Eskimo curlew did not survive the onslaught.

A little over four miles south from the channel sits South Monomoy's abandoned lighthouse, including the keeper's house, brick light tower, and generator house. For more than sixty years this light has been extinguished, but from 1828 to 1923 the light aided sailors navigating treacherous Pollock Rip. Once situated at the south end of South Monomoy near the original dune line, the light's present location indicates how dramatically the island has changed over the last century.

Gray seals in water. Monomoy Islands, Chatham.

the strip mining of horseshoe crabs: upsetting the balance of nature

Monomoy visitors are likely to see at least one horseshoe crab, if only a strange, helmet-like shell washed up on the beach. More closely related to spiders and scorpions than to real crabs, the horseshoe crab has been around for 350 million years, predating even the dinosaurs. Frequently seen along the Massachusetts coast, they are most populous in Delaware Bay, where for millions of years they literally covered the beach during their spring spawning. Due to their recent popularity as bait for eels and conch, however, the crab has experienced a sudden and precipitous drop in population. From Florida to Maine, annual catch rates have soared from fewer than 100,000 pounds in the early 1970s to 5.1 million pounds in 1996. Trawlers scrape tens of thousands off the bottom in a single day. Due to over-fishing and habitat destruction, the horseshoe crab population in Delaware Bay has plummeted by 50 percent since 1990. Reports in 1999 of horseshoe crab catches in the thousands off Monomoy Island has raised concern among local environmentalists.

Why is the health of the horseshoe crab so important?

• *Horseshoe crabs are essential to the survival of migrating shorebirds.*

Each spring millions of migrating shorebirds travel from wintering grounds in South America to breeding grounds in the Canadian Arctic. It is thought that the birds time the grueling 7,000-mile journey to coincide with the spawning of the horseshoe crab in Delaware Bay. As many as 1.5 million shorebirds, including red knots, sanderlings, ruddy turnstones, and semipalmated sandpipers, arrive in Delaware Bay for a 2-week stopover to gorge themselves on crab eggs. To reach the Arctic in good shape for breeding, the birds must double their body weight during this period. No other food source gives them such an abundant and rich source of fat and protein.

Unfortunately, the calamitous dip in the horseshoe crab population greatly reduces the number of available eggs. Consequently, the population of migrating shorebirds has declined sharply since 1986. Shorebird counts on some Delaware Bay beaches are down *90 per cent*. It is most serious for the red knot, because each year 80 per cent of its North American population stops in Delaware Bay.

• *Horseshoe crabs are critical to making medical devices safe*
The blood of the horseshoe crab contains a substance (limulus amoebocyte lysate) that is used to make medical devices, such as surgical implants, pacemakers and prosthetic devices, bacteria-free. Without this substance, producing safe medical devices is extremely difficult and much more expensive. Fortunately, most horseshoe crabs survive the procedure that removes a portion of their valuable blood and returns them to the water.

• *Horseshoe crabs are essential to the balance of nature*
No one can quantify the long term impact of the crab's population decline, but it doesn't look good. According to Dr. Larry Niles, Chief of New Jersey's Endangered Species Program, "It's reasonable to believe that we could lose [migrat-

Continuing south to the end of the island, kayakers pass Powder Hole, once a viable harbor and the site of Whitewash Village, a fishing community that thrived from 1830 to 1860. Only one cottage remains today. The harbor is shoaled and abandoned and is now a brackish pond, home to white-tailed deer, muskrat, snakes, toads, and an abundance of gulls, terns, black-bellied and semipalmated plovers, red knots, sanderlings and semipalmated sandpipers.

As you approach the end of the island, look directly south. On exceptionally clear days, Nantucket can be seen twenty-three miles away. A good picnic spot is at Monomoy Point, on the south tip of South Monomoy. In the pond behind the dunes and on the beach,

ing] shorebirds from this hemisphere." Because the horseshoe crab matures slowly (it doesn't begin to reproduce until about age 10), the negative effect of the 1990s' huge catches remains to be seen.

If the horseshoe crab population continues to decline, the ramifications are immense. Any major change in bird population has unpredictable consequences for the biodiversity of several ecosystems. If the shorebird population plummets, the arctic arthropod population will likely explode, because the birds are an important predator. Shellfish populations in South America could also rise dramatically without natural predators. These events could kick off other less predictable effects that might alter the balance of nature hemisphere-wide.

• *What can be done to save the East Coast horseshoe crab?*
Catch limits are a good start. The National Audubon Society calls for a 60-80 percent cut in horseshoe crab catches in all East Coast states. Numerous proposals are before the Atlantic States Marine Fisheries Commission, and no doubt a compromise will be reached. Whether new restrictions will be tight enough to safeguard horseshoe crab and shorebird populations remain to be seen. We can only hope that the commission acts quickly, wisely, and conservatively to save this critical resource.

hundreds of birds can often be observed. The refuge has one of the largest gull colonies in North America (20,000 pairs of herring and great black-backed gulls!). Mid-July to mid-September is prime time for birders although fall migration can start as early as June for some species. Try mid-July to mid-August for the Hudsonian godwit and for peak shorebird migration.

On a good day, watchers can spot more than 100 species, including more than 40 varieties of shorebirds. This is a good showing, but it's a far cry from a few decades ago when hundreds of warblers would light on the islands. Loss of habitat in the warblers' summer and winter territories has greatly reduced their numbers. All visitors to Monomoy must abide by the many closure signs that protect nesting areas. Large portions of the refuge are closed seasonally to protect sensitive wildlife like the piping plover from human disturbance. Watch for signs.

Lastly, late-season kayakers may find themselves paddling with an impressive number of sea ducks. In late fall, tens of thousands of common eider, scoter, red-breasted mergansers, and brant can be observed just offshore. Fall kayakers may also catch the end of the raptor migration. Watch the skies for peregrine falcons, merlins, and northern harriers.

Those wishing to learn more about Monomoy's birds or its cultural and natural history can take a tour from the Cape Cod Museum of Natural History in Brewster (508-896-3867), or from Mass Audubon's Wellfleet sanctuary (508-349-2615). For information about closings, boating, and weather information, call the Monomoy National Wildlife Refuge headquarters (508-945-0594).

Directions to Launch Site: From Boston, take I-93 south to Route 3 south. Take Route 3 to the Sagamore Bridge to Route 6. From Route 6, take Exit 10 (Route 124). Drive south on Route 124 to Route 28 in Harwich. Turn east on Route 28 and drive to Chatham. Route 28 becomes Main Street in Chatham. Where Route 28 turns left (north) in Chatham Center, continue straight on Main Street about 0.6 mile to Mill Pond Road. Turn right on Mill Pond Road and continue to the landing at its end. Parking is roadside and limited.

Alternate Launch Sites: (1) Harding Beach, Chatham. Follow above directions to Route 28 (Main Street) in Chatham. About 1.5 miles after the intersection of Routes 28 and 137, turn right on Barn Hill Road. After 0.4 mile, turn right on Harding Beach Road and proceed to the town landing and beach at its end. If surf impedes safe launching and landing, try the above launch site or consult a local map for the many town landings within Stage Harbor. (2) Barn Hill Town Dock off Chatham Neck in Stage Harbor. Drive Main Street to Stage Harbor Road and take a right. Follow Stage Harbor Road to Port Fortune Lane and turn left. Follow to landing at end.

Camping: Camping is prohibited on North and South Monomoy Islands.

trip 35 **HERRING RIVER, WEST HARWICH**

Level of Difficulty: Easy; protected water

Round–Trip Mileage: 4.0 miles to West Reservoir. Add 1.0 mile to explore reservoir.

Attractions: Freshwater marsh, bird-watching, fishing

Precautions: Paddle upriver with a peaking tide for greatest ease of movement and flexibility of course. Bring bug repellent.

Charts: Although NOAA 13237 and 13246 cover the Herring River, their scale is too small to be useful. Butterwurth's detailed street map (covering Brewster, Harwich, Chatham, and Orleans), offers more information. Butterwurth maps are widely available at stores throughout the Cape, or call 508-790-0971.

Tidal Information: While it is easier to paddle *with* the tide, the current is fairly mild at this point in the river. High tide in Harwichport is 1 hour and 15 minutes after high tide in Boston. Assume about a 30-minute delay for high tide in the river at the reservoir. Mean tidal range, 9.0 feet.

Launch Site: Town Landing at Route 28 bridge, Harwich. Free parking.

THE SOUTHWEST CORNER of Harwich is home to one of the most extensive freshwater marshes on Cape Cod. The Herring River flows through the West Harwich Conservation Area and gives paddlers an opportunity to view the gentle beauty and elusive inhabitants of the marsh. Kayakers follow the narrow tidal river through conservation land to a freshwater reservoir. The paddling is easy, although shorter kayaks have a better time negotiating the

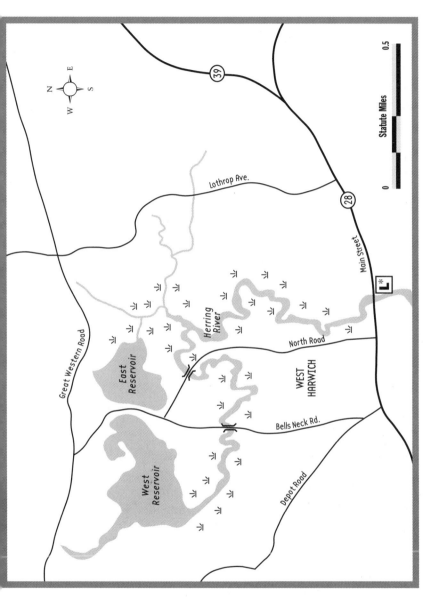

Trip 35: Herring River, West Harwich

river's tight curves. A portage over the dike and into the reservoir allows paddlers to search for the plentiful painted turtles that reside there. This is a good family or beginner paddle.

From the boat launch, turn right (north). The river grows less saline as one progresses toward the reservoir. After passing a restaurant and a few houses on the left bank, the scenery turns decisively natural. The distance to the reservoir, as the crow flies, is only a little more than a mile. Given the curvaceous path of the Herring River, however, it is about 2.75 miles by kayak. These are relaxing, lovely miles, nevertheless.

A few smaller streams branch off the Herring, and at high tide paddlers can briefly explore their meanderings. Mostly, kayakers will want to keep to the main channel, for it is narrow enough. Take advantage of the slow progress to search for the many birds that find food and shelter in the marsh. Raptors like red-tailed hawk and northern harrier are frequently seen hunting above the rodent-filled grass. In the wooded islands of the marsh reside great horned owls.

This area is also a good place to see great blue, green, and black-crowned night herons, as well as egrets. Paddle the river just as the first high tide of the day is falling to see the birds feeding by the

Paddlers on the Herring River.

banks. Watch also for swamp sparrows, marsh wrens, Virginia rails, and American bitterns.

One and a half miles from the put-in, paddle under a small bridge. The landing next to the bridge is a popular fishing spot for blue crabs. Paddle about 0.75 mile farther and pass under a second bridge. A half-mile from this bridge, reach the West Reservoir.

To paddle in the West Reservoir, kayakers have to lift their boats over the dike. The easiest spot to do this is probably on the left bank. The half-mile-long reservoir is rimmed with oak and pine, and its bank makes an excellent place for a tranquil picnic (but don't try this in duck-hunting season!). Paddle along the shore to search the nooks and crannies for painted turtles. Keep alert for snapping turtles also. Check the snags above the reservoir for osprey. Osprey are frequently seen, and there have been rare sightings of bald eagles.

After enjoying the reservoir, glide back down the river to the put-in. This paddle is especially nice at dusk, when the soft glow of the setting sun lights the marsh and colors the expansive sky.

Directions to Launch Site: From Boston, take I-93 south to Route 3 south. Drive Route 3 south across the Sagamore Bridge to Route 6. Take Route 6 east to Route 134 (exit 9) Take Route 134 south to Route 28. Drive east (left) on Route 28 2.2 miles to West Harwich. Cross the bridge over the Herring River and find the boat launch on the right. Driving west on Route 28, find the launch 0.9 mile from the intersections of Routes 28 and 39 on the left, just before crossing the bridge.

Alternate Launch Site: Irish Pub, Route 28, Harwich. With prior permission, kayakers can park in the large pub parking lot and launch just north of the Route 28 bridge described above. The pub is located across the highway from the town landing.

trip
36

GRAND ISLAND CIRCUMNAVIGATION, OSTERVILLE/COTUIT

Level of Difficulty: Easy; protected water

Round–Trip Mileage: 6.5 miles

Attractions: Salt marsh, bird-watching, fishing, sandy barrier beach for picnicking and swimming

Precautions: Watch for tide and wind-driven waves at West Bay's outlet to Nantucket Sound. Current runs at 1–1.5 knots.

Charts: NOAA 13229 (1:40,000), and NOAA 13237 (1:80,000)

Tidal Information: In Cotuit, high tide is 1 hour and 15 minutes after Boston high tide; low tide is 45 minutes after. To explore the marsh north of Prince Cove, paddle at high tide. Mean tidal range, 2.5 feet.

Launch Site: Prince Cove, Cotuit. Parking is free, but restricted to residents Memorial Day through Labor Day.

THE CIRCUMNAVIGATION OF GRAND ISLAND is a nice off-season trip, offering protected waters and pleasant, sandy places to picnic. The downside is that much of the route resembles a house tour of the rich and famous. Grand Island consists of steroid-fed Federal and Nantucket-style summer houses sitting conspicuously on intensely manicured lawns. Furthermore, Cotuit's oppressive parking restrictions are decidedly inhospitable to nonresident kayakers. Yet again, it's ultimately an enjoyable ride. Focus on the beautiful marsh north of the put-in; the protected barrier

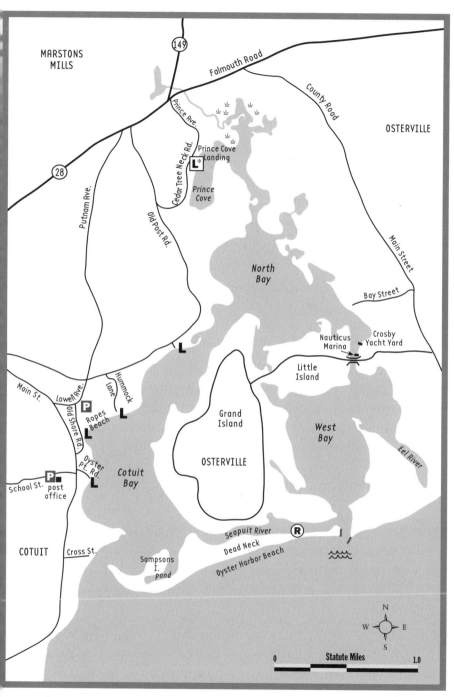

Trip 36: Grand Island Circumnavigation

beach between Grand Island and Nantucket Sound; and the clean, productive waters that made Cotuit the "oyster capital of New England" in the early 1900s.

Start the trip at Prince Cove. North of the cove lie acres of exquisite protected marsh which kayakers can explore at high tide. In late September the still water is a haven for waterfowl and herons. Viewed amid the surrounding scarlet maples, the scene is idyllic. To reach the marsh, paddle northeast to the cove's outlet (following buoys), then turn north (left) up a wide channel. After about 0.25 mile, follow the water west (left) into progressively narrower channels. Unfortunately, navigable water soon disappears and kayakers must head back to the main channel.

Back at the Prince Cove outlet, paddle south down a channel to reach North Bay. (Circumnavigating Grand Island is accomplished by moving through three bays—North, West, and Cotuit—and a river—the Seapuit—which surround the island.) About 0.5 mile from Prince Cove, reach North Bay. The bay opens up with drama. The centerpiece of the blue water is green, forested Grand Island, directly south. To the east (left) the yachts of the Crosby Yacht Yard and Nauticus Marina are visible. To the west (right) is the outlet leading to Cotuit Bay. The following describes a clockwise circumnavigation. Readers must consider the wind and tide when choosing the best direction for travel.

Paddle south into North Bay, heading for the white sails and hulls of the busy marinas. At the Crosby Yacht Yard in the late 1800s, Crosby cat boats, the quintessential Cape sailboat, were designed and built. Pass the boat yard, then paddle under a bridge connecting Grand Island with Osterville. On the other side of the bridge, continue through a short channel to enter West Bay.

At the very south end of West Bay, a breakwater frames the narrow outlet to Nantucket Sound. A buoyed channel leads straight down the center of West Bay, but kayakers need not feel so constrained. Paddlers can explore the mansioned shoreline of West Island and peek up the inlets that poke into the island at the top (northwest) and bottom (southwest) corners of the bay. Gunkholing kayakers can also explore Eel River at the bay's southeast edge. Then paddle down to the breakwater to catch a glimpse of Nantucket Sound. Watch for current-generated waves at the entrance, especially in an opposing wind.

Continue the circumnavigation by entering the Seapuit River at the south end of West Bay. The entrance to the river is just inside the breakwater. The barrier beach of Dead Neck protects the narrow and quiet Seapuit River, navigable at all tides. Find excellent picnic spots on the sandy beaches of Dead Neck owned by the Massachusetts Audubon Society (MAS). From mid-May through Labor Day, non-members must pay a fee to use the beach. Bring $5 or your MAS card. Those stopping on Dead Neck can follow a path through the dunes to visit Oyster Harbor Beach, which fronts Nantucket Sound. On a very clear day, Chappaquiddick can be seen to the south. Respect all man-made barriers. Much of the fragile barrier beach is currently being restored and is off-limits to recreation. Areas of the beach are also periodically closed to protect nesting least and common terns and piping plovers. More than one hundred pairs of least terns nested here in 1999. Watch where you step—especially from late May to mid-July!.

Paddle about one mile west down the Seapuit River to the more lushly vegetated west end of the barrier beach called Sampsons Island. Kayakers can explore a beautiful and quiet pond just south of where the Seapuit River empties into Cotuit Bay.

Entering Cotuit Bay, paddle north up the west side of Grand Island. To the left the white church steeple of the quaint town of Cotuit lords over the picturesque bay. Continue north and pass two public landings on the left in Cotuit (see Alternative Launch Sites, below). In the early 1900s, Cotuit was called "Little Harvard" because of its popularity among university professors. "Purchased" from the Native Americans for a kettle and a hoe, the town achieved notoriety in the 1850s for its oyster beds. Cotuit Bay stretches about a mile northeast to reach North Bay.

At North Bay, the circumnavigation is complete. Kayakers can follow the buoys back to their cars at Prince Cove.

A circumnavigation of Grand Island under a full moon is highly recommended. On that trip, however, kayakers must brave the ghost of Hannah Screecher. Some say her screams can be heard on quiet evenings around the island. Legend has it that Captain Kidd buried treasure on the island which has never been found. It is said that the captain buried his lover, Hannah Screecher, with his gold, so that her spirit might guard it. In an ironic betrayal of her lover's misdeeds, Hannah screams to be discovered, along with his misbegotten booty. Good luck, matey!

Directions to Launch Site: From Boston, drive I-93 south to Route 3 south. Take Route 3 south across the Sagamore Bridge to Route 6. Drive east on Route 6. To reach Cotuit from Route 6, take Exit 5 for West Barnstable (Route 149 south). Drive Route 149 south about 3.9 miles to its junction with Route 28. Directly across Route 28 is Prince Avenue. Take Prince Avenue 0.4 mile to the town landing on the left. There are only a few parking spaces and all are resident-only Memorial Day to Labor Day.

Alternate Launch Sites: There are several town landings in Cotuit, and all provide resident-only parking from Memorial Day to Labor Day. There are, nevertheless, two alternatives for summer access. 1) Town Landing at Ropes Beach. Follow the above directions to Route 28. Turn right on Route 28 and proceed 0.5 mile to Putnam Avenue. Turn left on Putnam or Lowell Avenue and drive south about 2.0 miles to Old Shore Road (Putnam Avenue runs right into Old Shore Road). Drive just 0.1 mile on Old Shore Road to the landing at Ropes Beach. Drop the boat off and find parking back 0.1 mile on Putnam or Lowell Avenue by the side of the road. (2) Town Landing at Oyster Point. Follow above directions to Route 28. Turn right on Route 28 and proceed 2.1 miles to Main Street. (Opposite the intersection of Routes 28 and 130.) Turn left on Main Street, and drive south 1.75 miles to Oyster Point Road on the left. (Note that School Street is directly opposite Oyster Point Road on the other side of Main Street.) Turn left on Oyster Point Road and find the town landing at the end of the road. Drop boats off, then drive back up to Main Street, across to School Street, and park in the lot of the post office just 0.1 mile up School Street.

trip 37   WASHBURN ISLAND AND WAQUOIT BAY, FALMOUTH

Level of Difficulty: Easy; protected water

Round-Trip Mileage: 4.5 miles to Washburn Island (with portage), 5.5 miles without portage; 6.75 miles to tour Waquoit Bay

Attractions: Island for camping and picnicking; salt marsh; bird-watching; fishing; sandy barrier beach for picnicking; clean, shallow water for swimming

Precautions: For those circumnavigating Washburn Island, watch for waves and current at Waquoit Bay's outlet to Nantucket Sound. Tidal current can run at 1.4 knots (ebb) and 1.5 knots (flood) at Dead Neck. A good chop can develop when wind and current are opposed.

Charts: NOAA 13229 (1:40,000), and NOAA 13237 (1:80,000)

Tidal Information: Mean tidal range, 1.5 feet. Paddle at high tide to explore Washburn Island inlet and marsh.

Launch Site: Falmouth Town Landing on Childs River, East Falmouth.

A VISIT TO WASHBURN ISLAND by kayak is a must-do Cape adventure. For novices, shallow Waquoit Bay offers miles of protected paddling. For more-advanced paddlers, a circumnavigation of Washburn Island can include challenging conditions in Nantucket Sound. For nature-lovers, the trip visits three significant natural areas including Washburn Island, South Cape Beach State

Park, and the Waquoit Bay National Estuarine Research Reserve. It is nicest by far in the off-season, but it can also be heavenly midweek in summer when paddlers can swim in the inviting waters. Camp at one of Washburn Island's eleven wilderness campsites for the ultimate experience. Kayakers who love to fish will also enjoy this trip.

Start at the public boat ramp next to Edwards Marina on the Childs River. Paddle about 0.5 mile south to the end of river. At the south end of the river, paddlers looking east can see the eroded west side of Washburn Island. The densely developed banks of the Childs River stands in sharp contrast to the protected forests of the island. Pinyon pine, oak, wild roses, and a healthy crop of poison ivy cover the island. The only homes visible are osprey nests. Take a sharp left and paddle northeast up the Seapit River.

Paddle around the north side of Washburn Island. The shallow clear water provides excellent views to sea life below. Waquoit Bay provides shelter, spawning, and nursery grounds for more than 50 species of fish, including eel, flounder, trout, herring, bluefish, striped bass, scallops, clam, and blue crab.

The Commonwealth of Massachusetts recognized the importance and beauty of Waquoit Bay's natural resources in 1979 by designating the bay an Area of Critical Environmental Concern. Two years later, the state acquired Washburn Island when developers threatened to build fifty homes and a golf course on the island. In 1988, further protection and funding came when the federal government added Waquoit Bay to the National Estaurine Research Reserve system.

Today the reserve encompasses 2,500 acres of open water, barrier beaches, marshlands, and uplands, including the 28-acre reserve headquarters (visible at the top of the bay next to the Waquoit Yacht Club), 330-acre Washburn Island, and 500-acre South Cape Beach State Park. Waquoit Bay is the centerpiece of the reserve, approximately two miles long and one mile wide, with an average depth of three feet. Washburn Island forms the western boundary of the reserve and the bay. Barrier beaches extending from the island and South Cape Beach protect the bay from Nantucket Sound, creating a superb area for small boats and water recreation. (Visit the reserve's headquarters to learn more about the bay, watershed, and research programs and to enjoy the reserve's magnificent grounds and hiking trails.)

From the north tip of Washburn Island, kayakers can venture across the bay to explore its shoreline and attractive coves and inlets.

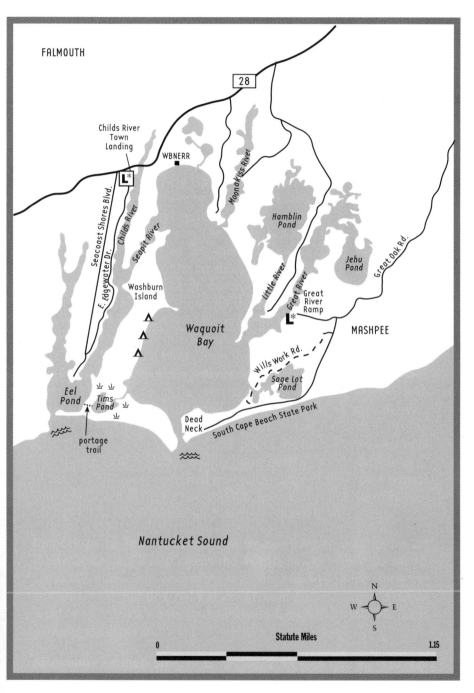

Trip 37: Washburn Island and Wasquoit Bay

Such a tour would be approximately 6.5 miles round-trip. Alternatively, stay west and hug the shoreline of Washburn Island for an equally attractive but shorter 4.5 miles tour.

Paddling south along the island's east side, one gets a glimpse of the island's campsites set beneath the pines. Where kayakers camp today, Native Americans once fished and hunted. The Mashpee Wampanoags, the "people of the first light," claim their people lived at Waqouit Bay "since time." Their stone flakes and arrowheads are still found on the island today.

In spring and summer, watch for signs restricting beach access due to nesting piping plovers. In recent years, the threatened birds have built several nests on the island. Other island wildlife include red fox, skunk, raccoon, box turtles, and several types of harmless snakes.

Paddle south almost to the end of the island. Kayakers can picnic on the sandy southwestern tip of Waquoit Island or paddle southeast to Dead Neck, part of South Cape Beach State Park. The two flank Waquoit Bay's outlet to Nantucket Sound. This area is an extremely popular fishing spot for stripers.

If there is sufficient water, paddlers should visit Tim's Pond, a marshy body of water at the south end of Washburn Island. Where the island's sand spit juts out into the bay to the southeast, look west for a channel heading into the island. At an hour and a half on either side of high tide, there is enough water to enter the narrow channel and explore the lovely pond. At high tide, it's a beautiful place. Look for osprey and a variety of water-loving birds, including herons (great blue, green, and black-crowned night), geese, swans, and ducks. Watch the thousands of tiny fish in the eelgrass beneath your boat. After touring the quiet pond, paddlers can exit the way they came or portage the short distance to Eel Pond.

There are three options to get back to the Childs River. The first is to portage. Find the short, straight path through the rugosa roses near the southwest end of the pond. Walk briefly under the pines to the west facing shore. Put in at Eel Pond, then paddle north about a mile to reach, once again, the mouth of the Childs River. Continue north 0.5 mile to the town landing on the left.

The second option is to paddle out of the pond and back to the bay through the inlet where you entered. Once in the bay, return to the boat ramp simply by retracing your route up the east side of Washburn Island, then south down the Seapit River. Or, for those

Nitrogen and Coastal Waters: A Deadly Mix

Flashback to a muggy summer day at Waquoit Bay. The weather has been hot and overcast for days. The water is warm and murky. Dead fish and shellfish decompose on the shore, killed by a deadly lack of oxygen in the water. What caused this catastrophic event? Eutrophication, or the depletion of life-sustaining oxygen by an overload of nitrogen. Who caused this massive die-off? We did.

As development increases along the coast, we increase the amount of nitrogen that enters coastal waters through surface run off, septic systems, ground water, and atmospheric deposition (e.g., acid rain). Nearshore waters are among the most fertilized places on earth, their nitrogen content surpassing most farmers' fields.

Why is nutrient loading so harmful? The same nutrients or fertilizer that promote green growth on one's lawn, promote growth of algae and seaweed beds on the water's surface. In some estuaries, large mats of seaweed grow 3-feet deep. Such vegetation blocks sunlight from reaching the estuary's bottom. As a result, eelgrass beds, an important habitat for fish and shellfish, die off. In a healthy estuary,

who enjoyed paddling in Tim's Pond, visit Sage Lot Pond at the east end of Dead Neck, before heading back.

The third option for experienced kayakers is to paddle around the outside of Washburn Island. To complete this circumnavigation, exit Tim's Pond the way you came, then paddle east to the outlet of Waquoit Bay. Paddle out the breakwater at the end of Dead Neck and paddle west in Nantucket Sound along the barrier beach 1.0 mile to the narrow inlet at Eel Pond. Paddle north through the entrance and continue through Eel Pond, keeping the west side of Washburn Island on your right. At 1.2 miles from the inlet, reach the Childs

eelgrass beds provide shelter, as well as ideal spawning, nursery, and feeding grounds. In Massachusetts, eelgrass beds are critical habitats for winter flounder, scallops, and blue crabs.

What can be done to reverse nitrogen loading and the damage it wreaks? Halting runaway development along the shoreline is one solution, because paved surfaces, landscaped lawns and septic systems increase the nutrient load. Vegetated buffer zones, restored wetlands, use of native plantings, boat pump-out stations, water conservation, and improved septic systems provide some relief. Zoning restrictions, public acquisition of open space, and community sewage treatment systems can also help immensely.

From Buzzards Bay to the Merrimack River, our land use greatly influences the health of our coastal waters. Local environmental groups play an essential role promoting public education and community-wide solutions. In Waquoit Bay, Citizens for the Protection of Waquoit Bay (CPWB) is a nonprofit organization concerned with the health of the area's waters. CPWB is also the Friends Group for the Waquoit Bay National Estuarine Research Reserve, sponsoring their educational programs and seminars. For more information, contact CPWB, P.O. Box 3021, Waquoit, MA 02536.

River. Bear left, paddle up the Childs, and arrive at the landing after another 0.5 mile. Be sure to take wind, current, and wave conditions into consideration before venturing out of the bay.

Guided kayak tours to Washburn Island are offered by Cape Cod Coastal Canoe and Kayak (508-564-4051 or 888-CANOE-93) and Adventure Tours, Edwards Boat Yard (508-548-9722).

Directions to Launch Site: From Boston, take I-93 south to Route 3 south. Drive Route 3 south across the Sagamore Bridge. From the Sagamore Bridge, drive Route 6 to Exit 2 (Route 130). Drive Route

130 south to Route 28 in Mashpee. Turn right on Route 28 and drive to Falmouth. Watch for signs for Edwards Boat Yard, and turn left on East Edgewater Drive. The town landing is on the left.

Alternate Launch Sites: Great River Town Landing, Mashpee. From Route 28 in Mashpee, at the rotary, turn south on Great Neck Road. This turns to Great Oak Road after its intersection with Red Brook Road (about 2.5 miles from the rotary). Continue south on Great Oak Road, then turn right on Town Landing Road, and proceed to the landing and parking area at its end. Parking is very tight on summer weekends. If the parking lot is full, try an obscure put-in at the end of a dirt road by driving back out to Great Oak Road, turn south (right) and drive a few blocks to Manitoba Road. Turn right on Manitoba, then take the next left onto Wills Work Road. Drive to the end of the road, through the woods, to a put-in at the beach.

Camping: Washburn Island has eleven wilderness campsites available from March 15 through October 15. Campsites can be reserved up to six months in advance by calling 877-I-CAMP-MA. For more information, contact www.state.ma.us/dem/whatsnew.htm #RESERVE. A few of the campsites can be reserved through the office of the Waquoit Bay National Estuarine Research Reserve. For information, call 508-457-0495, or check their website at www.capecod.net/waquoit. Reserve early for summer weekends.

BUZZARDS BAY

trip 38 MARION HARBOR AND BIRD ISLAND

Level of Difficulty: Easy to moderate; protected and open water

Round-Trip Mileage: 7.0 miles to Bird Island; add about 4–5 miles to the round-trip distance to explore Great Hill Point or Aucoot Cove

Attractions: Bird Island (lighthouse and beach), protected harbor, salt marsh, bird-watching, island beaches, swimming

Precautions: Prevailing southwest winds can generate whitecaps in harbor south of Ram Island, especially on an outgoing tide. Yacht traffic in harbor can be heavy in summer, especially on weekends.

Charts: NOAA 13236 (1:20,000), NOAA 13229 (1:40,000), NOAA 13230 (1:40,000)

Tidal Information: High tide is 10 minutes after Newport high tide. Mean tidal range, 4 feet.

Launch Site: Island Wharf, Marion Town Landing, Marion. Free parking.

"PRETTY" IS THE OPERATIVE WORD** for Marion. From its quaint, well-heeled streets to its precious tree-lined coves, kayakers can find attractive settings wherever they wander. The highlight of the trip is a visit to Bird Island and its lighthouse, just a half-mile from the mouth of the harbor. Visit in fall when yachtsmen

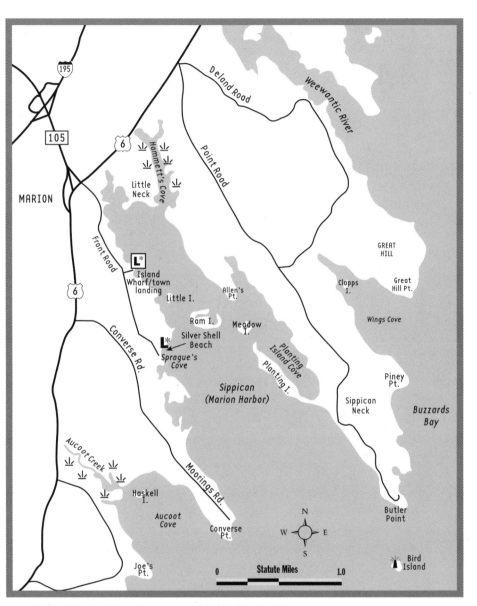

Trip 38: Marion Harbor and Bird Island

are back to work and terns have finished nesting. Through September and October, Buzzards Bay waters stay reasonably warm, and kayakers can have the whole lovely place to themselves.

When kayaking in Buzzards Bay, paddlers must watch the wind. Because Marion Harbor opens to the southeast, its outer half is vulnerable to the prevailing southwesterly winds. For the flattest water, paddle early in the day. Strong afternoon winds are the rule, and conditions become rough quickly. The only refuge from the prevailing wind is the area north of Ram Island and the upper reaches of Marion Harbor. Don't be fooled by the serene nature of Aucoot or Wings Coves—neither is protected from southerly winds.

From the put-in at Island Wharf, paddle right (southeast) toward Ram Island. On the right, pass the Beverly Yacht Club and its many moorings, occupied in season by a rich selection of sailboats. To the left, gracious homes sit high atop rolling green lawns. From the mid-1800s to the early 1900s, Marion was a swanky summer playground for the rich and famous. Former U.S. President Grover Cleveland spent four summers here. Many of the beautiful harborside homes hearken back to these golden years. It was during these years that Elizabeth Tabor, a well-to-do widow, established the Tabor Academy as well as many other cultural and educational institutions in Marion. The academy's handsome red-brick buildings can be seen from the northern end of the harbor. While weaving south through the harbor's moorings, look for the ninety-two-foot, two-masted schooner *Tabor Boy*, a training schooner owned by the academy.

Pass to the left (east) of privately owned Ram Island, staying clear of the marked boat channel that runs along the west side of the harbor. The low-lying island to the left, just south of Ram, is Mead-

buzzards bay kayaking

Buzzards Bay is one of the least known areas for kayaking in Massachusetts. Those who ignore its considerable beauty, challenging waters, and uncrowded spaces are missing out. For local expertise in finding some hard-to-reach locations along the south coast, join Buzzards Bay Kayak for guided tours to the Elizabeth Islands, Mattapoisett, New Bedford, Fairhaven, and more. Kayakers who arrive with their own kayaks paddle for only $35. Buzzard's Bay Kayak also offers expert instruction from ACU and BCU qualified instructors. For more information, call 508-996-8885.

ow Island. Kayakers can land and picnic on this bit of shell, sand, and marsh grass. Passing Meadow Island, paddle southeast out of the harbor, watching for rocks and shallow water between Meadow and Planting Islands. From Planting Island to Butler Point, wood-shingled houses stand shoulder to shoulder, elbowing each other for space along the sea wall. Watch for barely submerged rocks at the end of Butler Point.

From Butler Point, it is only a 0.5-mile paddle to the lighthouse at Bird Island. Especially at low tide, the water is very shallow. On calm days, enjoy the crystal-clear view to the ocean bottom in this half-mile stretch, reputed to be an excellent fishing area. The beach on Bird Island's north side provides easy landing. In summer, however, nesting common and roseate terns occupy the island, and kayakers will want to steer clear. Bird Island is a very significant nesting area in Massachusetts, supporting almost 1,600 pairs of common terns and 1,300 pairs of roseate terns in 1995. Midsummer kayakers should circumnavigate the island, appreciating the thirty-six-foot whitewashed lighthouse from a safe distance. Nesting terns will divebomb intruders who stray too close.

Those paddlers up for additional exploring can head north from Bird Island back to the coast of Sippican Neck. Sippican was Marion's original name before it was changed in the mid-1900s to honor Revolutionary War hero General Francis Marion. Following the coastline to Piney Point, kayakers can head into the shallow waters of Wings Cove at high tide. Paddle deep into the quiet cove. Low water uncovers an island as well as a rock garden between the island and the cove's south side. The far end of the cove is quite pretty, as the forests of Great Hill Point hide the mansion that occupies its northern side. Kayakers can find a beach and hills of pine and oak. Paddle around to the outer side of Great Hill Point to view the mansion known locally as the "castle."

Returning south to Marion Harbor, paddlers can also explore Aucoot Cove, lying just south of the harbor's entrance. The cove is lovely to visit at high tide, because paddlers can explore the tidal creeks that flow through the large marsh at the end of the cove. The houses surrounding the cove are set far back from the water and are hidden by trees. A wonderful picnic can be had on tiny Haskell Island by finding the small beach on its northern side. Watch for rocks.

Upon returning to the harbor, paddle up its south side. Pass a few public beaches and many beautiful homes. About two miles from the harbor mouth, reach the put-in. For more quiet exploring, kayakers can continue north past the launch and paddle east of Little Neck to Hammett Cove. Though only about a half-mile long, the cove is a pleasant diversion that's well sheltered from the wind. Watch for osprey, herons, and egrets.

Before or after paddling, hungry kayakers should visit the Marion General Store. Established in 1841, it is the real thing. Located on Front Street just 0.1 mile from Island Wharf Road, this authentic general store offers delectable fresh bread, unusual cheeses, and other picnic-ready treats.

Directions to Launch Site: From Route 128, drive Route 24 south to Route 195. Drive Route 195 to Exit 20 (Route 105). Take Route 105 south, following signs for Tabor Academy in Marion. Pass the intersection of Route 6 with Route 105. Continue one mile on Route 105 past this intersection to Island Wharf Road on the left. Turn left and find the wharf and ramp at its end. Launch from the beach next to the wharf.

Alternate Launch Site: Silver Shell Beach, Silvershell Road, Marion. Off-season, kayakers can launch off the beach. From Island Wharf, above, drive 0.8 mile south on Front Street to its end at Silver Shell Beach.

trip 39 WEST ISLAND AND LITTLE BAY, FAIRHAVEN

Level of Difficulty: Easy to moderate; protected and open water

Round-Trip Mileage: 7.0 miles to circumnavigate West Island; add 1–2 miles to explore Little Bay. A full exploration of Little Bay and Nasketucket River (without paddling around West Island) is about 6.5 miles round-trip in protected water.

Attractions: Islands for picnicking, sandy beaches, swimming, bird-watching, fishing, salt marsh

Precautions: Prevailing southwest winds can generate rough water on southwest side of West Island. Rocks off the island's southwest shore and Rocky Point create hazards, especially in rough water. Note that the summer's prevailing southwest winds usually increase in the afternoon. Watch also for tide rips off Rocky Point. Lastly, be aware of swift current flowing under narrow bridge between Long Island and West Island. Paddle with the tide.

Charts: NOAA 13229 (1:40,000), NOAA 13230 (1:40,000), NOAA 13218 (1:80,000)

Tidal Information: High tide is 7 minutes after Newport high tide. Mean tidal range, 3.8 feet. High tide offers the best opportunities for exploring the nooks and crannies of Little Bay.

Launch Site: Sconticut Neck State Ramp, Seaview Road, Fairhaven. Parking fee.

PADDLING AROUND WEST ISLAND offers challenging water, beautiful beaches, good birding, warm seas, great scenery, and easy access. Diversity is the area's strong suit, and kayakers of all abilities can take advantage of its challenges and charms. Spend an entire afternoon exploring the protected coves of Nasketucket Bay, or play in the waves and open water off Great Island. Come and enjoy. This is a great place for a summer outing when the crowds on Cape Cod drive most paddlers away.

Plot your trip based on the direction of the tide. Plan to pass under the West Island Bridge *with* the current or at slack tide. Those wishing to explore the northern reaches of Little Bay or paddle up Bass Creek on Great Island must do so at high tide. Also consider the weather. Paddle around Great Island early in the day before the wind (and waves) pick up. In addition, the area around the West Island Bridge and marina becomes uncomfortably congested on summer weekend afternoons.

From the boat ramp, turn right (south) and paddle toward West Island along the eastern shore of Sconticut Neck. Numerous outcroppings, large and small, are visible in the bay. When the sun is at the right angle, the rocks gleam like tips of golden pyramids. Many disappear at high tide. Others, like Pea Island, are popular picnicking and camping sites. Continue south past two of these islands, Puppy Rocks (named for its use by boaters traveling with dogs) and Old Keel-lick Rock (an obvious reference to careless sailors). Then paddle around blue buoys which demarcate a scallop-seeding operation.

For a special treat on summer mornings, kayakers must head into the quiet cove southwest of the point of land called Round Island. The only buildings visible in the cove are a shack and an old farmhouse. If the tide is right, clammers will be digging for quahogs in this fertile spot. Arrive here early to see herons and egrets roosting in the trees at the west end of the cove. Scores of snow-white egrets sit high on tree limbs, radiant against the dark foliage, looking like exotic Christmas tree ornaments. A heavenly gift on a warm July morning.

From the cove, round the north tip of Long Island and then, depending on the tide and weather conditions, proceed clockwise or counterclockwise around the island. The description here follows a clockwise route. (Those who want to remain in the protected waters of Little Bay can skip the following three paragraphs.) From the tip of Long Island, paddle around the north side of West Island. West Island, lying east of Sconticut Neck, was named for its owner, Stephen West. Round its narrow northern side, then continue down

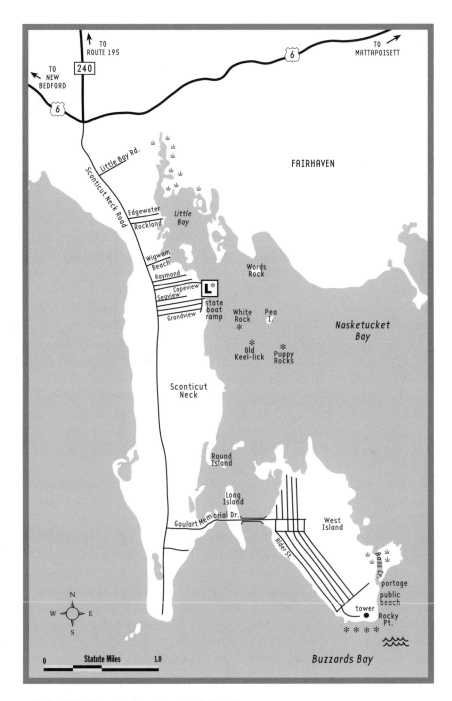

Trip 39: West Island and Little Bay

its marshy eastern shore. Near the southeastern end of the island, kayakers at high tide can take an interesting shortcut through Bass Creek to the beach on the island's southeastern side.

To find Bass Creek, aim for a sandy cove bordered by trees at the southeast end of the island. As you approach, the sand appears split by a grassy area. Paddling up to the grassy area reveals a creek. Passable at high tide, Bass Creek allows kayakers to paddle south about 0.25 mile through the marsh. The creek ends at the back of a beach, and it's an easy carry to put in on the other side. This is an excellent place for a rest stop. Kayakers can choose to stay on the quiet marsh side or head over the sand to the popular public beach. Those who enjoy a more straightforward route can skip Bass Creek and continue to paddle around the outside of the island.

The large public beach on West Island is marked at its southern end by a WWII gun tower. It's a beautiful crescent-shaped beach with wide, soft sand and expansive views. On clear days, look south to the Elizabeth Islands, seven miles away. Southeast of the tower, at Rocky Point, the rock-studded shore presents hazards for paddlers. The rock garden just south of the point is a treacherous place in surf, so steer wide if wind and waves are up. Also watch for riptides around the point.

Continuing the circumnavigation, paddle north up West Island's more developed east side. This is the least scenic and most congested part of the trip. (In fact, kayakers might opt for heading back around the island the way they came, especially if conditions around the point are too much to handle.) In any event, from Rocky Point it's just over a mile to the West Island bridge. Watch the boat traffic, then paddle under the low, narrow bridge, preferably with the current.

Paddle past a busy marina and north toward the boat ramp to explore the bay. Watch for the graceful flight of terns, which nest on the bay's islands. Pass the boat ramp and explore Little Bay's quiet estuary. Paddling north up the west side, pass a private sandy island on the right, used by Girl Scouts. Across from the island is a small plot of land, wedged between houses, called Wigwam Beach. Wigwam Beach is a Sconticut Indian burial ground. The Sconticut Indians summered on Sconticut Neck and enjoyed the plentiful marine resources, including shellfish, haddock, and flounder. An Indian village probably thrived, at least seasonally, at Little Bay. Sconticut descendants still come to the burial ground to pay their respects.

Continue north to the far end of the cove to paddle up the narrow tidal Nasketucket River. Kayakers can pass under a low bridge and travel up the river a short distance, guaranteed of some solitude along the river's twisting course.

Paddling back into Little Bay, cross the water to the bay's west side. At the northwest end of the bay, find active osprey nests and tidal inlets where bird life is abundant. Look for a variety of herons, oystercatchers, and egrets. Heading south along the west shore, depending upon the tide, paddle above or within the bay's rock gardens. When ready, paddle back across the bay to the boat launch on its western shore.

Rental kayaks, equipment, instruction, and tours (including guided fishing and moonlit tours) are offered by the Kayak Shack, located at Earl's Marina on Long Island, on the causeway (Goulart Memorial Drive) to West Island. Experienced paddlers John and Yvonne Sabourin are ready with boats and advice to aid visiting paddlers. Contact them at 508-984-7137. Buzzards Bay Kayaks also provide excellent tours around West Island. For more information, call 508-996-8885.

Directions to Launch Site: From Route 128, drive Route 24 south to Route 195 east. Drive Route 195 east to Exit 18 (Fairhaven/Route 240). Take Route 240 south to its end (at Route 6), where it turns into Sconticut Neck Road. Proceed south on Sconticut Neck Road about 2.3 miles to Seaview Road on the left. Turn left on Seaview Road and proceed 0.4 mile to the State Boat Ramp at its end. Small parking fee. Free parking along Seaview Road.

trip SLOCUMS RIVER,
4 0 DARTMOUTH

Level Of Difficulty: Easy to strenuous; protected and open water

Round-Trip Mileage: 7.0 miles to mouth of Slocums River (Demarest-Lloyd State Park); 14.5 miles to Allens Pond

Attractions: Quiet river paddling, bird-watching, salt marsh, Demarest-Lloyd State Park (sandy beach), swimming, fishing, open-water paddling in Buzzards Bay

Precautions: Prevailing southwest winds can generate rough water at the mouth of the river and along the coast west of Barneys Joy Point. Take care entering and exiting Allens Pond because strong rips and waves can occur at the inlet at midtide. Plan to paddle *with* the tide entering and exiting the pond.

Charts: NOAA 13228 (1:20,000), NOAA 13229 (1:40,000), NOAA 13218 (1:80,000)

Tidal Information: High tide is 30 minutes after Newport high tide. Mean tidal range, 3.8 feet. River is navigable at all tides but is best midtide or higher. High tide (2 hours either side) recommended for paddling Allens Pond. High tide at west end of Allens Pond is delayed 3 hours. Tide differentials at Allens Pond are subject to change depending on dredging of channel.

Launch Site: Town Landing, Russells Mills, Dartmouth. Free parking.

A TRIP DOWN THE SLOCUMS RIVER is a beautiful study in contrasts. Paddlers start in an intimate, slow-flowing river, float to the wide-open, sandy spaces of Demarest-Lloyd State Park,

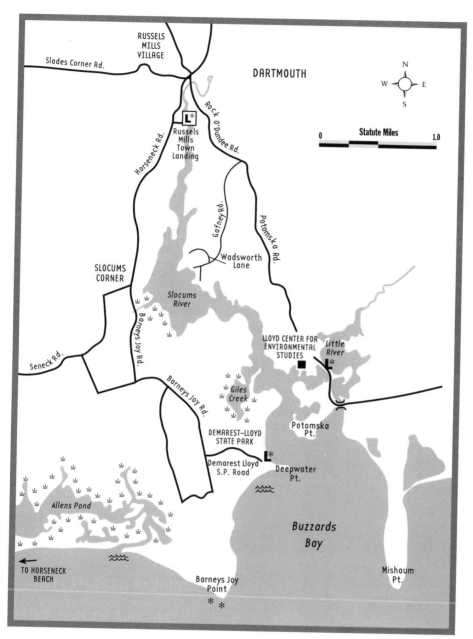

Trip 40: Slocums River, Dartmouth

plunge into the perennially choppy waters of Buzzards Bay before finding refuge in jewel-like Allens Pond, a salt marsh rich in beauty and wildlife tucked behind the dunes. The trip is fun and demanding, easily occupying a fine summer's day. Deliciously uncrowded on weekdays and in fall, the Slocums is a hidden treasure easily found.

A wise choice for novices is to paddle only the river portion of this trip, thus staying in protected water for a short but satisfying seven-mile round trip. For those novices who want to poke their bows into the bay, a good, but far from foolproof, way to avoid rough water is to paddle in the morning. Early morning kayakers (often) avoid the southwest winds that kick up most summer afternoons, creating the infamous Buzzards Bay chop.

The trip begins in the sleepy Slocums. Amid a welcoming committee of ducks and geese, launch from the put-in at Russell's Mills landing, and turn right (south). Though today bucolic, in the 1700s Russell's Mills village was a center of industry where water-powered mills ground grain, cut wood, and processed wool. Shipbuilders even operated a shipyard near this tiny landing. Today, the upper Slocums is deliciously quiet, bordered by a few homes, half hidden by trees, and by granite rocks, half submerged. As one moves south, the river widens and small islands appear. Watch for herons and other birds feeding along the shore.

About a mile from the put-in, the river broadens significantly. To the west, a large farm looks down on the river. Wooded banks give way to rolling fields. If kayakers follow the west bank of the Slocums River, they arrive at a creek flowing into freshwater wetlands, navigable for a short distance. The main flow of the river bends east. Paddle past a weathered dock where cormorants stand motionlessly atop wooden posts like carved owls. Again the river becomes narrow as it turns east and then south.

After three-quarters of a mile, the Slocums suddenly opens again to reveal a long spit of sand (Deepwater Point) directly south and a deep pocket of marsh to the west (right). Flowing through the marsh, Giles Creek is a fine detour. The broad creek provides access into the salt marsh on the backside of Demarest-Lloyd State Park. Watch the edge of the marsh for herons, gulls, and egrets and the skies for hawks and osprey. At low tide check the mud flats for hordes of fiddler crabs, a small crab with one huge, fiddle-shaped claw. Paddle Giles Creek now, or save this detour for the return trip.

To the left, an arm of the Slocums River heads east. If kayakers turn east, they pass the well-camouflaged Lloyd Center for Environmental Studies, a fifty-five-acre property comprising salt marsh, forest, and freshwater wetlands. The center offers educational programs and conducts research on the coastal and estuarine environment of southeastern Massachusetts. The Lloyd Center's grounds provide nesting habitat for birds and trails for visitors 365 days a year.

endangered buzzards bay

Many areas of Buzzards Bay, particularly some of its most scenic coves, harbors and river mouths, suffer from excess nitrogen input. Excess nitrogen adversely affects water quality and leads to a chain reaction of negative impacts known as eutrophication. Eutrophic conditions (oxygen loss) cause poor water clarity, stressed marine organisms, and even fish kills. (See page 283.) Two of the most endangered water bodies are the Slocums River (Trip 40) and the East Branch of the Westport River (Trip 41).

The Coalition for Buzzards Bay is dedicated to the restoration, protection and sustainable use and enjoyment of Buzzards Bay and its watershed. The Coalition's Baywatchers Program uses volunteers to test water quality in 28 major coves and harbors. This data is critical to identifying those areas most at risk and to determining effective solutions. Other Coalition programs include public education, the Bay Lands Center (promoting the protection of critical habitats), and advocacy projects.

To learn more about Buzzards Bay, contact The Coalition for Buzzards Bay, P.O. Box 3006, New Bedford, Ma 02741, 508-999-6363, www.savebuzzardsbay.org. Membership in the Coalition supports their important work, and members receive quarterly newsletters, merchandise discounts, and invitations to special events.

Among the center's many programs are naturalist-led paddling trips in the area. (For information, call 508-990-0505 or log on at www.ultranet.com/~lloydctr.) Kayakers are welcome to picnic on the shore or sample one of the trails. Look for the center's canoe rack on the northern bank, after turning into the eastern arm. Watch for the partially submerged remains of a stone dike.

Continuing south to the mouth of the Slocums, kayakers must pass between the sandy spit of the state park and rocky Potomska Point to the east. Beyond Potomska Point the scenery changes dramatically. From the river's dark browns and greens, kayakers jump to a bright palette of blue, tan, and glistening white. To the west, Demarest-Lloyd State Park's sandy beach (wide at low tide and more than a mile long at low tide) provides a great place for picnics. Shade is available at tables set back from the water. Views southeast from the beach include the long line of the Elizabeth Islands separating Buzzards Bay from Vineyard Sound. Watch for waves breaking in the shallow water just east of the shore. Watch also for least terns in the park, as well as on adjacent Barneys Joy Point.

From Demarest-Lloyd State Park, paddle south to round Barneys Joy Point. Watch for rocks and rips around the privately owned headland. Pass the point, and paddle west along the shore. Rock turns to sand, and dunes appear. Farther up the shore to the west, the crowded houses along East Horseneck Beach are visible. After paddling about a mile from Barneys Joy Point, reach a break in the sand, found just west of a high dune. The inlet to Allens Pond is not apparent until you're right on top of it.

Paddle into the inlet (watching for breaking waves) and east up a shallow channel flanked first by dunes, and then by marsh. As one follows the channel north, the marsh opens like a flower. The narrow channel widens to 165-acre Allens Pond, stretching about a mile in length. A number of conservation groups, including Massachusetts Audubon and the Dartmouth Natural Resources Trust, were instrumental in protecting two-thirds of the land surrounding the pond (more than 700 acres) from development.

Allens Pond is "one of the most pristine coastal areas in Massachusetts" and is a critical link for birds traveling along the Atlantic seaboard. Year-round the bird life is vibrant. In spring and summer, observe small flocks of roseate terns, a federally endangered species. Also nesting along the barrier beach in the spring and summer are threatened piping plovers and least terns. During the spring and fall migration, a wide variety of migratory shorebirds feed on the flats along the pond's edge. From April to October, observe osprey on the pond's three nesting platforms, and in winter short-eared owls, horned larks, and snow buntings visit the marsh, grasslands, and dunes. The importance of this area for threatened and endangered species has placed it high on Massachusetts Audubon's priority list for purchasing additional acres to safeguard the integrity of the pond.

Enjoy the pond, but watch the tides to avoid getting stranded in low water. Exit the pond the way you came. If breaking waves at the mouth of the inlet obstruct passage, kayakers can beach their boats on the side of the dune and carry over. When walking over the sand, however, avoid stepping on fragile dune grass. Once back in Buzzards Bay, retrace your path east to the Slocums River and north to the put-in. Those who launched off Potomska Road on the Little River must paddle east of Potomska Point to find the inlet to the Little River.

Stop at Davoll's General Store in Russell's Mills village for a peek at an authentic general store circa 1776. The six-room store, complete with U.S. Post Office, is located at the intersection of Russell's Mills and Slade Corner Roads, once the center of a thriving eighteenth-century village.

Directions to Launch Site: From Route 128, drive Route 24 south to Route 195 east. Drive Route 195 to Route 88 south. Drive Route 88 south about 7.2 miles to Hix Bridge Road. Turn left and drive 2.7 miles to Division Road. Turn right on Division and proceed 1.0 mile to Slades Corner Road. Turn left and drive 1.5 miles to Horseneck Road at Russell's Mills. Turn right and proceed to the landing in a small park, 0.2 mile on the left. From Fall River or New Bedford, take I-195 to Exit 12 south. Cross Route 6 and continue 0.25 mile to a fork. Bear left at the fork onto Chase Road. At the end of Chase Road, turn right onto Russell's Mills Road to the village. At the village, follow directions, above.

Alternate Launch Sites: (1) Demarest-Lloyd State Park, Dartmouth. This put-in is located at the mouth of the Slocums River. Follow directions above to Division Road. Turn right on Division and drive south to its intersection with Horseneck Road. Take a left on Horseneck and then a right on Allens Neck Road. After Barneys Joy Road enters on the left, continue straight about one mile to

Demarest-Lloyd State Park. Park in the lot farthest north, where there is a short carry to the water at high tide (but a moderate carry at low). Note that the park is open only from Memorial Day through Labor Day, 10 A.M. – 6 P.M. on weekdays and 8 A.M. – 6 P.M. on weekends. Call 508-636-3298 for more information. Entrance fee. (2) Potomska Road, Dartmouth. This put-in is also located near the mouth of the Slocums River. Follow the above directions to Russell's Mills village. Drive Slades Corner Road to Russell's Mills Road and turn left, then immediately right onto Rock-O'-Dundee Road. Drive 0.9 mile to Potomska Road and follow Potomska Road 2.0 miles to a pullout for a few cars on the right (the pullout is 0.3 mile after the entrance to the Lloyd Center). Park along the road on the right and launch into the Little River on the left side of the road within a few hours of high tide.

trip
41

EAST BRANCH OF THE
WESTPORT RIVER

Level of Difficulty: Easy to Hix Bridge, strenuous to Route 88 bridge; both protected water

Round-Trip Mileage: 7.0 miles (Head of Westport to Hix Bridge); 14.0 miles (Head of Westport to Route 88 bridge and north side of Horseneck Beach)

Attractions: Bucolic rural scenery, wide tidal river, excellent bird-watching (especially osprey). Fall foliage and warm water make this an excellent late-season paddle.

Precautions: Avoid low tide at the head of the river as the water falls to less than one foot. Watch for partially submerged rocks and trees in the river, especially near the head. Boat traffic increases as one nears Westport Harbor. Approach the Route 88 bridge with caution, as currents are strong under the bridge. Lastly, watch the wind. Strong southwest winds develop most summer afternoons and paddling against them can be difficult. Be aware that strong winds and a falling tide can create difficult waves, and even whitecaps, on the river. Kayakers are less likely to encounter strong winds in the morning and evening. Listen to local forecasts before departing.

Charts: NOAA 13228 (1:20,000), or NOAA 13218 (1:80,000)

Tidal Information: High water in Westport Harbor is 10 minutes after Newport high water, and low water is 40 minutes after Newport low water. Furthermore low water at the head of the Westport River is about three hours after Newport's low water, at the Hix Bridge about 2 hours after Newport, and at the Route 88 bridge, about 1 hour after Newport. Avoid paddling within two hours of dead low tide at the head of the river. For greatest ease of travel, run *with* the tide. The Westport River's current is relatively mild, nevertheless, so one can easily paddle against the current if necessary. Mean tidal range is 3.0 feet at Westport Harbor.

Launch Site: Head of Westport River Landing, Westport; free parking.

RIDING THE WESTPORT is a relaxing and delightful trip where boat traffic is light and the scenery inviting. Given favorable tidal currents and light wind, kayakers can enjoy an easy paddle through a beautiful rural landscape. Pleasant in summer and exquisite in fall, the trip offers kayakers a glimpse into the rarely-seen-from-the sea pastoral Massachusetts countryside. It also gives paddlers the opportunity to see osprey as well as a variety of other estuarine birds. For the best osprey viewing bring binoculars!

For the easiest trip, plan to ride *with* the tides. Although it's possible (with one important exception) to paddle against the current, it is easier, of course, to run *with* it. The exception concerns the Route 88 bridge and the constricted channel just west of the bridge. Kayakers of novice and intermediate abilities should *not* attempt to paddle against the current under the bridge (it can run three to four knots and is strongest while ebbing). Take time to calculate the tides by using the differentials noted on page 296 in Tidal Information. Also be aware that winds generally are lightest in the morning, build in the afternoon, then diminish toward evening. In summer winds usually blow from the southwest. Consequently, a strong southwest wind can greatly affect kayakers because it blows directly upriver. In the fall, wind direction generally changes to the north. Check the local forecast before launching.

The following describes a trip beginning at the Head of the Westport River. (Those launching from Westport Harbor can follow the description in reverse.) From the put-in at the Head, turn left and paddle downriver; upstream the river is too narrow to paddle. For a brief distance, stone walls enclose the slow-moving, tea-colored river like a canal. Gradually the river widens, the banks turn to marsh grass, and the houses become farms. Rows of corn appear beyond the reeds, and an occasional cow strolls on gently rolling pasture. It is pretty country, and the river is wide enough to dispel

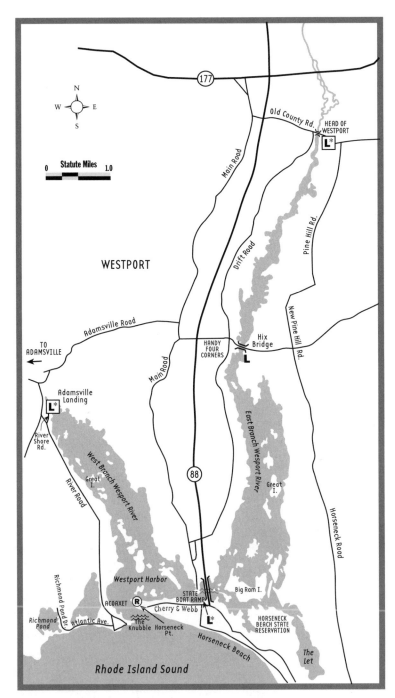

Trip 41: East Branch of the Westport River
Trip 42: West Branch of the Westport River

any claustrophobia. Keep a lookout for a variety of ducks, great blue herons, egrets, red-tailed hawks, and osprey.

Unfortunately, all is not quite as copacetic as it appears in this provincial scene. The farms that give the river its bucolic charm adversely affect its water quality and harm its value as a habitat for fish and wildlife. Runoff from agricultural lands contributes significantly to the river's high fecal coliform and nitrate levels. The nutrient-rich sediment causes eutrification, which affects the clarity of the water, and the bacteria from human and animal waste in runoff has forced shellfish beds to close from the Head of the Westport to Hix Bridge, about 3.5 miles south. The Westport River Watershed Alliance is an active proponent of water quality and resource conservation for both branches of the Westport River and is working hard to address these problems (see inset).

After about 3.5 miles, reach the Hix Bridge. Kayakers can take a break at the put-in on the left (east) bank after the bridge. This is a popular place to fish for blue crab. (For the uninitiated, the bait of choice is a chicken drumstick!) South of the bridge, the river loses its pastoral tranquillity. Its banks are more crowded with houses, and boat traffic increases. About 0.5 mile after the bridge, the width of

Hix Bridge, East Branch of the Westport River.

rescuing the river: the westport river watershed alliance

The mission of the Westport River Watershed Alliance (WRWA) is "to restore, protect, celebrate and sustain the natural resources of the Westport River and its watershed." This is a heady goal for a small watershed association based in a town that has more land in farming and acreage in estuary than any other town in the state. Indeed, it is an essential one as well. Paddling the quiet waters of the Westport River above Hix Bridge, one would never guess that its water quality has slipped below that of the Charles River in Boston. The chief culprit is agricultural runoff, especially from large dairy farms. Storm-drain discharge of surface and road runoff and improperly maintained septic systems contribute as well.

In order to reach the laudable goal of restoring the Westport River to fishable and swimmable status by 2005, the WRWA launched a "rescue the river" campaign. Components of its efforts include:

the river doubles and remains broad (nearly a mile wide) until you reach the Route 88 bridge.

Scattered throughout the river below Hix Bridge are small islands. Although they are highly attractive to land on, all are privately owned. Paddle among the islands and observe the numerous platforms constructed for osprey nests. These platforms, constructed by local residents, host many inhabited nests, and summer paddlers can readily observe the adult in the nest and often his or her offspring. Osprey generally mate for life and return to the same nest each year.

The Westport River is home to the largest concentration of breeding osprey in New England. These magnificent fish hawks have

* Urging enforcement of Westport's Domestic Animal/Livestock Regulation to limit entry of manure into the river;

* Supporting town efforts to remediate storm-drain discharge to the river;

* Sponsoring river cleanups and Adopt-a-Watershed programs;

* Monitoring water quality through monthly water sampling for fecal coliform bacteria;

* Collaborating with town committees to develop long-range plans for open space and recreation; and

* Educating the public about the health of the river and promoting both individual and community stewardship through public education and volunteer programs.

To help the WRWA, a nonprofit citizens' group, call 508-636-3016 and become a member. To find out more about the river and the threats it faces, visit the WRWA website at www.wrwa.com, or write WRWA, Wing Carriage House, 1151 Main Road, P.O. Box 3427, Westport, MA 02790-0703.

wingspans up to six feet, a black bandit's mask, and a remarkable way of swooping up fish in their sharp talons. For a good view, use binoculars. If an osprey appears agitated by your presence or leaves the nest to circle your kayak, retreat—you have approached too close. Do not allow these birds to expend precious energy chasing you away. Both male and female osprey have the exhausting summer-long task of supplying their two to four hungry offspring with a daily average of *seven* pounds of fish.

Many believe that the most beautiful section of the Westport River is the area south of Hix Bridge, from Great Island south to the back of Horseneck Beach. This, indeed, is a wonderful area to explore, filled with islands and marsh life. The wind can kick up chop, but

Horseneck Beach protects the water from receiving significant surf. The only drawback is the noise from the Route 88 bridge, which carries thousands to the popular state beach each summer weekend. In high season, this drone can disturb enjoyment of the waterway, but the highway quiets significantly midweek and off-season.

Kayakers can paddle west, under the bridge to explore Westport Harbor and the West Branch of the Westport River. For details, see Trip 42. To return to the Head, simply retrace your route upstream.

Directions to Launch Site: Take Route 128/I-93 to Route 24 south to Route 195 east. Drive Route 195 east to Route 88 south. Drive Route 88 south for about 3.8 miles to Old County Road (a sign at the traffic light indicates Head of Westport). Turn left onto Old County Road and proceed 0.9 mile to the small bridge over the Westport River. Cross the bridge and turn right immediately at an outdoor-equipment store. The small landing and parking area for the Head of the Westport is just behind the store.

Alternate Launch Site: State Boat Ramp, located at the south end of the Route 88 bridge. This is a difficult put-in for novices because the current is strong directly off the ramp. Launching and landing at slack time is recommended. A better option is launching from the F. L. Trip and Sons Marina, located about 0.5 mile west of the State Boat Ramp (next to the Westport Yacht Club). The current's pull is considerably less at this location. Call ahead to gain permission to park and launch from the marina (508-636-8885). They are most likely to welcome kayakers on weekdays and off-season.

trip 42 WEST BRANCH OF THE WESTPORT RIVER

Level of Difficulty: Easy to moderate; protected water

Round–Trip Mileage: 7.0 miles to mouth of Westport Harbor; 4.0 miles additional round-trip to explore Big Ram Island and lower East Branch of the Westport River

Attractions: Excellent bird-watching (especially osprey), picnicking on sandy beach or shady island, swimming

Precautions: Strong current in the vicinity of Route 88 bridge and at Westport Harbor entrance. Strong opposing southwest or southerly wind (especially with ebb current) can generate hazardous waves at harbor entrance.

Charts: NOAA 13228 (1:20,000), NOAA 13218 (1:80,000)

Tidal Information: See Trip 41. High tide is 10 minutes after Newport, low tide 40 minutes after. At low tide, the West Branch of the Westport River is very shallow and difficult to navigate. Low tide at the head of the West Branch (Adamsville) is about 40 minutes after low tide in Newport. Mean tidal range, 3.0 feet.

Launch Site: Adamsville Landing, Adamsville, MA. Free parking.

THE WEST BRANCH of the Westport River provides hours of tranquil paddling as well as the opportunity for some challenging open-water kayaking outside Westport Harbor. For paddlers seeking warm, protected waters, fabulous osprey-viewing, island-hopping, and sandy beaches, the river is an excellent choice. Visit in fall when the water is still several degrees warmer than Massachusetts Bay, the summer boaters and beach-goers have departed, and the foliage glows warmly on the river's densely wooded banks.

A view of the West Branch of the Westport River.

Begin in Adamsville at the small town landing. Mid- to high-tide launchings are preferred, because the river is considerably easier to negotiate in high water. If paddling at low tide, stay close to the left (east) bank of the river. A deeper channel meanders down that side and, while difficult, it is possible to paddle at an average low tide. To aid your navigation, local residents maintain channel markers, June through October. The great advantage of the river's shallowness is the scarcity of motorboat traffic.

About one mile from the put-in paddlers arrive at Great Island, the largest island in the West Branch, marked by three colorful flags at its northern end. *Please note:* The island is privately owned, and although once open to kayakers and picnickers, it is now closed to the public. For more information, contact David Cole at 508–636–6594 (a member of Westport River Watershed Alliance).

As you travel downriver, note the abundance of osprey nests. Through the efforts of local bird-lovers, particularly Gil Fernandez of

Allens Pond, nearly 100 nesting platforms were raised, and the majority support active nests. The Westport River boasts an 80 percent occupancy rate, with some osprey pairs returning to the same nest for more than ten years. To view osprey, visit between April and October. In late October, the birds return to warmer waters on the Gulf coast and off Central and South America. Watch the magnificent birds from a respectful distance. If a bird moves off a nest to warn you away, retreat at once. Be especially considerate before July 1, when osprey have young chicks in the nest that need the parents' full attention and protection.

As one travels south, Westport Harbor comes into view. During the summer, the harbor is filled with masts and motorboats. The pull of the current becomes noticeable as one approaches the harbor.

Where the west branch of Westport meets the harbor, there are two options. A fine detour of about 2 miles round-trip is to paddle east (left) under the Route 88 bridge and into the beautiful area between Big Ram Island and the back of Horseneck Beach on the lower East Branch of the Westport River. There is good paddling around the island, with the opportunity to see a variety of birds feed-

View toward Great Island, West Branch of the Westport River.

ing in the marsh. Once under the bridge, rocky islands glow golden in the sunlight and quiet waters abound. The islands and blue water are reminiscent of Maine, except the water is fine for swimming!

On the way back west, pass again under the bridge, anticipating the strong current. Heavy traffic increases the risks dramatically for kayakers. Paddle defensively, watching for small boats pulled out of control by the current. A good place to rest after passing under the bridge is the eddy to the left (south) just after the state boat ramp and Moby Dick Marina. Kayakers can find refuge here from the traffic and current. Then hug the north side of Horseneck Beach and paddle west along its shore to Horseneck Point.

The second, shorter option is to paddle straight across Westport Harbor to Horseneck Point. The sandy beach at its end provides a good place to rest. Hunt for shells, or picnic along the popular beach. Paddling west to the far shore of Acoaxet is also recommended. One can land near the elephantine rock formation at its tip, hop over the tide pools, and climb up the rock for Buzzards Bay views. Watch the current when paddling to the west. Novices should avoid paddling near the mouth because of strong current and breaking waves when the wind blows from the south.

If conditions allow, experienced paddlers can paddle out of the harbor. The coastline to the west is quite beautiful. It is rocky and rugged but sprinkled with small sand beaches. Be aware, however, that the Westport River runs at four knots out of the harbor. Pass at slack tide or *with* the current. Once out of the harbor, turn west and pass the Knubble, a grand summer home built by one of the founders of Woolworth's (now converted to condos). Explore a bit, then retrace your route back to the harbor. Paddling east along the front of Horseneck Beach is not recommended due to frequent breaking surf.

Directions to launch Site: From Routes 93/128: Take Route 24 south to Route 81 south near the MA/RI border. Drive Route 81 about 8.3 miles to its end in the tiny town of Adamsville. Turn left and then take the first right after 0.1 mile onto Westport Harbor Road. Proceed 0.25 mile to Adamsville Landing on the left. Free parking at the put-in.

Alternate Launch Site: F. L. Trip and Sons Marine in Westport Harbor; see Trip 41 for directions.

appendix a **RESOURCES FOR SEA KAYAKERS**

KAYAKING IS BEST LEARNED, practiced, and enjoyed in the company of others. To link up with sea-kayaking clubs, tours, instructors, symposia, and other associations, consult the lists below. Also included in this chapter are local environmental organizations. These nonprofit groups draw their strength from citizens, like sea-kayakers, who care deeply about the health and quality of their local environment.

Instruction

Good instruction is the key to safe and enjoyable kayaking. Paddlers will go farther and faster, with less effort and less risk of injury, when paddling correctly. To gain confidence in rough water, learn rescues, and conquer Eskimo rolls, kayakers should seek professional instruction.

Fortunately, fine instruction is available at many venues in Massachusetts. As with any instructional program, small class size and experienced instructors are paramount. Demand both, since instructional workshops are often expensive. Lastly, plan ahead, because many programs fill up quickly.

The following outfitters and organizations offer a variety of instructional programs:

North of Boston

- Adventure Learning, 67 Bear Hill, Merrimac, MA 01860; 978-346-9728, 800-649-9728; www.adventure-learning.com.

- Eastern Mountain Sports, 210 Andover, Peabody, MA 01960; 978-977-0601. EMS offers an occasional free clinic, call for details.

- Essex River Basin Adventures, Inc. (ERBA), 66R Main Street, P.O. Box 270, Essex, MA 01929; 978-768-ERBA, 800-KAYAK-04; www.erba.com.

- Kayak Learning Center, 15R Stone Street, Beverly, MA 01915; 978-922-5322

- North Shore Paddlers Network (NSPN), P.O. Box 306, Merrimac, MA 01860; www.nspn.org. NSPN sponsors both formal clinics and gatherings for learning new skills. Information available on the website.

Boston and Areas West

- Charles River Canoe and Kayak, 2401 Commonwealth Avenue, Newton, MA 02166; 617-965-5110; www.ski-paddle.com

South of Boston

- Billington Sea Watercraft, 41 Branch Point Road, Plymouth, MA 02360; 508-746-5644

Buzzards Bay

- Buzzards Bay Kayak, P.O. Box 144, Fairhaven, MA 02719; 508-996-8885

- The Kayak Shack, Earl's Marina, 56 Goulart Memorial Drive, Fairhaven, MA 02719; 508-984-7137

Cape and Islands

- Kayaks of Martha's Vineyard, P.O. Box 840, West Tisbury, MA 02575; 508-693-3885; www.kayakmv.com

- The Paddlers Shop, Riverdell Marine, 420 Shore Road, Monument Beach, MA 02553; 508-759-0330; www.capecod.net/rivendell/ paddler.html

- Ripple Creek Kayaking, 1 South Shore Drive, South Yarmouth, MA 02664; 508-776-9036; rckayaking@capecod.net

Rhode Island

- The Kayak Centre, 9 Phillips Street-Waterside, Wickford, RI 02852; 888-SEA-KAYAK; www.kayakcentre.com/funn/; email: funn@kayak-centre.com.

- Ocean State Adventures, 99 Poppasquash Road, Bristol, RI 02809; 401-254-4000; www.kayakri.com

Maine

- H2Outfitters, P.O. Box 72, Orr's Island, ME 04066; 800-20-KAYAK; www.H2OUTFITTERS.COM

- L.L. Bean, Inc., Outdoor Discovery Schools, Freeport, ME 04033; 800-341-4341, ext. 26666; www.llbean.com.

- Maine Island Kayak Co., 70 Luther Street, Peaks Island, ME 04108; 800-796-2373; www.maineislandkayak.com.

Paddlers can supplement on-water lessons with fine instructional books and videos. A full bibliography of materials is found on page 330. A short list of excellent kayaking books and videos includes:

Instructional Books

- Dowd, John. *Sea Kayaking: A Manual for Long Distance Touring*. Seattle: University of Washington Press, 1997

- Foster, Nigel. *Nigel Foster's Sea Kayaking*. 2nd Edition, Guilford, CT; Globe Pequot Press

- Hauson, Jonathan. *Complete Sea Kayak Touring*. New York: McGraw Hill, 1998

- Hutchinson, Derek. *The Complete Book of Sea Kayaking*. Guilford, CT: Globe Pequot Press, 1995

- Seidman, David. *The Essential Sea Kayaker, A Complete Course for the Open Water Paddler*. Camden, ME-Int'l Marine Pub: 1997

- Washburne, Randel. *The Coastal Kayaker's Manual*. Guilford, CT: Globe Pequot Press, 1998

Instructional Video

- *Performance Sea Kayaking, The Basics and Beyond*. Performance Video 800-259-5805

Kayaking Clubs

Joining a kayaking club is one of the best ways to improve your skills, meet other kayakers, and find new paddling partners. The larger clubs offer workshops, slide lectures, websites, message boards, newsletters, and instruction.

- Appalachian Mountain Club, Southeastern Massachusetts Chapter, Murial Thomas, Chair 508-428-3593; www.outdoors.org

- Boston Sea Kayak Club, c/o BSKC Membership Coordinator, 47 Nancy Road, Newton, MA 04267; 617-246-1337; www.bskc.org. Spring through fall, BSKC sponsors dozens of trips and instructional clinics throughout Massachusetts.

- Cape Ann Rowing Club, P.O. Box 1715, Gloucester, MA 02025; 508-927-1834

- North and South Rivers Watershed Association, P.O. Box 43, Norwell, MA 02061; 781-659-8168; www.nsra.org

- North Shore Paddlers Network, P.O. Box 306, Merrimac, MA 01860; www.nspn.org. NSPN offers a fabulous website, an active message board, and an extensive schedule of regional trips, as well as year-round clinics and gatherings for kayakers of all abilities. This very inclusive group invites kayakers visiting the area to join them on club trips.

Kayaking Symposia

Kayaking symposia offer paddlers a chance to test the latest kayaks, attend lectures, participate in on-water workshops, and meet other paddlers. They present excellent opportunities for kayakers of all levels of experience to improve their skills; upgrade equipment; and become safer, more knowledgeable paddlers. Every summer there are two symposia held in New England:

- Boston Kayaking Symposium: This fledgling symposium was held on Thompson's Island in Boston Harbor, and offered all of the above, just a ferry ride from downtown Boston. Contact the Wilderness House, 1048 Commonwealth Avenue, Boston, MA 02215; 617-277-5858 for news on the next one.

- L.L. Bean Atlantic Coast Sea Kayak Symposium: Held in July each year, this symposium offers a weekend of classes, demos, and workshops for the whole family in picturesque Castine, Maine. Contact L.L. Bean Outdoor Discovery Schools, Freeport, Maine 04033; 800-341-4341; www.llbean.com.

Kayaking Tours

The following outfitters offer guided kayak tours. Choose from bird-watching, moonlight, whale-watching, family, and naturalist-led trips. Contact:

- Adventure Learning, 67 Bear Hill, Merrimac, MA 01860; 978-346-9728, 800-649-9728; www.adventure-learning.com

- Adventure Tours, Waquoit Kayak Company, Edward's Boatyard, 1209 Route 28, East Falmouth, MA 02536; 508-548-9722; www.waquoitkayak.com

- Billington Sea Watercraft, 41 Branch Point Road, Plymouth, MA 02360; 508-746-5644

- Cape Cod Coastal Canoe and Kayak, 36 Spectacle Pond Drive, East Falmouth, MA 02536; 508-564-4051; 888-CANOE-93; www.paddlecapecod.com

- Charles River Canoe and Kayak, 2401 Commonwealth Avenue, Newton, MA 02166; 617-965-5110

- Essex River Basin Adventures, Inc. (ERBA), 66R Main Street, P.O. Box 270, Essex, MA 01929; 978-768-ERBA, 800-KAYAK-04; www.erba.com

- Fun Seekers c/o Eric Guftafson at Jack's Boat Rental, Route 6, Wellfleet, MA 02575; 508-349-1429

- Ipswich Bay Ocean Kayaking, 121 Jeffrey Neck Road, Ipswich, MA 01938; 978-356-2464; www.ipswichma.com

- Kayak Learning Center, 15R Stone Street, Beverly, MA 01915; 978-922-5322

- The Kayak Shack, Earl's Marina, 56 Goulart Memorial Drive, Fairhaven, MA 02719; 508-984-7137

- Kayaks of Martha's Vineyard, P.O. Box 840, West Tisbury, MA 02575; 508-693-3885

- Off the Coast Kayak, 3 Freeman Street, Provincetown, MA 02657; 508-487-2692, 1-877-PTKAYAK

- The Paddlers Shop, Riverdell Marine, 420 Shore Road, Monument Beach, MA 02553; 508-759-0330; www.capecod.net/rivendell/paddler.html

- Ripple Creek Kayaking, 1 South Shore Drive, South Yarmouth, MA 02664; 508-776-9036; rckayaking@capecod.net

Connecting Online

Check out the following websites to learn more about regional kayaking, to purchase or sell equipment, and to connect with other kayakers. New organizations and websites are rapidly emerging (and some disappearing), so this list, unfortunately, may grow old shortly after publication.

- Appalachian Mountain Club; www.outdoors.org

- Atlantic Coastal Kayaker; www.shore.net/~ack

- Boston Sea Kayak Club; www.bskc.org

- Canoeing and Kayaking Info-Paddling Net; www.paddling.net

- Metropolitan Association of Sea Kayakers (MASK); www.seacanoe.org/default.htm#bc

- North Shore Paddlers Network; www.nspn.org

- Northeast Paddler's Message Board; www.npmb.com/index.htm

- Rhode Island Canoe/Kayak Association; www.ricka.org

Rental Equipment Outlets

The following companies rent kayaks for hourly and/or day use. Call ahead to inquire about reservations and availability.

- Charles River Canoe and Kayak, 2401 Commonwealth Avenue, Newton, MA 02166; 617-965-5110

- Billington Sea Watercraft, 41 Branch Point Road, Plymouth, MA 02360; 508-746-5644

- Eastern Mountain Sports, Anchor Plaza, 211 Lincoln Street, Hingham, MA 02382; 781-741-8808

- Eastern Mountain Sports, Cape Cod Center, 1513 Iyanough Road, Hyannis, MA 02601; 508-362-8690

- Ipswich Bay Ocean Kayaking, 121 Jeffrey Neck Road, Ipswich, MA 01938; 978-356-2464

- Jack's Boat Rental, Bull Pond, Wellfleet, MA 02575, 508-349-7553; Nickerson State Park, Brewster, MA 02631; 508-896-8556

- Kayak Learning Center, 15R Stone St., Beverly, MA 01915; 978-922-5322

- Kayaks of Martha's Vineyard, P.O. Box 840, West Tisbury, MA 02575; 508-693-3885

- The Kayak Shack, Earl's Marina, 56 Goulart Memorial Drive, Fairhaven, MA 02719; 508-984-7137

- Nauset Sports, Route 6A, Orleans, MA 02653; 508-255-4742

- Palmer River Canoe & Kayak, Taunton River Base, Route 44, Raynham, MA 02767, and Palmer River Base, 206 Wheeler Street, Rehoboth, MA 02769; 800-689-7884, 503-336-2274

- Waquoit Kayak Company, Edward's Boatyard, 1209 Route 28, East Falmouth, MA 02536; 508-548-2216

Environmental and Conservation Organizations

Kayakers rely upon clean water, safe beaches, and a healthy natural environment. As most kayakers know, Massachusetts waters could really use some help. Less than half of the state's rivers and streams meet Clean Water Act standards for fishable and swimmable waters. Sewage discharges and surface runoff pollutes many of the state's beaches, harbors, and waterways. Kayakers can make a difference by joining one of the local environmental clubs listed below. All have a critical need for volunteers to monitor water quality, adopt streams, participate in beach cleanups, or work on the local level for clean water, river protection, wetland preservation, and improved wildlife and fisheries habitat. Contact one of the following (or start your own!):

- Appalachian Mountain Club, 5 Joy Street, Boston, MA 02108; 617-523-0636; www.outdoors.org

- Charles River Watershed Association, 2391 Commonwealth Avenue, Auburndale, MA 02166; 617-965-5975

- Citizens Protection of Waquoit Bay, P.O. Box 21-W, Waquoit, MA 02536

- Conservation Law Foundation, 62 Summer Street, Boston, MA 02110; 617-350-0990; www.clf.org

- Eel River Coalition, 52 Clifford Road, Plymouth, MA 02360

- Environmental League of Massachusetts, 14 Beacon Street, Suite 714, Boston, MA 02108; 617-742-2553

- Essex County Greenbelt Association, Inc., 82 Eastern Avenue, Essex, MA 01929; 978-768-7241; www.shore.net/~ecga

- Hands Across the River, 222 Union Street, Room 202, New Bedford, MA 02740; 508-979-5910

- Ipswich River Watershed Association, P.O. Box 576, 51 South Main Street, Ipswich, MA 01938

- Issak Walton Fish Association, Old Swamp, 31 Pine Street, South Weymouth, MA 02190

- Massachusetts Audubon Society, 208 South Great Road, Lincoln, MA 01773; 781-259-9500

- Merrimack River Watershed Council, 181 Canal Street, P.O. Box 11377, Lawrence, MA 01842; 978-681-5777

- Neponsett River Watershed Association, 2468A Washington Street, Canton, MA 02021; 781-575-0354

- North and South Rivers Watershed Association, P.O. Box 43, Norwell, MA 02061; 781-659-8168; www.nsrwa.org

- Parker River Clean Water Association, P.O. Box 823, Byfield, MA 01922; 978-462-2551

- Salem Sound 2000, 210 Washington Street, Suite 9, Salem, MA 01870; 978-741-7900

- The Trustees of Reservations, 572 Essex Street, Beverly, MA 01915-1530, 978-921-1944

- Westport River Watershed Alliance, P.O. Box 3427, Westport, MA 02790; 508-636-3016

appendix b USING MARINE CHARTS

Reading Charts

Latitude and longitude: No matter how many charts you purchase, they are worthless unless you know how to read them. The most basic concept to master is an understanding of latitude and longitude. On a globe, the horizontal lines represent *latitude* (think of the horizontal rungs of a ladder), which measures the distance north or south of the equator. It is described by degrees, starting at 0 degrees at the equator and moving to 90 degrees at either pole. Lines of *longitude* run vertically, like slices of an orange, and measure the distance east or west of Greenwich, England. It starts there at 0 degrees and runs to 180 degrees at the opposite side of the globe. Each degree of latitude and longitude is divided into 60 minutes (60'). Each minute is divided into 60 seconds (60").

What kayakers have to remember is that one minute of *latitude* equals one nautical mile. This knowledge allows easy determination of distances on any chart by checking the latitude marks that run up the sides. Knowing this equivalence frees kayakers from having to unfold large charts to locate the key. A nautical mile is 6,000 feet, or just over one mile measured on land (1.15 statute mile).

Secondly, kayakers must know how to use latitude and longitude to find specific locations on a chart. Current tables describe the strength of a current in a particular location by giving its coordinates in latitude and longitude. The location of certain hazards may also be described in this manner. To find a point on a chart by its coordinates, look for the identified latitude on the vertical edge of the chart (latitude is always given first and is followed by a designation N or S) and then find the degree of longitude along the top or bottom of the chart (longitude is given second and is followed by E or W). The intersection of these lines will be the identified location. For instance, the current table for Pollock Rip Channel specifically gives the strength of the current at Butler's Hole, located at 41-33-00 N x 69-59-00 W. Translated, this means that Butler's Hole is located at the intersection of 41 degrees, 33 minutes, 0 seconds latitude north and 69 degrees, 59 minutes, 0 seconds west.

Interpreting Abbreviations and Symbols: NOAA employs a panoply of confusing symbols to depict important landforms, lights, rocks, buoys, etc. To break the code, obtain NOAA's comprehensive guide to symbols and abbreviations called *Nautical Chart No. 1*. This is a good reference book to own, and it costs only $2.50. To get you started, nevertheless, the following describes the most commonly encountered icons and terms.

Color: White on a chart depicts deep water (more than ten meters deep). Blue represents shallower water and green the intertidal zone, or foreshore. Green areas will be covered with water at mean high water and uncovered at low tide. Land that is always dry at mean high tide is represented in tan. Buoys and lights are depicted in purple and green.

Rocks, islands, and other hazards: Try to commit the following icons to memory, for they are important symbols for kayakers to learn.

Rocks are indicated by asterisks, crosses, and sometimes, if very large, by circles of green or tan. Just how the rock or small island is represented is very critical. A plain cross (+) indicates a rock that is below water at mean low tide. If the cross, however, has four dots at its corners ( ), it will be awash at low tide. A dotted line around such a cross ( ) emphasizes that it is a hazard to navigation. A cross with no dots on its corners but surrounded by a dotted line ( ) indicates a submerged rock that is also considered a navigational hazard. If there is no number beside it, its depth is unknown.

Asterisks can represent intertidal rocks, those that are covered by water at high tide but uncovered at low tide. Often charts indicate the height of the rock above the water at low tide. This is represented in one of three ways. The most common is by an underlined number in parentheses [e.g., (5)], meaning the rock stands five feet above the water at low tide. Note that the paren-

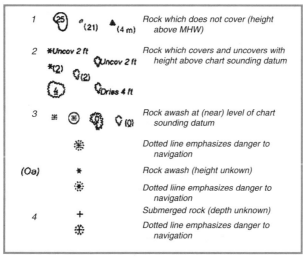

Examples of rock symbols from NOAA chart No. 1.

theses and underlining is critical to this interpretation. Secondly, there may be a notation next to the asterisk stating "dries 5 feet." The "drying height" is the height of the rock above the lowest tide. Third, the chart might read "uncovers 5 ft." This again means the rock rises five feet above the water at low tide. If these notations appear on or next to a green dot, they indicate a large intertidal rock or island. If an asterisk is surrounded by a dotted line (✳), it represents a hazard to navigation.

Asterisks also represent rocks that are never covered with water. In this case, the number in parentheses next to the rock will not be underlined. Hence "(5)" means that the rock stands five feet above the water level at high tide. Similarly, a number in parentheses next to an enclosed yellow area indicates the height of a large rock or small island. The box on page 323 illustrates the various combinations of symbols that kayakers may encounter.

Coastline features: Charts also indicate—fortunately with much more clarity—the nature of the coastline. The illustration on page 325 shows how steep, sandy, stony, marshy, and muddy shoreline are depicted.

Lights and buoys: Buoys are usually indicated on charts by green or purple diamonds, although they occasionally appear as other shapes as well. Green diamonds represent green buoys and purple diamonds usually signify red buoys. Red buoys are placed on the right of the channel as one comes into a harbor (think of the mariners' adage "red returning right"). Green buoys mark the left side of the channel. A purple dot indicates a lighted buoy. There may also be notations on the chart to indicate the buoy's number, its color (R=red, G=green, B=black, RG=red and green striped), and its shape (N= nun-shaped or pointed top, C= can-shaped or flat top). The word "BELL" or "GONG" specifies the sound emitted by the buoy.

Lights on lighthouses or structures are marked with a purple exclamation mark (or teardrop shape) emanating from a black dot. The dot indicates the exact location of the light source. Next to the purple mark is a notation that tells how often the light flashes, its color (white if not specified), how high it is above the water, and from what distance the light could be seen on a clear day. For example the notation "F G 130 ft, 10M" on Marblehead Light means the green light is always on, it is 130 feet above the mean high-water line, and theoretically it can be seen from ten nautical miles. Note that because kayakers sit so low on the water, the information regarding visibility cannot be relied upon. In addition, although the order remains consistent, not all information for lights is always listed. For instance, the light on Black Rocks in Lynn Harbor carries the notation "FL G 6s 9M '9.'" This indicates that a green light flashes every six seconds, it can be seen from nine nautical miles, and there is a "9" painted on the structure. A third example is "Alt Fl W & R 111ft, 13M"

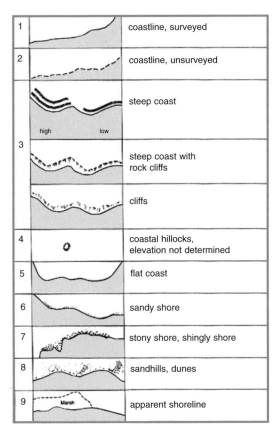

1		coastline, surveyed
2		coastline, unsurveyed
3	high low	steep coast
		steep coast with rock cliffs
		cliffs
4	✿	coastal hillocks, elevation not determined
5		flat coast
6		sandy shore
7		stony shore, shingly shore
8		sandhills, dunes
9	Marsh	apparent shoreline

Samples of coastline features from NOAA chart No. 1.

which marks the lighthouse on Bakers Island in Salem Sound. The notation reveals an alternating light flashing white and red, a lighthouse 111 feet tall, and a light which can be seen from thirteen nautical miles. Notations may also be found next to lighted buoys indicting the nature of the light.

appendix C   CHECKLIST OF ESSENTIALS

- ❑ Personal Flotation Device (PFD)
- ❑ Clothing (dress for the water temperature)
- ❑ Flotation bags
- ❑ Paddle float or other self-rescue device
- ❑ Pump or other bailing device
- ❑ Dry clothes stored in waterproof bag
- ❑ Water and food
- ❑ Spare paddle
- ❑ Signaling device
- ❑ Chart
- ❑ Whistle
- ❑ Compass
- ❑ First-aid kit
- ❑ Towline
- ❑ Duct tape or kayak repair kit
- ❑ Waterproof matches or lighter
- ❑ Weather radio (for multiday trips)

GLOSSARY OF
SEA-KAYAKING TERMS

BEAM: The width of a kayak measured at its widest point.

BEAUFORT WIND SCALE: A table that indicates how various wind speeds affect the state of the sea.

BOOMER: An intermittent offshore breaking wave that occurs when swells hit submerged rocks or reef. Potentially hazardous to kayakers.

BOW: The front end of a boat.

BRACE: A paddling technique used to stabilize a tipping kayak. Low and high braces are two examples.

BREAKDOWN PADDLE: A two-piece paddle that comes apart in the middle and can be set up as a feathered or unfeathered paddle.

BULKHEAD: A sealed compartment fore or aft of the cockpit in a kayak. Used for flotation and storage, with access via deck hatches.

CHINE: The edge of a kayak. The transition area between hull and deck.

COAMING: See *cockpit.*

COCKPIT: The opening in the deck of a kayak where the paddler sits. The curved lip around the edge of the cockpit, used to secure the sprayskirt, is called the coaming.

DEAD RECKONING: Distance calculated from time on the water and estimated paddling speed.

DECK: The covered area of a kayak over the bow and/or stern.

DEPTH OF A KAYAK: The vertical measurement from the hull's lowest point to its highest.

DIRECTIONAL STABILITY: The ability of a kayak to maintain a straight forward direction when moving. See *tracking*.

DUMPER: A wave that breaks with explosive force onto a beach. Occurs most often when the beach drops off precipitously.

EDDY: The area behind or downstream of an obstruction in the main current, where water swirls in a direction different from that of the main flow.

EDDY LINE: The transitional area between the main current and an eddy current. See *eddy*.

FEATHERED PADDLE: A paddle whose blades are set a roughly right angles to each other.

FERRY: A technique used to cross a current to minimize trail downstream.

FINAL STABILITY: Describes a boat's resistance to tipping once the boast has been leaned to a point beyond its *initial stability*. Determined by hull design. Also called *secondary stability*.

FLARE: A term used to describe a hull cross section that grows increasingly wider as it rises from the waterline toward the gunwales.

GRAB LOOP: A short rope or grab handle attached to the ends of the bow and stern of a kayak. Most often used as carry handles.

HATCH: The access port on front or rear deck.

HULL: The body of a kayak. The area that has the greatest impact on how the boat handles in wind and water.

HULL CONFIGURATION: The shape of the *hull*.

INITIAL STABILITY: Describes a kayak's resistance to leaning. Sometimes described as its degree of "tippiness."

K–1: A one-person kayak.

K–2: A two-person kayak.

LEE SHORE: The shore that receives an onshore wind and wind-generated waves.

NAUTICAL MILE: A distance equal to approximately 1.15 statute miles.

PUT-IN: The location where you put your boat in the water at the start of a paddling trip. See *takeout*.

ROCKER: The upward curvature of the keel line from the center toward the ends of a kayak. Increased rocker allows for quick and easy turning.

ROLL: A self-rescue technique to right an overturned kayak in the water without leaving the boat.

RUDDER: The flat-bladed steering device mounted at the rear end of the kayak and controlled by foot pedals.

SECONDARY STABILITY: A hull's tendency to stabilize as it's leaned to one side. See *final stability*.

SKEG: A fixed-direction blade set in a boxed slot in the keel of a kayak which can be lowered various degrees into the water. Takes the place of a rudder in primarily British or Canadian-made kayaks.

STATUTE MILE: A mile as measured on land (1,860 yards). A nautical mile is approximately 1.15 statute miles.

STERN: The back end of a boat.

SURF: Large breaking waves along a coastline or tidal area. Also a technique for riding large waves in a kayak.

TAKEOUT: The place where you take your boat out of the water at the end of a paddling trip.

TANDEM: A two-person kayak. See *K-2*.

TRACK: The ability to move a kayak forward in a straight line.

UNFEATHERED PADDLE: A paddle whose blades lie on the same plane.

VOLUME OF A KAYAK: Describes the overall carrying capacity of a given hull shape.

YAW: The tendency of a kayak to swing right and left with each paddle stroke.

BIBLIOGRAPHY

Bull, Shirley and Fred. *Paddling Cape Cod: A Coastal Explorer's Guide.* Woodstock, VT: Countryman Press, 2000.

Burch, David. *Fundamentals of Kayak Navigation.* Old Saybrook, CT: Globe Pequot Press, 1993.

Cape Cod Bird Club & Massachusetts Audubon Society. *Birding Cape Cod.* Wellfleet, MA: Massachusetts Audubon Society, 1994.

Duncan, Roger F. and John P. Ware. *A Cruising Guide to the New England Coast.* Dodd, Mead & Company, 1979.

Gill, Paul G. Jr. *The Onboard Medical Handbook.* Camden, Maine: International Marine, 1997.

Hutchinson, Derek C. *The Complete Book of Sea Kayaking.* Old Saybrook, CT: Globe Pequot Press, 1999.

Kales, David and Emily. *All about the Boston Harbor Islands.* Hingham, MA: Hewitts Cove Publishing Co., Inc., 1989.

Massachusetts Coastal Zone Management. *Coastal Access Guide.* Boston: MCZM, 1992.

O'Brien, Greg. *A Guide to Nature on Cape Cod and the Islands.* Hyannis, MA: Parnassus Imprints, 1990.

Seidman, David. *The Essential Sea Kayaker: A Complete Course for the Open Water Paddlers.* Camden, Maine: Ragged Mountain Press, 1992.

Tougias, Michael. *Exploring the Hidden Charles. A Guide to Outdoor Activities on Boston's Celebrated River.* Boston: Appalachian Mountain Club Books, 1997.

Venn, Tamsin. *Sea Kayaking along the New England Coast.* Boston: Appalachian Mountain Club Books, 1991.

Washburn, Randel. *The Coastal Kayaker's Manual. A Complete Guide to Skill, Gear and Sea Sense.* Old Saybrook, CT: Globe Pequot Press, 1993.

White, Robert Eldridge. *Eldridge Tide and Pilot Book.* Boston, MA: Robert Eldridge White, 1990.

Wilson, Alex. *Quiet Water Canoe Guide: Massachusetts, Connecticut, Rhode Island.* Boston: Appalachian Mountain Club Books, 1993.

INDEX

ABOUT THE AUTHOR

Lisa Gollin Evans is an avid sea kayaker and author of four other wilderness guide books, *An Outdoor Family Guide to Rocky Mountain National Park*, *An Outdoor Family Guide to Lake Tahoe*, *An Outdoor Family Guide to Yellowstone and Grand Teton National Parks*, and *An Outdoor Family Guide to Acadia National Park* (The Mountaineers Books). Evans has also written an award-winning book for children, *An Elephant Never Forgets Its Snorkel* (Crown Books). Between books, Ms. Evans practices environmental law in the Boston area. She lives with her husband and three daughters in Marblehead, Massachusetts—a terrific place to sea kayak.

ABOUT THE AMC

Since 1876, the Appalachian Mountain Club has helped people experience the majesty and solitude of the Northeast outdoors. We offer outdoor skills workshops, guided trips, and lodging options for all levels of outdoor adventuring. Our conservation programs include trail maintenance, air and water quality research, and advocacy work to preserve the special outdoor places we love and enjoy for future generations.

Join the Adventure!

Take a hike, ride a bike, paddle a canoe. We believe that people who enjoy breathing fresh air, climbing mountains, splashing in streams, and walking on trails have more fun and take better care of the outdoors. Join the fun today. Call 617-523-0636 for membership information.

Outdoor Adventures

From beginner backpacking to advanced backcountry skiing, we teach outdoor skills workshops to suit your interest and experience. If you prefer the company of others and skilled leaders, we also offer guided hiking and paddling trips. Our five outdoor education centers guarantee year-round adventures.

Huts, Lodges, and Visitor Centers

With accommodations throughout the Northeast, you don't have to travel to the ends of the earth to see nature's beauty and experience unique wilderness lodging. Accessible by car or on foot, our lodges and huts are perfect for families, couples, groups, and individuals.

Books and Maps

We can lead you to the best hiking, biking, skiing, and paddling destinations from Maine to North Carolina. With more than 50 books and maps published, we're your definitive resource for discovering wonderful outdoor places. For ordering information call 1-800-262-4455.

Check us out online at **www.outdoors.org**, where there's lots going on.